Return to Earth

Book Three of the Peter Chronicles

AL MINER and LAMA SING

CoCreations Publishing

Return to Earth: *Book Three of the Peter Chronicles*

Cover art and book design by Susan M. Miner

Library of Congress 2017944989

ISBN 9781941915073

1. Lama Sing 2. Psychics 3. Trance Channels 4. Life After Death
5. The Peter Project
I. Miner, Al II. Lama Sing III. Title

Printed in the United States of America

For books and products, or to write Al Miner,
visit our website: **www.lamasing.net**

Contents

CHAPTER 1

Back to Visit Abe

MARCH 31, 1992

As we prepare to rejoin our companions and Peter in realms beyond the Earth, we wish to say to you that, in all of those works that have gone before, we have always asked of the Father that these might surround you as lights to illuminate your pathway, to enhance your quest for the nature of your own spirit's uniqueness, and to grace the path when seeking to better know Him. So it is with this thought that we now turn back to our colleagues.

Having been in song in the Realm of Laughter, where they displayed to Hope the wonders and joys of the manifestation of such an emotion as is found in finite realms, we find that they have just returned to the lush expanse of greenery in Peter's Garden Realm. Our group is sitting leisurely in a circle upon the grassy knoll.

Peter is gazing at Hope, whose countenance or cloak seems to be much more aglow, displaying many more subtleties of color as the after-effect of the sojourn in the Realm of Laughter. "Well, Hope, I suppose you now have a greater understanding of some of the aspects of dealing with finiteness and creativity in that expression. Is that so?"

Hope still carries the same gentleness and calm to her countenance. "I have a considerably greater comprehension of the essence of what you call emotion and greater insight into what activities might produce such reactions in entities expressed finitely. But I have several questions to present to you, Peter."

There is a quick smile and wink from Zachary, as though

to say, *Well, Peter, she's turned the tables on you. Now it's your turn.*

Peter acknowledges the silent communication from Zachary with a smile and turns back to Hope. "Please do ask your questions, dear ... Goodness! I almost called you 'dear lady' again, Hope. I guess that provides an example of how things work in finiteness. They become a habit. They become so familiar that one tends to get comfortable in them, and then there they are, a part of your daily life, like an old pair of shoes. But do ask away. I'll respond as best I can, supported by my colleagues, here." He glances around the group.

Again, Peter notes that what he hears from her comes as utter softness, like a gentle spring breeze. "If I may ask, Peter, what is it that causes such a state as the Realm of Laughter to dissipate? Why do you substitute laughter with some of your other emotional expressions that I noted here and there in our experiences together? It would seem to me that, once having found a desirable emotion, one would choose to remain in it."

Peter fidgets and glances over at Zachary who, as is his custom, is on an elbow, fidgeting with the greenery beneath him. He looks up at Peter and shrugs as if to say, *There's a good one for you, Pete. Let's see how you handle this one.*

Peter can't help but smile at that. "Well, Hope, let's take the Earth, for example. When you're in a physical body in the Earth, it seems that there are so many things to deal with. Each day is filled with, well, let's say, activities. Some are expected, some are known and familiar, and some are surprises or accidents. Each of these, then, triggers ... Hmm. How *does* it work? I guess they trigger a string of memories, familiarity, and that familiarity seems to cause a reaction to different situations. So they draw on their past and their experience and use that to deal with anything that's before them."

A little tinkle of laughter comes from Zachary. Peter glances over and realizes that what he's expressed hasn't been clear at all, at least not to Hope, who is seated courteously, attentively studying Peter, striving to grasp the essence of what he is saying.

Paul turns around, and Peter can see that his face is illuminated with humor, as well. He looks at Elizabeth beside him, and she is smiling to encourage him. Rebecca, seated rather serenely, is nodding, as though confirming Peter's comments. He takes some reassurance from this, for at least one in the group seems to understand his explanation.

Hope breaks Peter's mental assessment. "So, if I perceive this correctly, Peter, it is as though one has a collection of these emotions, as you call them, and depending upon what they are enduring or experiencing, they choose from this collection to fit the occasion. Is that reasonably accurate?"

Peter himself even chuckles at this, for it sounds like people in the Earth have an inventory in their head with a little person who walks along studying the shelves and selects one or another according to the situation. "Well, Hope, I guess I have a lot to learn to be efficient at communicating with entities such as yourself. It's difficult to define these things, not only to you but also for those in the Earth. I'm not sure what I can say that would give you a better understanding,." He turns to Zachary. "Do you have a suggestion, Zack? You are so adept at these things."

Zachary is still looking down, gently brushing the greenery to and fro, almost as though he were speaking to it. "If I were you, I'd show her, Pete. You know, like you and I do. Showing and doing is far better than attempting simply to explain something. Or didn't you think so?"

"You're certainly right, Zack. I did, I learned a great deal that way. Far more than I ever could have by sitting around hearing someone talk about it. Could you show us, then?"

"Sure thing, Pete. Does that suit you, Hope?"

Hope responds like flowing music, color, and light. "It would seem that would be quite helpful, Zachary, if it isn't any inconvenience to you."

Zachary simply nods, studying her. Peter can almost hear his thoughts, *Goodness, we have a lot to teach this one, don't we?* Peter realizes this is true, and Zachary shields a wink at Peter by glancing off to the side.

"If it wouldn't be a bother, Zachary" Paul interjects, "Might we, on the way, stop and see Wilbur? If you'll recall, I mentioned I do need to stop there and renew my presence with a number of them there, not the least of which is Wilbur. By the way, Peter, he's been asking about you."

Peter is naturally excited by this and rises to his feet.

As he does, Hope asks, "Is this one of those occasions where you have selected an emotion to suit an event?"

Peter laughs. "Yes, I guess you could say that, Hope. It is a reaction within stirred by a memory. You see, I remember Wilbur and how fond I am of him and his realm and much more. Probably more than I fully understand at present. But you'll understand more when we visit him. He'll be so enchanted to meet you. Is this acceptable, Zack?"

Zachary has also risen at this point and is brushing his cloak, as Peter has seen so often. "Why, of course. We have eternity, don't we?"

This brings a ripple of laughter from all, even Hope.

"Goodness, that's a lovely sound, Hope."

"Why, thank you, Peter. I learned it from your Realm of Laughter. It has a wonderful feeling within me, as though something opens when I laugh, and I like it very much."

"Well, you see? That's just what I mean. You brought the laughter forward when the rest of us did because you remembered it."

Hope looks at Peter. "I understand. Thank you."

Zachary, now finished with the rather ceremonious brushing and cleansing of his cloak, moves casually over to Hope. "If you don't mind, Hope, let me take a look about you and make sure things are as they should be for us to move into Wilbur's realm."

Instantly, Peter offers, "Oh, Zachary, might I do the honors here?"

"I was hoping you would."

Hope looks to Zachary and then to Peter. "Am I to be honored? If so, for what purpose?"

Laughter cascades from all of them, and Peter speaks quietly in the direction of Zachary. "You certainly are correct, Zachary. There's a great deal to be shared with this one." He turns back to Hope. "You see, Hope ... well, your presence would be just too bright, too powerful."

Examining herself, she turns back to him and fixes her perception (you would think of this as her eyes) on Peter, clear, incredibly deep and shining. "Will I offend someone with my presence?"

"No, no, not that at all. It's just that, in these other realms of expression, sometimes they're, well, let's see. Correct me, anyone, if I err in this. But sometimes they're not vibrating or don't have the energy that you do. If you were to move into their realm, unusual things could occur. I'm not sure what they all are, but either you might not be seen, or you might be just ... well, too bright for their comfort."

Peter takes a quick look at Paul, who smiles and nods, and then at Zachary. "That's about as well put as I could do myself, Pete. Is that an acceptable understanding for the moment, Hope?"

"Yes, if it's what I am to know. This honor, then, what shall it be?"

"No, no, Hope. That was a sort of play on words. I simply mean that it's an honor to provide a cloak for you, and I think it's appropriate that Peter would be the one to so do."

He then motions to Peter who, remembering the past procedures well, goes within himself, creates the thought and brings it forth. As he does, he moves about Hope and covers her with an energy like spun light from his own essence. He comes around to the front and looks closely at her. "How does that feel to you, Hope?"

"Just fine, Peter. It has a warm, loving feeling. I know it to be of you. Thank you for the honor. It is a lovely one." Zachary is smiling and rocking on his heels, looking like a teacher would, pleased to watch a student perform so well. He then announces, "Shall we?" and swings to the forefront with Peter and the others following.

Zachary then reaches his hand up into the air. Peter notices with humor that Hope does the same, evidently believing this is what she should do. A sound comes forth, created by Zachary's up-stretched hand, and instantly behind that another is heard. It is Hope's.

This delights Peter and the others, as well, and one by one they all follow suit, their hands in the air, creating lovely sounds as they move into the luminous mist. Peter notes that Zachary has chosen this particular pathway. He remembers it must be for the purpose of moving entities not experienced in such realms of expression to and from these realms with the greatest probability of ease.

He hears softly inside his consciousness, *Correct, Peter. At least for the first trip or two, it's always a good idea. This is referred to as a pathway of light, or the tunnel of light if we were moving from the Earth to elsewhere. It's always a good choice for the first journey.*

Soon they are all gathered before the luminescence of the Crystal Workers' Realm. Peter marvels at how much more beautiful it is. Things seem to be in much more order, and as he looks around the greenery and the pathway, the greenery has a lushness that rivals his own Garden Realm. He looks at the structure. It is as he has always remembered it, seamless, smooth, and beautiful, but now it is radiant.

They pause and gather to talk briefly, and Zachary notes Peter's awareness of the change. "I told you, Pete, there were many more involved in our commission than I could express to you. Wilbur and all the others in this realm were no exceptions. Their efforts were with us all the while."

"So, this is a sort of return for their service?"

"You could say so, Pete. The Law of Return, you know." Zachary turns to Hope. "This is the Crystal Workers' Realm, Hope. As you have gathered from our conversation, those who dwell here contributed to what I call 'the commission' that involved you."

"Yes, I know, Zachary. I heard them and felt their prayers. I know them."

Smiling, Zachary turns to Peter. "There, see?"

Peter shifts himself this way and that, glancing between Hope and Zachary. "Forgive me, Zack. See what?"

"Well, it's like this. Everyone who contributes to a work in God's name becomes a part of God's Law while doing so. And God's Law states that as one gives, it is given to them. Wilbur and all the others here gave all that they knew to give to Hope, and to us as we served on the commission. As the grace of God flowed through them to Hope by their free will, they also received. That's what I meant by 'see.' See?" With a smile, he turns and calls over his shoulder. "Come along. They'll be waiting. They're sure to know we've arrived, with all the racket we made coming here," and he chuckles.

They move into the opening of the Great Hall, and Peter is taken aback, almost stopped in his movement, at the sheer beauty of the Crystal Workers' Realm.

Still along the one wall—the north wall, as he would think of it relevant to the Earth direction—are the magnificent crystals, but there are many more of them, gathered in small groups here and there, all aligned in certain directions.

It appears that the large chamber has been expanded and he marvels at the predominance of the purple hues coming from the groups of crystals. While he notes these colors and the sounds emanating from them, he hears a bold voice.

"Welcome, Peter, Zachary, Paul ... all of you. Come, please. Join us."

Peter is startled as he realizes it is Wilbur, literally aglow. Glancing around the room, he notes many others are equally so. He rushes to embrace Wilbur, and Wilbur laughs. "We heard your song, Peter. It was beautiful, and we knew it was you. We are so joyful to have you with us again. You remember my colleagues here. We wish to thank you from the center of our being for the privilege of being able to participate with you in the commission."

"It is I who thank you, Wilbur, and all of you. I know that it was only with the love and dedication of all of you that we were able to fulfill our intent."

Wilbur cannot restrain himself. "Oh, Peter, I can see you've made it."

Peter looks at him inquisitively. "Made it? What do you mean?"

"You've made it to oneness with God, haven't you?"

Peter is totally disarmed at this and stands momentarily without thought or word.

Zachary chimes in. "Yep, Wilbur, he made it."

"We feel so honored that you would return from such a position of oneness to visit us and there are so many things I would ask you, my friend. But you have guests here. Please do share them with all of us." Wilbur motions and the others who were standing back a distance come to join the group, which now has gathered in the center of the room.

"Well, of course, you remember Paul, and no one ever needs to introduce Zachary." Zachary merely grins and looks down. "And do you know Rebecca and Elizabeth?"

"Oh, yes, I remember them well."

"Well, then, let me now introduce to you Hope."

Wilbur stands. Intently and serenely he gazes into her countenance. "On behalf of all of my colleagues, we welcome you. We are so joyful that you emerged from your position of inward reflection, and for our small part of the commission."

As though it were a musical aria, the response from Hope

flows as simply thought-forms, music, color, and so much more. "I saw the beauty and sincerity of your intent. I know not by way of what mechanism you directed your intent, but I know the outcome as God's pure spirit and light. I know it to be good and know therefore all of you to be good workers in His name. I feel great honor and what you call joy within me to be with you."

Wilbur now guides Hope over to the crystals and begins to explain how they work to her. "So once we define a particular intent, we use the crystals we had past associations with when incarnated in the Earth and also in other realms. It is a means of focusing and tuning our prayer, our intent, to the recipient of our work. In the case of your commission, we joined to focus with all of our spiritual consciousness upon the commission, that it would be surrounded by the presence of God's Light. Peter, you may have discerned it as color and the movement of light and such, for we were using the entire spectrum of the crystals and energy levels of vibration that we are familiar with."

Wilbur turns to speak directly to Hope. "I do not wish to imply that we are as limited as that sounds, although at one time, indeed, we were. We thought of the crystals as having some sort of power in and of themselves, and we sought ways to invoke that or to control that within the crystal and to make it perform for us. This misconception was more or less a memory from the period in the Earth called the Atlantean time. As a dear friend and leader from that time showed us, that wasn't it at all. It was the faith within one's being that was projected to and through the crystal, and the crystal then became a tool or mechanism to direct, to amplify, and to hold our intent. So we have all now grasped this. We have applied this truth, and it has elevated the consciousness of all in our realm.

"Since we have all agreed in harmony and joy to this realization, we and our realm have progressed considerably.

Although I do not have a measure by which I can tell you how much we have progressed, I know it to be considerable, just by the resonance of joy and the presence of His light within us."

Murmurs of delight from all the others here affirm what Wilbur has explained.

Throughout all this Peter has stood admiring the visible growth and progression of his friend Wilbur.

Zachary leans in from Peter's left. "See? That's what I meant outside. That's what I was trying to tell you, Peter. We all gain."

"I do see, Zachary. That's pretty terrific stuff."

Of course, this exchange is known by all of the others, and laughter fills the room.

During the laughter, Hope moves over, much more composed than the rest, to stand close to the crystals. "Wilbur," she notes softly, "the crystals are emitting sounds."

Wilbur, also now more composed, moves to where Hope is standing, before an immense crystal, radiating light from within its being, pulsing, wave upon wave of energy coming from it, which produce sound and light that ricochets about the room.

Wilbur explains in the same tone of voice as Hope's. "We have so acclimated ourselves to these crystals, each of us, that they are as an extension of our being. Therefore, our laughter resonates through and from within the crystals. We have placed many, many Earth centuries of work into and through these crystals, always in God's name, but never fully understanding the function and the truth behind what we were doing. Only since working with and for you, dear Hope, have we made this discovery. So you see, we have much to be thankful for and much to honor you for, regarding our growth."

Hope looks at Wilbur, and he feels a flood of warmth move throughout him. He notes Rebecca standing nearby and extends an embrace to her, and then wraps an arm about Hope, and there they stand.

"I knew there was more, Rebecca. I knew that from long ago. I also know that there is more to be shared with Hope. I am in absolute support of your work, Hope, as are all of us here." He looks around and realizes that the others have come to gather about them. "I also know Zachary intends to share with you some valuable experiences. But before you leave, we all wish you to know that we will, in our newly recovered awareness, contribute all we can to those activities. And should you encounter any of the entities who are interacting with those in the Earth we've been working with, it would be our great joy if you would communicate that to them."

He looks at Zachary who nods an affirmation that it will be explained.

Hope turns back to Wilbur, with the melodious sweetness of her expression. "These things you ask I will do. You have all contributed much to my understanding of this realm of expression, and I am joyful in the center of my being for having known each of you." She then dispatches a bit of pinkish light to each of them, which Peter instantly recognizes to be her angelic essence.

Peter wonders for a moment how she was able to do that through his cloak and looks at Zachary who is shaking his head as if to say, *Not now, Peter. Don't ask now.*

Nodding, Peter accepts, and Zachary gathers them up. After exchanging further wishes of farewell for the present, they move outside of the Crystal Workers' Hall. Peter takes a last look over his shoulder, marveling again at its radiance and at the greenery. Before he can turn back, he hears the gentle tinkling of Zachary's trademark, and off they go again.

They are in a sphere of luminosity. Peter discerns that the movement is very swift but yet a great distance. He can feel more and more of an essence, something strange, as though it were attempting to attach itself to him somehow, yet it seems to fall effortlessly from the periphery of his being, his cloak. Zachary moves over beside him. "You detected that?"

"Are you referring to the ... whatever it is I felt subtly pulling on the outside of my being? Yes, I did."

"Do you wish to answer it?"

"You mean it's a call of some sort?" Peter studies Zachary's more serious countenance. He notes that the others are observing them, listening.

Before he can ask further, Hope responds. "Do what you are called to do, Peter, always. I would have it no other way."

Zachary, smiling now, turns to Hope. "That is kind and generous of you, Hope, but this isn't a call from the Father."

Nodding in understanding, Hope remains silent.

"But duly noted, Pete. If you wish to answer the call, Hope can learn from this experience as well as she could any one of the others I had available as choices."

All the while they have been moving. Now Peter discerns that they have begun to slow slightly, continuing to slow until Peter feels as though they are motionless.

Now he feels a sort of finger of light, soft, warm. He detects nothing hostile or errant about it as he tries to perceive it. In fact, it has a bit of a golden glow that is familiar to him, reminding him somewhat of the entity in the Hall of Wisdom. "I don't feel anything disturbing about this, Zachary, but rather a kind of good feeling. Is it being directed specifically at me?"

"It is indeed directed at you, Peter, and only you, for it is a message and the person sending it is unaware of us being with you since he is in the Earth."

"Well, I don't know much about the person so far, though I do I know it's a 'he in the Earth.' What more can you tell me?"

"I didn't mean to lead you, Pete. I was actually trying to stay out of your way and allow your free will to choose."

"Well, I choose to know what this is all about."

"That's you, Pete, direct and to the point." Zachary, chuckling a bit, glances at Hope.

She then draws upon the memory of the Realm of Laughter and issues forth a bit of her own, and they all have a moment of merriment at this.

Zachary turns back to Peter. "It is your friend who remained behind when you departed the Earth. You remember him?"

Pausing to search within himself, Peter exclaims, "Abe! We're talking about Abe?"

"Yes."

"How is it that Abe is calling me?"

"Through prayer."

"Why is he calling me?"

"Well, that's for you to discover, Peter. Why not visit him?"

The thought of visiting Abe draws forth a myriad of memories for Peter. He is instantly flooded with the warm memory of his mate, his family, his friends, and much more. All this makes a colorful radiance come from Peter.

Hope notices this. "That is very lovely, Peter. Those are memories that you are drawing from within you?"

No one in the presence of Hope's gentle innocence can resist being melted by the sincerity of her being. Peter is no exception. "You know, Hope, I named you well when I called you Dear Lady, for you are both of those. But to answer your question, yes these are memories. Come closer and perhaps you can experience them first hand.

Hope moves adjacent to Peter, reaching out, as though you would think of someone extending their hand, to touch the memories. "These are lovely, Peter. You have so many of them, and they are filled with what you call goodness. Is that correct?"

"Correct."

"How do you know memories that would be to the contrary? Are there memories in opposition to laughter and joy?" Peter pauses to reflect. "Well, Hope, I guess not. Not now, anyway. Whatever they might have been, I have forgotten them, or they have fallen away like leaves from a tree in its season."

Peter looks over to see Paul nodding, as though complimenting Peter's choices, remaining silent but supportive.

"So, Pete, Hope, how about we visit Abe and see what's up?"

"I'd forgotten how you waste no time or effort, Zack. That's something I've always found endearing about you."

"Well, Abe's in prayer now, Peter, and this would be a good time to visit."

"We wouldn't be disturbing him?"

"Not at all. The prayer is directed to you. He would consider it an honor, a privilege, even a miracle, if you were to visit."

"A miracle?"

"Well, think about it, Pete. Put yourself in his place, had it been he who departed and you were there, quietly praying on his behalf or for him."

"Yes. Yes, Zachary. I do see what you mean. Let's go."

Zachary moves the entire group instantly into the chamber where we find Abe. On his head he has the small circular cap and in his lap some documents. He has, as well, his prayer shawl over his shoulders. The entourage studies the room. Candles are burning, and Peter feels their warmth as well as the warmth of the love from his dear and trusted old friend.

After Hope is given some explanations to a number of questions, Zachary turns to Peter. "Listen now, Peter. Very carefully, listen. Try to catch the flow of his prayer. You'll know it when you have it because it's like a gentle, warm light coming from the center of his being."

Hope moves to Peter's side. "If you would like, Peter, I will show it to you."

"You will show it to me? You can perceive it?"

"Yes, I can."

"How is it that you can see it and I cannot?"

She glances over to Zachary, and Zachary responds. "We can delve more into that later, but for now it's this simple: She hasn't as many memories, as yet, to block her perception."

"Okay. Yes, Hope, if you would, please show me."

Peter can see a soft, rose-colored shaft of light moving from Hope, reaching out and cascading down and around his friend. He notices that Abe appears to have aged, though he seems very much at peace. In that instant, Abe's body straightens.

"He feels that, Hope. Zachary, he's feeling that!"

"Indeed," responds Zachary. "He is a man of God."

Hope continues to cascade the soft rosy hue. Now Peter begins to discern something that looks like an undulating flow from Abe's being, just near the bottom of his rib cage. Zachary motions him to position himself in front of it. All the while, the group is probably three to four feet above floor level in Abe's "prayer room," as he calls it, which is an unused bedroom since his son moved out.

Abe straightens himself further as he feels what is going on. The group can perceive his thoughts: *I have reached God. I feel the presence of His angels!*

Joy nearly overwhelms Peter. He turns to Zachary. "I never hoped to be able to hear him again."

"Why not?"

"Well, I just didn't, Zachary."

Elizabeth now comes to Peter's side. "He is a wonderful friend."

"Yes. The best I ever had, present company excepted." Peter offers a smile to the group.

"No offense, Peter. We understand," responds Paul.

"Peter," reminds Zachary, "back to Abe, please. If you

want this message, now is the time."

Listening and focusing, Peter hears Abe.

"If you're out there, Pete, and if you can hear me, you're not going to believe what's happened. Remember my oldest son? I'm sure you do. You always favored him. Well, he and your daughter, Miriam ... They're going to get married! And I just wanted to talk to you. I hope it's okay with you and I hope our friendship can continue and grow stronger as our families join through this union of our children."

(The words that follow are difficult to translate because there is such an intense resonance between Abe and Peter, a deep field of love, and companionship exists between them. In essence, it boils down to this:

Abe is praying to Peter. True, he is praying to God, but he is talking to Peter, trying to explain and to tell him how pleased he is in spite of his Jewish heritage and Peter's family's Christian status. All this is aside, for Abe is, above all else, a man of God. He is trying to express to Peter how privileged and beautiful it is that their friendship might endure in the Earth for generations to come through the lineage of their two families, bound first by the love between them and now by the marriage between his son and Peter's daughter.)

Peter is reveling in the emotional bond and is also trying to reciprocate. Abe is silent and listening, rocking and uttering his soft prayer in a low, repetitive chant, half-sung and half-spoken.

Zachary has been studying Peter carefully. "Well, Peter, a wonderful turn of events, wouldn't you say?"

"Dumbfounding, Zachary. I had forgotten how much Mirry had probably grown, and that she and Abe's son ... Well, they were always close, but everyone thought of them as brother and sister. I never dreamed ... Oh, I'll bet her mother has had a delightful time. And Abe's wife, too."

"Both are very joyful about it. I checked while you were busy."

"I am truly touched. I only regret I cannot communicate with Abe."

"Well, let's see what we can do here," Zachary offers with a twinkle in his eyes.

"What do you mean, Zack?"

"Just give me a moment or two."

The group moves back a bit as Zachary comes to the forefront. Peter can see that he is studying the room, looking over at the candles that Abe has lit and glancing all about. There on a bureau is the photograph we had seen near the very beginning of our sojourn with Peter when Abe was praying, nearly begging, that Peter would not die. It is of Abe and Peter, taken many years ago, probably thirty, thirty-five years earlier when they first met.

"Do I have your permission to give him a confirmation?"

"Yes, Zachary. It won't interfere with him?"

Zachary smiles gently at Peter. "No."

Peter can hear Paul behind him. "Zachary has done this before. Remember, as he always says, one needs to be mindful for whom they work."

Peter nods and watches in wonder.

Zachary hesitates no longer. Abe has the door closed as well as the only window. The only illumination comes from the several soft, small candles, flickering light on Abe's face.

Peter watches as Zachary seems to be pulsing somehow, moving in strange ways that he cannot recall.

Suddenly, something moves from Zachary, passing over the candles, extinguishing the one in the middle, and over to the bureau, whereupon the photograph in the small frame falls over, as it had those years before, once again startling Abe, who looks up abruptly.

Abe stands and exclaims, "Thank you, Peter!"

We will need to conclude here because we are so close to the Earth. Since our Channel is there and the emotion in this event is intense, we are having difficulty sustaining this communication without the possibility of disrupting the Channel.

Therefore, we now call upon the Spirit of God to bless and surround all present, and to make whole and balanced all involved here, including this Channel and those in all the realms adjacent to the Earth who have participated in permitting this work to be fulfilled.

CHAPTER 2

A Wagon for Bobby

MAY 3, 1992

*As we prepare to rejoin Peter and his colleagues, we
have been requested to offer these comments on behalf of
Zachary, Paul, and several others who are, as yet, unidenti-
fied to you: For this and perhaps several of these future meetings, there will be a heightening of activity and significant
movement. Considerable detail will need to be passed over in
the next few "chapters" due to the rapidity of the movement.
Should this spawn the numerous questions from you regarding that detail, which we suspect will be the case, we will respond to your questions, should you request it.* [Ed. Note: The
Q&A readings can be found in their entirety in the books called
"Study Guides" that accompany the Peter Chronicles.]

*So now we return to join Peter and his friends. We find
them having left Abe's quarters and moved away from the
Earth, presently located near it but not actually within the
finiteness of it. For reference, you could say that they are at
that level of consciousness where new arrivals, those souls
who have recently departed the Earth, are entering the unlimited realms of existence and are first greeted. We remind you
that much detail will be moved through quickly due to the nature of the works just ahead.*

We find Peter speaking with exuberance, primarily to
Zachary, regarding the previous activity involving
the extinguishing of the candle and the tipping
over, once again, of the photograph on the bureau in Abe's
prayer room. "Would you call that an act of poltergeist, Zack?
Is that sort of thing accepted? You know, in view of the na-

ture of our works and the commissions and such, does *"He"* approve of such things?"

Constraining his humor, Zachary responds to Peter in equal seriousness as Peter's comment was to him. "To date, I've had no dressing-down, as you call it in the Earth, for having performed such actions."

With a wink at Paul, who is laughing quietly in the background, Zachary continues. "But you see, Peter, it is the circumstance that determines whether or not such activities can be performed within God's Laws. As you know, Abe is a man of God. His prayer room is like a sanctuary, made hallow by his faith and his prayers, and that has a purifying or neutralizing element. Any intent that is equally pure and performed, not out of a self-oriented intent but as an act of charity or grace, is certainly condoned. Understand?"

Studying Zachary, Peter nods, with numerous further questions passing through his consciousness.

Hope is the next to speak. "Peter, your friend Abe is such a lovely person. I would like to know more about him at his eternal level. What can you tell me?"

Taken off-guard by this question, Peter considers Hope's question. "Actually, Hope, I know little about that. I believe I saw Abe as I was leaving the Earth, did I not, Paul?"

"Yes, we did, Peter. Good that you recalled that."

"I would conclude," Peter continues, "that because Abe is a man of God that he has had numerous experiences of charitable and kindly activity in earlier incarnations. But as for specifics, I only have a vague recall of our past associations in previous lifetimes, and they wouldn't completely answer your question."

There is a pause, and Zachary speaks. "Hope, we can visit the records if you'd like at some point, and I will obtain that information for you. But if you will forgive me, Paul has something he needs to do as long as we are here within the, I'll call it, energies of the Earth. If the rest of you wouldn't mind, I would like to honor Paul's intent and turn this activity over to him for a time. Is that acceptable to you, Hope?"

"Yes, of course. And I will be gladdened to contribute as I can to any activities that are before you, Paul. You have but to identify those to me."

As ever, Peter is amazed by the immediacy of Hope's actions and reactions. To date, he has no recall of any instance where she has hesitated or questioned anything placed before her. As he notes this inwardly with admiration, she turns to look at him, and he instantly realizes that she is aware of his thoughts. She smiles and radiates a bit of rosy glow to him, and Peter, just a bit embarrassed, smiles in return.

"Paul," asks Rebecca, "how do you wish us to accompany you, perceived or unperceived?"

Peter, now more alert, for obviously, they are about to engage in something new or unique, listens intently.

"Thank you, Rebecca, for your consideration. There is no need for you to be concerned about that at the moment. Let us simply proceed, for the need is at hand for my presence elsewhere."

Much more swiftly than Peter can recall Paul ever acting before, he turns and assumes the lead, which is also surprising to Peter, for Zachary has almost always done so in the past.

The movement is brisk, and Peter detects a general air of familiarity to it, but nothing specific comes to his consciousness. Then Paul abruptly stops the group. "I ask all of you to prepare yourselves, for I must engage the consciousness of the Earth. It is entirely possible that you can contribute, and therefore I welcome you to be at my aide."

All quickly offer their affirmation, and without another word, Paul turns and moves off again. This time Peter detects that they are entering into greater density, not unlike that which he had just experienced when moving to rejoin Abe. As they continue, Peter's thoughts dance momentarily back to his beloved Mirry and Abe's son, Jacob, and thoughts of their union pass through his consciousness.

They are interrupted by Paul's gentle voice. "We have arrived. If you will pause here a moment, I must make contact with some associates."

Peter's attention snaps back to full alert status. As he has learned to do, he follows Paul with his consciousness, staying at a reasonable distance. Two beings of light move towards Paul, and in a moment they come together. Very soon, Paul calls him and the others, and Peter feels Zachary, Rebecca, Elizabeth, and Hope sort of sweep him along with them as they respond to Paul's call.

They are now before Paul and the two entities. Zachary greets them warmly, apparently knowing them, and turns to introduce the others. "Chen, let me introduce you to my friends. Here is Rebecca, Elizabeth, and this is Hope, and my friend Peter."

Chen turns to each one after the other and greets them. Peter is touched deeply by the sincerity he feels flow from Chen, who is expressing himself in a form recognizable by Peter as an Earth body. As Peter studies the depth and eternal glow emanating from Chen's eyes, Peter marvels at the radiance around him. But above all, he has a sense of well-being, of all things being at ease, a sense of peace.

Chen then turns to introduce the other entity. "This is my friend Edol. Edol is new here in our work, so I would like you to greet him with a welcoming sense of camaraderie."

Peter glances over at Zachary, thinking, *Does not Edol hear this? Is he not embarrassed?*

Zachary responds to Peter, unheard by the others. *No, he does not, Peter, any more than the others hear this communication between us. It is the right of individuality in action.*

Peter steps forward and embraces Edol, surprising even himself at his own boldness. Then he turns to introduce Hope, Elizabeth, and Rebecca, and they, as well, embrace Edol.

Chen speaks quickly then. "Paul, the time is near for

your commission here. We are ready to assist you, and others have gathered here who are also prepared to meet their wards or their commissions, as well." He then turns to Hope. "You are familiar with these works, Hope?"

"I do know of them. I have brethren who have served in this capacity. I am ready to serve with you however you might deem it appropriate. My friends here, Rebecca and Elizabeth, have also offered themselves to any commission where they might be of service."

All this blurs Peter's consciousness. *What brethren is Hope speaking of? And how is it that Chen knows these things about Hope?*

Before Peter's questions can be answered by anyone, Chen asks, "And you are the Peter of Hope's commission?"

Startled, Peter begins to stammer. "Uh, well, yes, I, I guess I am, uh, known as ..."

Zachary interrupts, smiling. "Yep, he is one and the same. He is that Peter."

"Very good. Then you will assist, as well?"

Peter is now utterly disarmed. "Uh, Sir? Uh, Chen? I will gladly contribute wherever I can, but, uh, you should know that I have no idea what is transpiring here."

"Oh yes, of course. It is that Edol and I are waiting for several souls to depart from the Earth. The realm of consciousness that we are in is called Czechoslovakia. It is a time of conflict, and a number of souls will be departing, as have a number already. These several souls that we are waiting for are a part of our soul group work. Therefore, we have been commissioned to greet them and guide them from the Earth through the limiting realms to the light. Paul here also has one for whom he is preparing to do the same."

Paul simply nods in affirmation to Chen's comments.

Peter recalls these countries. "Might I ask why there is a conflict here?"

Chen yields to Zachary. "Much has happened in the

Earth since you departed, Pete. We can explain this to you later. The need now is immediate. Understand?"

Nodding vigorously, Peter cannot find words to speak.

Chen turns briskly and begins to move, Edol at his side, followed immediately by Paul, Rebecca, Elizabeth, and Hope, who are side by side. Zachary scoops up Peter's "arm" (as it were) and whisks him along.

Peter perceives density all about him. He sees shadows, wispy figures. He hears sounds. He feels energies, emotions. These experiences fall harmlessly off him, and his cloak begins to pulse and emanate a glow around him.

"Watch it now," Zachary reminds him. "Keep yourself in appropriate constraint. These are not our realms here. We've no right to interfere. We're merely passing through them."

Peter nods and turns back to observe the entities, waves of them, a veritable sea of faces peering at him, calling, beckoning. Then all manner of what Peter recalls to be Earth-realm emotions and attitudes can be felt whishing by him.

Suddenly the entourage moves into what Peter perceives to be a sphere of light. They come to rest and gather around with many others. He notes with awe that each seems more radiant than the other. Many of them come forward and greet Chen and Edol and all of the others, including himself. He marvels at the assembly of such beautiful souls with their radiant cloaks and their emanations. He can find very few words to define this. They are utterly sweet, forgiving and loving, and they emanate all-around wellness.

There is a sound, and Peter turns to see what it is. Two of the entities move quickly from the great sphere of light. He remembers having been to one such sphere, but his memories cannot continue, as his consciousness follows the movement of these two beings of light.

Off in the distance, a wispy stream of light is moving upwards, upwards until the two entities are each on either side of this rather weak-looking stream of light. Peter perceives the light draw unto itself and collect at a point between the two entities of light. In the twinkling of an eye (as might be said in the Earth), the two surround this weak orb with what Peter knows to be the cloak of their own spirituality. Slowly at first and then with increasing speed, they move upward. And then they are gone.

Another sound, and two more entities come. The scenario is repeated, again and again. Another sound is heard, this time very, very close. Peter studies it. It is not like the noise of an explosion, not like a pop or a bang. It is like ripping fabric, stretched to its limit until the molecular structure utterly gives way.

He notes in his consciousness that he must ask about this, but before he can think any other thoughts, Paul begins to move, slowly at first, his luminosity growing. It is as though Peter is vacuumed up in the sort of tailwind of Paul's movement. Whoosh! And Paul, along with Peter, Zachary, Rebecca, Elizabeth, and Hope are surging through darkness, time and space. Moving, moving ...

Peter begins to see a dull grayish-white filament, an undulating stream of light moving slowly upwards, a thread of light moving through a tunnel of darkness.

"This is the veil of separation, Peter," he hears from Zachary. "Paul is moving to meet this soul, this person, who has just 'died' in the Earth."

The next moment, Peter sees Paul at the side of this very dim light. Hope, Rebecca, and Elizabeth swoosh in and are now surrounding the light.

Peter hears another sound he cannot quite equate. This time, it is like something coming together, a feeling more than a sound, as if something has assembled itself from having been separate. In that moment, where the ribbon or stream of light was previously, now there is a rather weak luminous sphere. Peter observes Paul slowly surrounding it with light, and Hope, Elizabeth, and Rebecca continuing to move around

Paul and the sphere. Here and there, Peter perceives the three sending little rivulets of light out into the darkness. He cannot quite understand why, but he notes with curiosity that they seem to do this in different directions.

Then, he sees that Paul, along with Elizabeth, Rebecca, and Hope, are beginning to rise. As he starts to follow, he feels Zachary's touch. "We'll follow them in a moment, but first I think it would be good for you to watch."

"Watch what?" asks Peter, somewhat frustrated by his friend. "There is nothing to be seen but utter darkness, this veil of ... what did you call it?"

"I guess it's a veil of death, for lack of a better term, Peter, though that has a rather harsh connotation to it, don't you think?"

Peter begins to reflect inwardly, and Zachary pauses, awaiting Peter's re-emergence. Several moments pass. "I don't yet understand why, but it's enough for me to know you believe there is value in our remaining here."

"Good."

Peter notes that Zachary is more intense than normal, his outer periphery very energized. As he looks about himself to perceive his own outer periphery, he realizes with curious interest that it is identical to Zachary's. Although he cannot recall having done anything to produce this, nonetheless, it is highly charged, very intense.

"Watch now, Pete. Look over here."

All of a sudden, there is another light wiggling its way up into the darkness, and another, and yet a third. But these are different somehow, and Peter watches intensely. As one ribbon of light moves upward, there is a sudden burst of light at its terminus, as though the light snaps into itself, forming a sphere. It reminds Peter of a retractable ruler. Then, all three spheres, brightly luminous, begin to slowly move and, to Peter's amazement, the direction is toward him and Zachary. Slowly, they gently drift to Zachary and Peter's position.

Astonished, he hears Zachary call out, "Greetings!"

"Greetings, Zachary," he hears from the first sphere, followed by the same from the other two.

Peter is in a state of abject wonder and curiosity.

"How fare you, Zachary?"

"Very well, John."

He hears similar comments from the other two.

"Your sojourns in the Earth went well, then?"

Zachary answers and a brief discussion takes place, then Zachary gestures to Peter. "This is Peter's first return to this level. I wanted him to observe entities such as yourselves who are returning from having performed benevolent sojourns in the Earth."

Instantly, the three spheres are very close to Peter. So close that, for a moment, he feels uncomfortable.

"I'm John, this is Beth, and over here is our friend ..."

There is a pause that grows awkward before the third entity speaks for itself. "I am not known specifically by a name any longer, Peter, for I have passed beyond that. But if you would like, you might call me Samuel, for I have borne that name at one time."

"Uh, yes, uh, Samuel, and well, all of you, I'm delighted to meet you. Uh, do I understand correctly that you have just departed from lifetimes in the Earth? I mean, you just, uh ... "

John answers, with a note of humor. "Yes, Peter. We just died. Frankly, I'm glad that's over. It was a joyous work, being in such service, but we will all be pleased to move out of finiteness again. If you don't mind, we would like to do that now. Would you care to join us?"

Peter hesitates. "Well, uh, you see, we have ... "

"We'd be glad to, John," interjects Zachary. "We were with Paul, who had a commission here and who is already ahead of us with several other colleagues. So yes, we'll journey with you, and we can talk once we reach our destination. Ready, Pete?"

Peter, in his consciousness, wants to say, *Ready? What are you talking about, Zachary? I haven't the vaguest idea what's gone on here in the last, I don't know, however long it's been. And you ask me if I'm ready?* But all that is spoken by Peter is, "Yes, I'm ready."

The movement is slow at first and then increases in speed. Peter notes that, as the speed increases, the darkness begins to change. The frequency of the appearance of other entities and the thought-forms (which he now knows are expressed in the form of energized bands of color and sound) is diminishing. Then, as he perceives lightness and radiance, he realizes how dense and intense the realms in which he had just been actually are, for he now has a comparison.

Their movement has become remarkably fast when Peter notices an abrupt sound and sensation, an essence that passes over his being. From past experience, he knows this to be one of the, as called, veils, the demarcations that separate realms of expression. Before he has time to reflect on this, the group comes to a stop. A brilliant white mist surrounds them, and then Peter feels movement forward again and a rush of joyousness. For a moment he thinks it is the Realm of the Angels. The essence flows through him, pulsing, quickening, charging, energizing, purifying, enlightening, blessing, and so forth, until there is simply absolute bliss. *We must have returned to the Realm of the Angels!*

Peter is so startled by what happens next that he stops and gasps. Zachary, who is just a bit ahead, has turned to look at Peter, smiling, with his hands on his hips. Zachary is in a physical form! He knows it to be Zachary, for he knows the essence of Zachary. He turns to look at the three others. They, as well, have taken on physical bodies. Quickly, he looks down at himself, and he sees his hands, his body. "Zachary! What's happened? Are we back in the Earth? Am I … am I re-born?"

Zachary, constraining himself but visibly finding humor

in all this, walks over to him and, as though to illustrate the answer to Peter's question, slaps a hand on his shoulder, nearly knocking Peter down, for he is utterly unprepared. "How's it feel, Pete? You know, the good ol' physical form, finiteness, and all that sort?"

Before Peter can respond, momentarily very surprised by all this, Zachary continues, more gently, more serious. "Peter, I know things are happening quickly here, but that's out of necessity. Where we are now and what you perceived to be movement through what we've referred to as a veil was a shift from the Earth realm of finite consciousness to the next immediate realm of expression. Since this is the realm where many, many entities go soon after they depart the Earth, it is, as you might expect, expressed in a form, a structure that is most comfortable and acceptable to them.

"They think they have just died. This is the next realm of progression from the Earth for those who need to pause. For some, it will be a brief stay. Others will remain longer. Here, there is the privilege of tending to their needs, encouraging them, guiding them." He studies Peter, who is looking down, flexing and wiggling his fingers and toes. "Are you uncomfortable there, Pete? This isn't permanent, you know. It's just that, if we're going to be here and help Paul and the others, it's sort of the dress code here."

Peter is lightening up now and looks into his friend's eyes, and then his face shows the crinkle of a grin. Finally, he begins to laugh, and Zachary joins him.

Their laughter subsides, and this time it is Peter who slaps Zachary on the back. "Zachary, you are, without question, the most exciting individual to be with of anyone I have ever known. There is always some new experience. Everything with you is always in a state of change and learning."

Zachary shrugs, feigning an *I have no idea know what you're talking about* look. "I'm just doing what comes natural, as they say. And I like to keep moving. Don't you?"

"I guess so, Zack."

"Well, let's not tarry here. We actually do need to get moving. If you notice, we're alone. John and the others have gone on ahead." Zachary begins to stride off, then turns to wait for his friend. Peter is remembering the motions of walking. "An awkward mode of transportation, isn't it, Pete?"

Peter laughs at how true it is. He had forgotten how effortlessly they typically move. Now he is reminded of the feeling of being finite.

Zachary puts an arm under Peter's elbow, as though he is trying to hold him up, and they chuckle and meander down a lovely path. It seems to Peter to be finely crushed pebbles. There is green to the right and left, a few beds of flowers here and there, a few trees, and so on. Then, just ahead, he sees Paul standing, looking as though he is speaking to someone. He realizes it is Hope and gasps at her beauty. She is utterly radiant.

Hope looks up at Peter, smiling as she notes his thought. He feels a bit of her pinkish energy bounce off him and then stops several, hanging several feet in front of him. He reaches a hand out to touch the rosy glow.

"That's right, Pete," comments Zachary off to his side. "You still have your cloak. All of us do, only they can't be seen in the literal sense. In fact, even the new arrivals do."

Paul is waving at them as they continue on. Peter marvels at Paul's youthfulness, thinking he looks to be in his late teens or early twenties. Paul just smiles and nods, he, too, having perceived Peter's thought.

Peter then wonders what Elizabeth and Rebecca look like and he looks around to see. There is Rebecca, flowing black hair falling onto her shoulders and eyes with such a depth of loveliness. She is smiling at him with a wondrous softness, and Peter thinks, *They're all just so beautiful. Just radiant.* Then he hears a resonance within himself, and as he focuses on that, he hears, *You look quite lovely, as well, Peter.* Immediately, he recognizes the essence to be Elizabeth. "Thank you, Elizabeth."

Paul touches Peter's shoulder. Peter notes again how strange it feels, this finite expression. "This is my commission, Peter." Peter looks beside Paul and studies the person there, who seems to be growing younger right before him. "He was wounded in a battle and, as you know, I have just brought him here. He is not entirely, what you would call, conscious at the moment. I will remain here to assist him as that consciousness grows and he needs help, answering his questions, helping him understand ... you know, like we all did with you some time ago."

There is still a look of fatigue and even fear on this one, yet his eyes are firmly closed.

"Why doesn't he open his eyes, Paul?"

"He is frightened. He's afraid that his life on Earth wasn't sufficient and that perhaps he will not be 'accepted in Heaven'."

This comment strikes a chord in Peter, for he can remember such thinking, such attitudes and beliefs, and he realizes something he hadn't considered for a long time.

Paul addresses Peter's thoughts. "Heaven is more an attitude of one's consciousness, one's spirit and acceptance, than a place, Peter. Heaven is where the joyful of heart exist, wherever that might be in any realm. But if you wish to know if there is a 'heaven' per se, I would have to answer that question with a yes."

"Where is it, Paul? I don't mean to take you away from your commission here, but he seems half asleep, anyway."

"No problem, Peter. I am helping him here, even as we speak."

"You are?"

"Of course."

"What are you doing? I don't see you doing anything."

Paul laughs softly as Zachary answers. "You're expressed finitely here, but you are infinite, aren't you?"

"Yes, I would say so. Based on my recent experiences, I would have to say a definite yes."

"Well then, use your less finite perception. That's all."

Peter realizes then how quickly he had adopted the expressions of finiteness that, for a few brief minutes (Earth measure), he had relinquished his infinite capacity. As he realizes this, he also sees that it takes a bit of focusing to draw it back. "How strange, Paul! I have two or three questions pending before you already, and there's so much more I want to understand. I thought once I had reached the level of the Angels, I would know everything. But it doesn't seem so."

Peter can feel the radiance of Hope falling upon his being, and also that from Rebecca and Elizabeth.

Suddenly, he sees Paul surrounding the commission with his essence. "Paul, I can see what you are doing! I literally see it from my higher perception. It's a shimmering collection of light or energy surrounding him now. I see where little dashes of light move inward towards him, and then the rest seems to circle around and around him. Is that how you're helping him?"

"Yes, Peter. That is how I am helping him."

Studying Paul closely and Paul's commission, Peter reflects and thinks about the many concepts that people incarnate in the Earth have about the process of death, remembering for a moment his own. Then he turns back to Paul. "Why did this entity come here and I went somewhere else?"

"You know that answer, Pete. That's an easy one." Again, it is Zachary answering, who has moved to stand beside him. The group is now in a loose semi-circle around Paul's commission.

"Peter," explains Paul, "I would like to make a suggestion. I'll be here for awhile to be present to afford him whatever his needs are. I have pledged to do so. But you and the others might wish to wander around here a bit and talk to some of the other workers. Maybe visit some of the places and see what goes on here."

"Really? Could we do that?"

Zachary laughs. "He wouldn't offer if you couldn't do it, Pete."

"Oh, true. I guess all of this is just a bit much for me to grasp so quickly."

Zachary nods to Hope, Rebecca, and Elizabeth. "What of you three? Do you wish to remain here or join us?"

Peter is surprised to hear Hope say, "I have pledged to help Paul, so I will remain here. Perhaps I'll have the opportunity to explore a bit later."

Rebecca and Elizabeth indicate that they will remain, as well.

"Well, Pete, it's you and me again, the two adventurers. Off we go, then."

Still dazed by the rapidity of all of this, Peter nods somewhat half-heartedly. "Uh, yes. Off we go."

"No need to make a big deal out of any of this, Pete. If each little sojourn impacts you so strongly, goodness, you're going to be in a state of constant fatigue and imbalance." Zachary pauses for Peter to absorb that comment.

Suddenly, Peter bursts out laughing, and Zachary, laughing himself, puts a hand on each of Peter's shoulders. "You've got it, Pete. You're eternal. You can't get fatigued, and you can't get out of balance. You can believe that you are those things but, in fact, they can't happen to you. You can believe it so strongly that it becomes your reality. But if you remember to laugh and find humor and joy, those sorts of illusions won't linger long around you. Got it now?"

"Yes," still laughing a bit, "yes, I've got it, Zachary. Thank you for your patience with me. With everywhere I've been and all I've seen and done, I ought to remember some of this by now."

Zachary takes Peter's arm, and they begin walking.

"Well, don't be hard on yourself, Pete. You may have been to the 'Realm of the Angels' and realized your … "roots", but you are still functioning from a level that is Peter. And rightly so, for that's the way He wants it. I believe that's the way you want it, too. That's the way of your greatest potential service as a worker of commissions, as a teacher, as a guide."

"Me? A teacher? A guide? That's bit mindboggling."

They laugh and continue walking along, each with a hand on the other's shoulder, chatting, stopping to admire some plant or some bit of craftsmanship. They come upon several people who are, as best Peter can discern, working in a garden.

Peter bends over to have a closer look. "Lovely flowers."

"Why, thank you," answers one. "You know the thing about growing flowers here is they don't seem to require any care. I've only been here for, I don't know, several months or so maybe. But, well, I just love to plant things here. Before you know it, they've grown, and they're blooming and no bugs, not a one. Haven't seen a bug on anything here."

"My, that is amazing. And I have never seen finer flowers anywhere."

Obviously very proud of Peter's compliment, the entity smiles and goes back to smoothing the soil around the base of a small seedling.

"That was nice, Pete. That was a nice thing to say to that chap, and I know you meant it. And they are lovely, aren't they?"

"Yes, Zachary. We'll have to go back and check my Garden Realm, make sure none of the flowers are missing."

Zachary's laughter is spontaneous. "Now that's my Pete. That's the old Pete. We're going to have a good time here. You'll see. Fine folks work here. Some you'll be surprised to meet. And others … well, you'll see."

"You know, Zachary, you can sure be cryptic."

"Me, cryptic? I'm not sure that's a compliment. Deep,

profound, wise, far-sighted, those things I can relate to. But cryptic?" And they both break out in laughter again.

"You two sure seem like good friends," comes a small voice off to the side.

Peter, curious, turns and stops in his tracks, for there before them is a small boy, probably eight or nine years old. Zachary is quick to respond. "Oh, yes. We're good friends. Have had lots of fun times together. And who might you be?"

"My name was Robert, sir, but my friends called me Bobby. You can call me that, if you'd like."

"Well, Bobby, have you been here long?"

"No, sir, not long at all. I think I just arrived yesterday."

"I see. And what are you doing here?"

"I'm waiting for someone to come and get me."

"Hmm. Have you no one here for companionship?"

"Oh yes, Sir! I have many friends. But, you know, I get lonely for friends my age and size. I'm told that's where I'm going next."

"Ah, yes, I know the place well. You'll love it. It's wonderful. I have many friends there, and I promise, you will have a marvelous time. By the way, when you get there, mention my name and some of my friends will be quick to come to help you with anything you need."

"Thank you, sir. What's your name?"

"Oh, forgive me, Bobby. My name is Zachary, and this is my friend Peter. We're just visiting here, so that's why we haven't seen you before."

"Well, Mr. Zachary and Mr. Peter, I'm happy to meet you. And I will tell them that my friend Zachary said me to mention his name to them. I'll tell that to everyone I meet."

"Very good. You do that, and you might be surprised at what will happen."

Bobby turns to look up at Peter. "Mr. Peter, will you come and visit me?"

Surprised, Peter looks over at Zachary and gets a wink and a subtle nod. He looks down at Bobby. "Why, I'd love to, Bobby. Thank you for inviting me. Is there anything that I might bring you when I visit?" remembering his manners from the Earth.

"Well, since you asked, Mr. Peter, I would like a wagon. I never had one, and I always wanted one."

Zachary bends over to Bobby. "A wagon?"

"Yes, sir, I would love to have a wagon."

"You've never had a wagon?"

"No, sir. We couldn't afford one because my mother was sick, and my father, he couldn't be there very much. He had to go places and do things ... work, I guess."

"Wait right here a moment." Zachary takes several steps away from Peter and the boy, stops and turns. "What color?"

"Red, sir. Red is my favorite."

Zachary resumes his stride and disappears around a hedgerow. Before Peter barely realizes he has gone, Zachary is coming back from around the shrubbery, pulling a bright red wagon behind him. His face is beaming. "How's this one, Bobby?"

"Oh, sir!" Bobby runs over to Zachary. "That's just like what I wanted. How did you know?" His little hands caress the sides and wheels and all about.

"Well, you might say a little bird told me," winking at Peter. "Look, Bobby, we've got to go a little ways down the path here. I'll make sure that the one who's coming to get you will know where you are. But how about if Peter and I pull you for a bit in your shiny new wagon?"

"Oh! That would be terrific! Thank you."

Bobby clambers into the wagon, and Zachary and Peter begin to wander down the path with Bobby chattering away, swinging his arms with glee as he rides along in his beautiful new wagon. Here and there along the path are people. They smile and wave. One of them calls out, "Hi, Bobby. What a great wagon you have there." Bobby calls back to the individuals by name, as though he knows them well.

After a time, Zachary comes to the top of a little hill and turns to Bobby. "Look here, Bobby. You've got the perfect place to roll your wagon. You just point it towards the bottom of the hill, climb in, and hold the handle like this, and you can steer. When you get to the bottom, someone there will help you bring it back up." Zachary waves to several people now gathered at the bottom of the hill, and they wave back. One of them calls out, "Let her go, Bobby. Run her down the hill."

Bobby jumps into the wagon. "Thanks, Mr. Zachary. Thanks, Mr. Peter. I love my wagon. Remember, Mr. Peter, visit me. But now you don't have to bring a wagon."

Laughing, Zachary gives Bobby a little nudge, and down the hill he goes, laughing and waving.

"Well, that was fun, wasn't it, Pete?"

"Yes, it really was. I haven't seen a child for so long. It was so refreshing. It was touching, too. What's he doing here and where's the one who's picking him up"

"They're just waiting, Pete. It's like he's getting some medication. He won't stay here long. Once that 'medication' takes hold completely, he'll be moving on. He's destined to rise much higher."

"Medication?"

"Yes. You know, sort of a colloquial term, but in essence it's literal. You see, Bobby was incredibly lonely in his life and lacking in most all areas. He was in a household that barely provided him with the barest necessities. But his spirit, as you saw, is sterling in character. The *medication* he is being given is friendship, love, compassion, caring. Once he's adapted to that and has completely moved out from the inner chamber that he built around himself while in the Earth as a protective mechanism, and he allows himself to be fully expressed, that's when he'll be taken on. He's not here because the one who will take him on is busy or anything like that.

He's here because of the need for his 'medication.' And you see the entities now gathered around him at the bottom of the hill?" gesturing to them.

"Yes."

"Well, if you'll look carefully and perceive with not just your finite perception, you'll see their cloaks. They're not all residents here. The three by him over there are all here for Bobby, all three of them, and you can probably understand why. He is a very beautiful soul. As he gradually progresses, as he comes to know his infinite nature, he will go to some of the very higher realms. And remember, you promised to visit him, so that's where you'll find him."

"Higher realms?"

"Yes, indeed so."

"Higher than the Realm of the Angels?"

"Oh, yes, Pete, by our standards, indeed higher."

"That is very intriguing. I can hardly wait."

So, dear friends, as you've probably noted, the movement during this meeting has been brisk. If you have questions about any specifics, we would welcome them.

CHAPTER 3

A Heavenly Hospital

MAY 28, 1992

We are reminding you here of two points: One, though we ourselves don't use or have need of terms and references, we employ those that we believe will invoke the greatest overall understanding for you. Two, in order to gain continuing deeper understanding and to help him to move past the reasoning and logic he was accustomed to while expressed in finiteness, experiences are provided for Peter in lieu of lengthy explanations.

Putting these two points together, terms and experiences, the "Control Center" was playfully so named by Zachary for Peter. It is not that there is a big white cloud in the sky somewhere with an entity sitting at dials controlling this or that. But there are gathering areas, connecting links of sorts for those who serve others, wherein the best course for such service can more or less be coordinated. Zeb is an example of one who is interacting at such a gathering place, acting as a sort of coordinator. All such entities and "service centers" act in accordance with the will and purpose of God. We hope this is of assist to any who might question the existence of a Control Center.

Now, as we prepare to engage Peter and the group, we wish to let you know that, once again, there may be occasions where some rapidity of activity will again take place. Rather than delay conveying the information to you in order to more fully explain, we shall present the events as they occur and anticipate your questions on anything on which you wish further information.

P eter and Zachary are moving along the pathway. They
have just sent their new friend, Bobby, joyfully down
the hillside in his shiny new wagon, who is laughing
and squealing with delight all the way.

"Zachary, you must know that I have lots of questions."

"Indeed, Pete. So let's take a brief pause, and you can
question away." Motioning to a point just ahead of them that
seems specifically designed to suit their needs, Zachary
guides them into a lovely ivy-covered arbor, not unlike one
Peter recalls having visited before. "Here's a good spot, Pete.
Seat yourself and let's just relax and enjoy the view, and I'll
do the best I can to answer your questions."

As Peter settles himself upon a lovely hand-carved
bench, gazing out over the landscape before him, he notes
many individuals and groups here and there busy about various things he cannot clearly discern.

Just as he turns to ask Zachary about them, he is interrupted by the appearance of John, Beth, and Samuel. "Greetings, Zachary, we didn't want to leave without saying farewell for now. Peter, how are you doing?"

Surprised by their sudden presence, Peter has risen
quickly to his feet and extended a hand in the form of a handshake. John clasps it, then Beth and Samuel. "It's good to see
you again. Did you say you were about to leave?"

John nods. "Yes, Peter. We stopped here only briefly to
check on several friends from the just-completed incarnations
in the Earth. We each had several of them, and we felt our
appearance might encourage the process they are currently
undergoing."

"Do you have just a moment or two?" asks Peter, his sincerity flowing from him as shafts of clear light.

"Certainly. How might we serve you?"

"I have some questions about what you just went through
involving the Earth."

The three beam warmth to Peter that puts him completely

at ease. The spirit of camaraderie here is as old friends. Zachary has moved to make room for all to seat themselves. He is at one end of the semi-circular bench, Peter's new friends are in the middle, and Peter at the other end.

Samuel speaks first. "Perhaps I could comment on a few points that would answer some of your questions more quickly than a lot of verbal exchange might require."

Peter meets Samuel's eyes and instantly realizes that here is one who seems strangely familiar, obviously another who is capable of perceiving his thoughts clearly.

Smiling at Peter's realization, Samuel nods. "What you are thinking is true. You and I have met several times in the past and, if our friend Zachary here would care to accompany you to the Akasha or if you would like to turn inwards, you can re-gather those specifics, if it is of interest to you."

Peter is in silent wonder and joy at the anticipation of this.

"Allow me, then, to preface my comments with these statements that, since we have known one another in the past, it follows that we have known one another beyond the finite. Because of this, we have spiritual links that connect us that have created the sense in you of familiarity of me. It is upon this basis that I am drawing the information to respond to your unspoken questions and, of course, as always, if you wish to expand on these, please do.

"We returned to the Earth in order to perform certain benevolent acts specific to each of us," turning to acknowledge his companions, "and collectively, as a small group. There are other members of our group who are still in the Earth. They are functioning in various capacities, and once we return to a higher and less encumbered position of expression, we will resume our works with those yet in the Earth."

"Might I ask how many of you there are?"

"In our group, there are twenty-seven. Minus the three of us gathered here, twenty-four remain in the Earth."

"All in one place? Like Czechoslovakia or Poland, or one of those countries?"

"No, not all in one place, though a number remain in that general area. But they move about considerably, attempting to heal or make peace where they can."

Make peace? Peter wonders as he glances at Zachary.

Zachary explains to Samuel, "Peter is unaware of the conditions that have occurred there since his transition."

Nodding, Samuel turns back to Peter. "Much has changed since you departed the Earth, Peter. But to be brief, some considerable sense of freedom has transpired in what you know of as the Soviet Union. Many of the satellite countries, former dominions of the Soviet Union, are now struggling to express themselves as individual countries. The previous conditions actually caused some degree of camaraderie between opposing groups of theological or philosophical outlook. Now these groups have turned against one another to struggle for independence and individual recognition and all that sort of thing that is a part of the mechanisms in the Earth.

"It is to this purpose that some of our colleagues remain in those areas. But we have other colleagues who are on all the major continents in the Earth doing similar but variations of that type of work. Clear to this point, Peter?"

Peter nods slowly, for he does comprehend completely the message being given him, though he is startled at the news of such political change in the Earth.

"So it is, then, that we three and the others of our group, and a significant number of other groups not unlike our own, some much larger in number, are functioning in the same capacity, even as we speak."

"Truly? These groups like your own are all in the Earth benevolently?"

"Benevolence is the absence of a personal karma, Peter. In other words, it means that each of us has, in our own time and path, broken the links of karmic bond that individually involve us in finite expressions such as the Earth."

"What is your point here, Samuel? I'm afraid it passed over my head."

"Well, what I'm trying to convey here, Peter, is there is karma on the personal level, which is nothing more than the Universal Law of Cause and Effect. And then there is karma in the sense of choosing to be a part of a certain pathway or a certain area of growth or creation. While the one in the first instance implies a certain degree of personal responsibility and involvement, the latter is similar because it is by choice but that choice is much more knowledgeably made. It is to continue to perpetuate as much 'light' as we can to those of our brethren who remain bound by their personal karmic links to the illusion of finiteness. How's that? Does that help?"

Peter pauses only a moment as he is digesting the information. "Yes, I grasp that. Please continue, Samuel. You are answering many of the questions I was about to ask Zachary. I find it most fascinating."

"Good. At the point that we were prepared to depart from the Earth, we allowed ourselves to be a part of a conflict that took place not directly in Czechoslovakia but in a neighboring area. As a result, we offered the remainder of our lives for the enlightenment of those souls involved in that struggle."

"Excuse me a moment, Samuel. I need to understand this. You're saying that you three offered yourselves as an example or ... Do you mean you volunteered to *die* in order to help bring about peace?"

Samuel merely leans back now with his hands crossed upon one knee, and rocks slowly to and fro, nodding.

"Forgive me, but I fail to see how your individual sacrifices could do as much as if you continued to remain in the Earth but spoke out or did something in the more active sense to bring about peace. How does your death or deaths contribute to peace?"

"Very astute, Peter. Consider this: Unless some awareness is brought to the condition, the situation and its utter futility, its pointlessness, these people could continue on thusly for decades. Perhaps the hostility and animosity would not be expressed as violently as it is at the moment, but breeding nonetheless, like seeds sown waiting to be harvested in a future time. By offering up the remainder of those lifetimes, attention is drawn to the futility of such a direction and helps illustrate that like begets like: as they are meting out, they themselves receive in return, so none are actually gaining.

"But the publicity of our departures, and many others like us, has brought some focus of attention by multiple forces. There are incarnate forces as well as discarnate. The discarnates seek to return to the Earth to perpetuate an attitude of oppression or control. There are continual observers of such activities, and where there is conflict, they most assuredly are gathered by the droves. True, Zachary?"

"Indeed so. I might remind you, Peter, of the intensity of energies that you felt being repulsed by your cloak as we were moving to join our three friends here."

"I do remember, and that was one of the questions I had. Can you tell me more about that, Samuel?"

"That was a collection of souls who had departed from the Earth earlier, but who are bound by their desires to return to the Earth and gain power, to dominate, or create subservience. Like attracts like. Where they can find those things that satiate their needs, even if they are second-hand (as you call it), they will do so. That was what you passed through, a literal sea of entities, some of whose faces you saw as they sought to gain control over you. Their level of individual power was and is no match for your own awareness, even if it had been able to penetrate your spiritual cloak, which of course it could not. But they try. They must try, no matter what. They even seek to dominate one another and, finding that this is an eternal cycle that begins and ends and begins and ends, over and over again, they turn to other places, such as people in the Earth.

"If it could only be known to our brethren in the Earth what their thoughts attract. Their attitudes, emotions, and actions all attract entities of like intent. Even though some of them might mean well, in the sense of not causing harm or not dominating, if they involuntarily adopt such attitudes, they can attract these entities from what could be called the Sea of Faces who seek to fill their appetite for their various needs by associating with such actions.

"Fortunately, those who are well-intentioned and might have only momentary outbursts of such actions out of frustration or whatnot repel these entities easily. They are only there momentarily. But where this has become a way of life or habit for some, these entities can be found thickly expressed around them. Is this understandable?"

Peter nods silently, reflecting on the gravity of all this and its impact on those in the Earth. He responds quietly. "So I could conclude from this, too, that the converse or opposite is true? When someone in the Earth performs a selfless deed, a work of charity, or an act of kindness, they are then attracting souls of similar nature, as well?"

Samuel smiles, confirming Peter's conclusion.

Beth, who is seated between Samuel and John, interjects, "Forgive me for interrupting, but I might offer this in addition to what Samuel has conveyed: Love is an expression of universal nature. Love needs to be brought into greater illumination, where it has nothing to do with the physical, with things or situations or even people. It is a state of mind, a condition within, a sense of joyous well-being, that inspires the energy that is love."

"Thank you, Beth." Samuel turns to Peter. "This was her primary work. Beth was a missionary in this just-completed sojourn and was well skilled in medical training, as well. She was in a building that was struck by shelling while she was tending to the wounded in the midst of a battlefield, full knowing that this would possibly be life-threatening. That was her chosen work—to offer herself as silent testimony to the need for peace, love, and understanding, and she conveyed this message with total clarity. Perhaps not widely known in the Earth at the moment, but maybe in a time to come, her work will be known. Not to imply that we do our work because we seek such for ourselves, but only that such recognition would inspire others. Questions?"

Peter looks at the three entities before him. "You have provided me with an amazing gift in this information. No doubt after I reflect on it, I'll have other questions, but I don't want to hold you up just dabbling about." Then he laughs, followed by the joyous laughter of the others.

"Well said, Pete." Zachary rises and walks over to John, extending his hand. "John, it has been so good of you and your colleagues to come by to bid us farewell. I expect we'll see you shortly and many times beyond that, as our paths cross often, at least that shall be my prayer."

John looks gently at Zachary. "We share your sentiments, Zachary." He then turns to Peter. "And there is no question that we shall meet again, perhaps in the Great Hall, eh, Peter?"

"Really? In the Great Hall?"

"Indeed. We shall be there at the next gathering. We look forward to that and other opportunities where we may share with you. We are deeply moved by your compassion, Peter, and by the demonstration of your spiritual essence in your earlier commissions. These shall serve as examples for others, no doubt." He embraces Peter. "Well done, friend."

Beth and Samuel embrace Zachary and Peter. Peter feels a flow of glorious light, color, and sound from Samuel, who extends Peter at arm's length, a hand upon each shoulder. "Old friends, Peter. Friendship never ends. It only grows better. Is it not so?"

"Indeed," responds Peter. "My prayers will be with you

always, Samuel, and all that you do."

"I shall be warmed by that thought." Then Samuel moves to join Beth and John on the path where they turn with a farewell gesture, become light, and are gone.

Peter feels a bit as though he has lost something, gazing at the spot where the three disappeared.

"Lovely entities, don't you think?"

"Ah, yes, Zachary. Lovely. And something about them, I just feel sort of melancholy in this moment."

"Well, Peter, my friend, seat yourself and let's go over the crumbs or ... what did you call them? Leftovers?"

Peter bursts into laughter."

"Whatever they are, let's poke around in them a little and try to nourish that immense curiosity of yours as well as we can in the short time we have left here."

Peter's feeling of melancholy is immediately displaced by curiosity. "Short time left? What's that mean?"

"Well, I want you to visit some others here, and we've only traveled a short distance. And just look at all that you've experienced. Think about Bobby."

"Oh, that was so beautiful. Are there more experiences here like that?"

"Like that and different, each one unique, Pete. Would you like to poke at the crumbs or go exploring?"

"Enough said, Zack. Let's explore. We can work on the leftovers later."

With another burst of laughter from them both, they rise, arms over one another's shoulder, and stride down the path chuckling over this and that. This continues for a time as they greet entities here and there, look at their projects, and pause to engage in conversation once in awhile. Finally, we find them going down a bit of a hill and around a bend. Peter notes a lovely little structure that resembles a New England style home, painted a soft blue, trimmed in white, two-story but not too large.

"Well, Pete, here's a good place for us to step in and chat for a while. I have several good friends working here."

"I suspect you have good friends working everywhere, Zack."

Feigning some reflection, Zachary gazes off with a hand on his chin. "Hmmm. You could be right, Pete." He reaches his hand out to turn the shiny brass-like doorknob on an ornate windowed door, on the back of which hang white lacy curtains.

Peter looks into the large room before him and is taken aback.

"Quite different than you expected, eh, Pete?"

"Different? What's going on in here? These people in those beds ... this looks like a hospital!"

Zachary chuckles softly. "Well, Pete, it is, indeed, just like a hospital."

"Why, Zachary? Why a hospital?"

"You'll see why soon enough in a way that would far exceed my capacity to explain it to you. Come in and meet my friends, and possibly a few of yours, as well." Zachary strides into the room.

As Peter dutifully follows, he notes that the room is bright and immaculate, the surroundings giving the impression of a hospital ward. Perhaps one that would be dated somewhat from current Earth time, but nonetheless, clearly a place of healing or recuperation.

"That's it, Pete, healing and recuperation. There's no surgery here. There aren't any physical wounds, even though some of the people believe they still have them."

"Why?"

"Well, come over here, and I'll introduce you to a friend of mine who often works here, and perhaps he can help you with that question."

They move across the room and come to stand before an entity who is bending over someone in one of the beds. After a moment, the entity stands and turns, smiling. "Hello, Zachary. So good of you to call. We've had a number of people ask about you since your last visit. And who do we have here? Ah, yes, so this is Peter?"

"Excuse me, sir, but do I know you?"

"Well, actually, Peter, in the literal sense, no but in the spiritual sense, yes. Let's see now. If I were to just change a bit of myself this way and that and do this or that so that you could see me better as I truly am, you'd recognize me as ... "

"Zeb!" Peter shouts, and Zachary laughs.

"Hello, Peter. Nice to have you here. What do you think of the place?"

"What are you doing here, Zeb? Who's in the Control Center?"

"Well, you could say that this is a Control Center of sorts. And what I'm doing here? Well, come along and I'll show you."

Still astounded that this is truly Zeb, Peter follows along, but with a little uncertainty.

"Come on now, Pete. Relax. You're among friends." Obviously delighted at Peter's reaction to the discovery of him in the midst of this, Zeb stops and walks between two beds that are spaced generously apart. He reaches out to grasp the hand of the person who is lying in one of the beds.

To Peter, it appears to be a perfectly normal, healthy person. "Peter, I'd like you to meet ... What did you say your name was again?" jokes Zeb.

That brings some laughter from the person, and she speaks directly to Peter. "My name is Rosalie, as the good doctor here certainly knows. He's always teasing me like that. But I just love his sense of humor. Besides, he always brings me these lovely flowers," turning to a vase of flowers at a bedside stand. "You know, I don't know what he does to them, but they never seem to wilt. He changes them, but the old ones look as good as they did the day he brought them.

How do you do it, Doctor?"

Zeb smiles and winks playfully at Rosalie and then turns to Peter. "How does she look to you, Dr. Peter?"

Surprised, Peter studies Zeb and perceives another little wink as he hears, *Look, Pete. I don't mean to play games with you or anything like that, but this dear soul here thinks all of us are doctors. So you may as well get used to it. She'll consider you a doctor from this time forward until she moves beyond the current point of her consciousness. So I just cut through a lot of the intermediate stuff and called you doctor. And, you know, maybe you can help."*

All this takes place in a split-second of Earth time.

Peter nods with a soft smile. "Well, let me see ... "

He can hear Zachary commenting quietly in the background, "Yes, Doctor, do check. Do take a look at her."

Peter is fully aware that Zachary is having a delightful time with his current predicament. He moves awkwardly around to the other side of Rosalie's bed and reaches out to grasp her wrist, as he saw doctors do in the Earth.

"Oh, your touch is so warm and gentle, Dr. Peter. How nice of you to come and call on me. Dr. Zeb here has done so much for me. I feel much better. He says the cancer is completely gone, but I'm not sure. I just question whether or not that can possibly be. You know, these things are so often not curable. And after all, I haven't been here that long. Seems to me it should take longer to heal than this."

"Hmm." Peter looks off to the side as though he were listening for something, touches her forehead and looks into her eyes. "Well, Rosalie, I'm afraid I have bad news for you."

"I knew it. I just knew it. See, Dr. Zeb? I told you all the time. I can't be that well."

"No, no, Rosalie," Dr. Peter interrupts. "The bad news is that I am afraid I must agree with Dr. Zeb here. I would say that you are as healthy as anyone could ever be."

She stares at "Dr. Peter" with her mouth agape and her

eyes wide. Studying his face, she finds absolute truth, warmth, and sincerity returned to her. "You are serious, aren't you, Dr. Peter?"

"Yes, indeed, Miss Rosalie. I am completely serious. You have no more cancer."

Speechless, she looks from one doctor to the other. Zeb is nodding, holding her other hand and patting it as he does.

"Then I am truly well?"

"Yes, you are beyond truly well, Miss Rosalie. You are in a perfect state of expression."

"Perfect? I can't believe that. I'll never be perfect again. I don't deserve it, anyway. You know, all the things I've done in my life. Goodness. It's God's way of settling with me. You know, the truth in the Bible is, as you sow, that's what you reap. And I'm reaping ... a lot!"

Peter is surprised at her comments. Obviously, as he receives a glance from Zeb, this is the true malady of the entity: an inability to receive the Grace of God. Even though she lies in a perfect body, at complete ease, with total freedom of movement and an unlimited expression of God's existence to explore, she has purposefully confined herself to this bed. "Well, listen, Rosalie. I want to tell you a few more things. You've noticed, I'm sure, our colleague, the good Reverend Zachary, here."

"Oh, yes, I saw the Reverend immediately when he came in. You can always tell them. They have that look about them. A sort of holiness."

Zachary, glancing at Peter, struggling to retain a chuckle, shakes his head to the woman as if to say, *True, woman. True.*

Peter looks away and coughs a bit to cover a laugh. When he looks back at Rosalie, her face is aglow.

Zeb steps aside so that Reverend Zachary can come over to her bedside.

"Look here, dear Rosalie," counsels Reverend Zachary. "God does not want you to dwell in an attitude of self-imposed punishment. He wishes you and all of His Children to be joyful."

"Yes, yes. I know that, Reverend. But my sins ... well, they are just too great. No one could forgive them."

"No one?"

"I'm afraid not."

Zachary turns to Zeb. Peter can sense communication between them. He shifts inwardly and hears, *Zeb, is she ready to move on, do you think, or what's her status?*

Well, Zack, she has been at this point for a long while. I think it's time now to open her awareness a bit more.

Would you like me to assist you?

I'd be very pleased if you would.

Very well. Zachary looks back at her. "Miss Rosalie, I want to tell you something now, and I want you to hold my hand and Dr. Peter's hand over there as I explain this to you. You know, of course, that you are no longer in the Earth."

Again, Rosalie's eyes go wide and her mouth drops open. "No, no, no, no. That's not true. I'm just in some sort of a rest home. My children, they put me here. They never liked me, and I don't blame them. I was miserable to them. Crotchety, cantankerous, argumentative. When they needed help most, I didn't help them. So this is where I belong. Right here. This is my just reward. I know this is God's punishment."

"Rosalie, God does not punish His Children in the sense that you understand the Bible. He allows you to experience and to learn from your experience, knowing full well that some things you do won't always be the highest and best."

He glances at Peter. "But once you realize them to be less than the highest and best, as you obviously have, then God wishes you to free yourself from the unneeded burdens of guilt. The question of sin is not what you have considered, simply acts of wrongdoing. The greater sin is to limit oneself because of those things done in the past, thereby preventing you from doing good things in the present and future.

"Don't you think, dear Rosalie, that you are limiting yourself by remaining here? Wouldn't you rather rise and go about doing some good works? To show yourself, as an example to others and God, that you have learned and grown, and that you wish now to adjust your thoughts, attitudes, and actions to make them more joyfully fulfilling for others?"

Rosalie props herself up on an elbow. "Oh, Reverend, do you think that I am worthy of such grace?"

"I know that to be so," Reverend Zachary affirms.

"Would you ... could you, uh ... bless me, and take away my sins? Wash me clean?"

"I will do that and more," Zachary responds without a moment's hesitation. "But in return, I must ask you to arise and to go about those things that you know in your heart to be the best that you can do. But most of all, I ask you this one simple thing."

"Yes, yes. What is it, Reverend? What is it?"

"I ask you to forgive yourself. Release the past and go forward from this point with hope and joy. God wishes you to be joyful. Your joy enlightens and illuminates this world, this place of your current existence. If you would do that, you would be contributing a great deal to others. Who knows? You might even be able to assist Dr. Zeb here as he helps others who are in a worse state than you."

She looks to Dr. Zeb. "Oh, Dr. Zeb, could I? Might I?"

Studying her for a deliberate period of prolonged time, he answers, "Hmm. Well as I consider this, Rosalie, I think you're just the ticket. I have several patients who would certainly benefit from your presence and the light of your understanding. Once you learn to forgive yourself, you might be able to help them learn to forgive themselves, too."

"I'll do it," she states very vocally. "I will, I will. Cleanse me, Reverend. Heal me. Wash me of my sins, and I'll do all that I can and more."

Very ceremoniously, Zachary places his hand upon

Rosalie and utters something that Peter cannot fully hear, for Zachary has leaned over and is speaking softly into Rosalie's ear. She is lying outstretched, eyes closed, a rather angelic smile on her face.

Peter can see from his inner perception varying shades of darkness begin to move about and slowly dissipate, as though they were being drawn from her presence. An indeterminate amount of time passes, and as Peter shifts himself, studying the situation, he notes with wonder as Rosalie opens her eyes. In them, Peter can see the light of hope, a ray of expectancy.

Zachary straightens himself and extends his hand. "Rosalie, if you will allow me, I will assist you to arise."

Zeb moves to the other side to take her other arm. Slowly at first, Rosalie swings her legs off the bed and stands. "I feel marvelous. You have done wonders for me, Reverend. And you, Dr. Zeb and Dr. Peter. From this moment on, to repay you all, I shall work in ways that I am guided."

Zachary releases her hand. "That is not at all necessary, Rosalie. What we all urge you to do is to be joyful. Before you start your work, perhaps Dr. Zeb will take you to see one of the gardens from where he gathered those beautiful flowers. He has a good friend who raises them and gives them to Dr. Zeb to share with patients and other friends."

"Oh, that would be lovely, Dr. Zeb. You know how much I like flowers."

"Well then, dear Rosalie, my prescription to you at this time is that you go out with me now and I'll introduce you to several friends who have one of the most lovely flower gardens in all of this area. They would love to have you spend some time with them, and they'll show you how they raise the flowers. They're such delightful people. They were in your position before, and they've come a long way to reclaiming their complete health in every respect." Winking at Peter and Zachary as he makes the last comment. "See you later, my friends. Thanks for your assistance." Then he scoops up

Rosalie's arm and they stride towards the front door, with Rosalie chattering and fussing about her hair and her garments as they move. Zeb casts a glance over his shoulder as they exit the building and waves to Peter and Zachary.

Peter is standing before Zachary looking rather stunned. "I'm not sure what we all just did is, well, you know, kosher. Is it?"

"Did you do something that you are ashamed of, Peter?"

"No, but … I mean, letting her think I was a doctor and you a reverend. Isn't that like perpetuating a sham or a hoax."

"But Pete, aren't we intending to heal just as the doctors in the Earth do, and I as a reverend, seeking to bring spiritual healing, just as they do in the Earth? What differentiates us?"

"Training, for one thing. Credentials."

"Training in what? Credentials for what, Pete?"

"Well, you know. Medical school and all that."

Zachary's laughter echoes off the walls of the entire structure. "What kind of medical school do you need for a body that isn't a real body but is only the body of one's limitation at that point?"

Peter realizes, of course, that had he reflected on this to any length, he would have concluded this himself. "Ah, yes, good point, Zachary," and he joins in the laughter. "So what you're saying is what we just did was no different than we have done for others in earlier works. And as she saw us in this certain light, it was the way for us to address her needs?"

"Yes. You could have told her, Pete, that you weren't a doctor, and she wouldn't have believed you. I guarantee it. She believed you to be a doctor and me to be a reverend. And that's it. You could have taken a harsh approach and told her again and again that that's not so, and that she is no longer in the Earth and all that. But if you'll remember, she wouldn't accept that either.

"She has to be given what she is willing to receive at the level of her development. It's that way in all realms, actually, it's just that here the paradox is so dramatic for you that it seems incredulous and almost dishonest. But it's not. It's merely giving to the best of your ability at the level of the entity's acceptance. See? Now, if you walked around here claiming yourself to be this or that, your cloak would start to diminish in its luminosity and you'd probably end up going back to the Earth for another sojourn or two to get rid of that need, if it were one created out of a desire for personal power or that sort of thing. Got it?"

"Yes, I think so, Zachary."

"Well then, I'd like you to come upstairs, if you don't mind." He rounds a corner and strides up an expanse of stairs.

With Peter following, they enter another room. Here he can see all manner of different people, some appearing to be very young, some very old, and all sorts in between.

There are a number of entities walking about, obviously tending these people. Off in a corner, Peter recognizes his new friend Chen, who waves to them and motions them over.

"Hello, Peter. Good to see you again. Here's my commission. He's coming around rather nicely. I've just explained to him that he's no longer in the Earth and that he doesn't have a physical body. He's done quite well with that, and we've been over the affairs of his past experiences, looked at a few past lives and, of course, the just-previous one. Now he's resting comfortably. I think he'll do well and probably be able to be up and around in short order. Then maybe move on, or else take a position here if he chooses."

Absorbing all of this in detail, Peter inquires of Chen, "Did he have a difficult time in understanding death?"

"At first he did, Peter, but I took him back so he could relive the process and understand it better. Of course, not back to the physical finiteness where there was fear and pain and all that, but to the part where he left the Earth and passed through the various strata surrounding it. You know, about where we met. I explained all that to him again so that he could understand the progression of the soul's consciousness and the continuity of life as one progresses from the Earth onwards."

Studying the person peacefully lying before him, Peter turns to look at some of the others.

"Each of these," responds Chen to Peter's unspoken questions, "have varying levels of acceptance and realization. Most of them in this chamber are recent arrivals. Those you saw downstairs are long-termers. You both did a good job with Rosalie, by the way. I see that she's moving out now to be with her guides for a more permanent duration."

"She is?"

Chen nods and looks to Zachary. "You could show him and introduce him if you think that would expand on this for him, Zachary."

"Perhaps so in due time. But if you don't mind, give him a bit of a tour here, since you know most of these people on such a personal level."

"Be glad to." Chen steps in front of Zachary and takes Peter's arm. As he walks along, he mentions each person's name, their current level of acceptance, and introduces Peter to teachers and guides who are working with the people. When they reach the end of the room, he turns and asks, "Have you any questions, Peter?"

"Quite a few actually, Chen."

Zachary chuckles in the background. "As always."

Smiling, Peter agrees. "That's true. Always."

"Well, that's good," Chen responds. "The more you ask and inquire, the more knowledge you gather. You'll need it later on in your own works."

"I will?"

"Of course. We all do. That's why we have such a close bond between all of us workers."

"Workers? You include me in that category?"

"Well, of course. What would you call yourself?"

Pausing for a moment, Peter looks from one to the other. Zachary smiles at Peter. "Good question Chen's asked you. What would you call yourself?"

"Gosh, I don't know. I hadn't really thought about it."

"Well, what do you want to do, Pete? Would you like to go back to the Angelic Realm and, you know, just exist in a state of joyful fulfillment?"

"That was, of course, marvelous. But after meeting with the Master, I certainly opt to follow Him and work with you guys as best I can. But I don't feel qualified to be called a worker."

Chen leans in to Zachary. "He is as you described. He's at a good point of consciousness and balance. He'll do well. Turning back to Peter, "I want you to know that whenever I can assist, you can call on me, Peter, no matter where you are. I'll hear you and I'll come and help. Will you do this?"

Peter, a bit surprised, simply nods.

"Very good. Well, if you'll excuse me, I see a fellow stirring over there that I have been working on for some time. If he's going to move into a state of receptive consciousness, I want to be right there to maximize the situation. See you later. Thanks for stopping by."

Without waiting for comments, Chen moves briskly off to the opposite side of the room where Peter and Zachary first met him.

Peter glances slowly around. "These entities who are working here are so beautiful!"

"Yes, and each one unique. You might notice if you open your perception, some of them are *very* different than others."

Following Zachary's suggestion, Peter opens his perception. As he looks around the room again, he is surprised that there is a huge variation in the appearance of the spiritual cloaks. "Wow! Zachary, you're right." As his gaze moves around the room further, he stops and gasps.

Zachary carefully watches Peter, who finally takes his

eyes off the entity and turns to his friend. "Zachary, over there tending that man ... Isn't that ... ?"

Zachary's look confirms it all.

"I walked right by Him."

"Many do. They fail to recognize Him and often that's His choice. But He's at that person's side in this moment because the person is one of the faithful, and yet, hasn't awakened to his own limitation. The Master is there in answer to prayers and to that life of service that this person has given. Shortly, he will awaken. When he does, he will look into the face of the Christ. And they will be gone. Until then, the Master will stand at his side and care for him and heal him, as He is doing at this very moment."

"Oh, Zachary!" Peter is deeply moved. "I do. I do want to be a worker, just like the Master. I want to serve and to heal and to do what I can in His name."

"Good. Then let us leave and we'll get about your work."

We wish to point out several things here. Whether in this realm where Peter and Zachary are currently sojourning or in the Earth, each entity who exists lives to the limit of their spiritual acceptance of their own worthiness. It would be good for you to consider that, for as you understand the meaning behind the words we have just given, you will recognize a very powerful mechanism: The power is in the realization that you have been and always shall be free. You are the one that sets the parameters of your potential, your ability, and your accomplishments, from within your own being.

So we urge you to consider the experiences that have been given to Peter here and relate them to your own individual lives. Are there any areas of your life where you are like one of these patients, infirmed to a position of inactivity, just as though you were dis-eased? The dis-ease is your own limitation imposed upon yourself.

Many in the Earth are there to be the example, to be a light, to be a channel of blessings. Some will never be known as such, for that is their intent, their soul choice. They will sojourn throughout an entire lifetime, giving here and there, loving, encouraging, and being, ever, one with the Christ.

CHAPTER 4

Peter's Outer Limit of Experience

MAY 29, 1992

As you will recall from our last meeting, Peter encountered an experience of some revelation to him as he witnessed the presence of the Master, the Christ, at the side of one soul. The soul would not be considered among those of the Earth as having status, known only by a handful of those who were a part of this one's life, yet here we find the Master answering that call, tending to this one's needs in the most personal sense.

This so moved Peter that his decision was instantaneous to be a worker of such light and choose to follow the Master's path serving those who are in need.

Peter and Zachary are walking out the front door of the house that was described in our earlier meeting. As they move back along the pathway from where they had come, Peter cannot keep himself from turning back to look again and again with wonder at what he has just experienced, chattering away to Zachary, who is simply smiling and commenting briefly here and there.

They approach a gentle knoll, a broad expanse of lush greenery, and Zachary moves off the path and settles back on the grass. "Here's a lovely high place to rest a bit, Pete, and just gaze around this realm."

"Okay, Zachary, whatever you say."

Both settle themselves. Zachary reclines upon one elbow, as usual, brushes and caresses the grass.

Peter with his knees up and his arms clasped about them, rocks to and fro, looking about in wonder. "This is a beautiful realm, similar to the Garden Realm, though different in some way. And so many workers gathered here, it's difficult to realize that there are so many."

"How many do you think there might be?"

"Oh, I don't know, Zack. I hadn't really given it much thought."

"Well, there are quite a few souls 'round and about all the realms, not to mention those expressed in the Earth at the moment."

"I suppose there must be a certain ratio of workers for the souls in the realm of Earth and realms like this one, right?"

"It's not quite like that. As one becomes completely dedicated to the work and they become a willing worker, many things change."

"They do? In what way?"

"Well, such workers are guided carefully and beautifully into even higher realizations, and once they have these realizations, they become far less limited and many more things are possible."

"I want to be such a worker, Zachary. I have no doubt of it in my heart or mind. This is what I want to do."

"I know, Pete. I could see the conviction emanating from you and in the essence of your cloak."

"What you just said about the removal of those 'limitations', will that apply to me, as well?"

"Oh, yes, Peter. Why wouldn't it?"

Peter studies Zachary, as he seems somewhat expressionless, just rubbing the lush greenery beneath his hand. "I don't know, Zachary. It just seems to me somewhere within that I'm not really worthy to be given such attention as you and Paul and all the others have given to me. You know? And to be greeted so lovingly by the Master, who told me to rise and be at His side. These things don't rest easily in me. Probably a carryover from the Earth."

"Yes and no." Zachary, still less energetic than usual,

continues gently. "You see, Pete, each of us carries inwardly certain qualities of uniqueness that make us what we are. I know you understand that each is individually different, each soul is created in a light of uniqueness, but think about it this way for a moment: You have had many experiences for your consideration, have you not?"

"Yes, very many. Beautiful ones."

"What if you were to have ten or twenty or a hundred times those experiences already, and you knew of them at this moment?"

Peter thinks for a moment. "I can't actually say what I would feel like. I imagine I'd be more resolute in my decisions and probably less limited. Is what you're getting at?"

"That is correct, Peter. The fact of the matter is, you *have* had many times over the experiences that you consciously recall at this point. The others are available to you, should you wish to explore them. And we can certainly do that at some point.

"But those you recall at this point are the ones significantly contributing to, or providing opportunities for, your present point of consciousness. Most souls are dealing with their spiritual progression, or their incarnation, or whatever, on that basis. They are remembering what is purposeful, what is of service or support, or what is necessary for balance. The rest are sort of in a state of suspended animation for a time.

"Then, as they progress to another point, a fragment or two of experiences from here or there might move into the forefront as others move then into the background, not fully into a suspended or non-active state but less prevalent.

"It is important for a willing worker to be as prepared as possible to meet whatever challenge might be present in their commission. The further along one moves in their capacity as a worker, the greater becomes the potentiality of challenge. Greater control and awareness are required of them. See?"

"I think so, Zack. It's like earlier when you and I were

moving about with Paul and the others, and I found many things to be utterly amazing. Now these things have become a part of me, and I use them often and with comparative ease."

"Right. And you'll find other, perhaps you would call them, gifts or potentials within yourself and present in all of existence that you could not conceive of in this moment. As you discover these and become a part of them and they a part of you (without them unbalancing you or dominating your consciousness), you'll progress, and progress rapidly. Does that still make sense?"

Peter is looking down pensively. "I get the feeling that you are preparing me for something. Is that so?"

"Yes, Pete, I am trying to move your consciousness to a point of receptivity to what can be offered to you next."

"Are you concerned I may not be able to deal with it?"

"No, I have no such concern. But I do have a responsibility to give you all I can, to help and to support you in every way I can conceive of so doing before we move forward."

"Well, do you feel you've done that?"

This invokes spontaneous laughter from Zachary. His laughter infects Peter, and the two of them begin to roll about on the lush greenery beneath them, laughing.

They come to a rest. Zachary sits up and looks at Peter. "I just love that about you, Pete. You have such a completely honest and forthright nature. It seems to me that it would be impossible for anyone not to develop a profound admiration of you, at the least. Certainly a great love and admiration for those qualities that you possess so easily, so casually."

Peter knows Zachary has not made these comments idly. "Thank you for that. I know you're sincere."

Zachary rises, extends a hand to Peter and pulls him up. "Teamwork, see, Peter? Your hand and mine, pulling together seemingly in opposing directions, bring us both higher."

"I had never thought of that. I'd have to say that's true. A bit of the law of physics in there, too."

"Physics?"

"Yeah, you know, Zack, gravity, force and opposing force, and all that."

"Oh, I see." Now, to Peter's amusement and amazement, Zachary begins to float slowly upwards, until he is about three feet above the ground. "Yes. These laws, these laws of physics you are talking about. If I think I can rise, I can. And if I don't ... " thump, down to Earth he comes, "I can't. Is that what you're talking about?"

"I get the message, Zachary. You're reminding me of truth. Thank you."

"You're welcome. Now, we've got a short trip to take, and then we'll go back and check on Paul and the others and see what's up."

"Okay. Where are we off to?"

"Well, let's become formless, first. Just stay with me, and you'll see for yourself faster than I can explain it. Is that acceptable?"

"Very good." Peter turns inward. Finding the center of his being, he allows that to radiate outward, carrying with it his own consciousness, until he is expressed as a brilliant sphere of light, on the periphery of which is the obvious evidence of Peter in the form of his spiritual cloak.

He perceives Zachary to his side, expressed in similar form, and hears, "Follow me, Pete. Here we go."

They move so swiftly upwards that Peter realizes they have traveled a great distance in a split second. Their movement even seems to accelerate, and Peter denotes band after band of changing energies and differing forces or expressions. It is like passing through sets of multiple layers of color, each set of rainbow-like layers differing from the previous set, the colors becoming brighter and more luminous.

Finally, Peter feels them slowing, until they come to a vastness of golden light and Zachary moves more slowly. He calls out. "Pete, stay right behind me now, and we'll move through this with appropriate respect."

"Respect?"

"Yes. The best term I can find to fit the situation."

"Are you saying the other realms we went through didn't deserve our respect?"

"Not at all. Except that, here, we are reaching our upper limit of expression. Therefore, we must respect this position as being delicately balanced as we are capable of expressing."

"Wow! You mean this is the outer limit or end of where I might go? The border or boundary of my potential?"

"Something like that, though don't dramatize it too much, for you are always growing, so this can be anticipated to move proportionately. Follow that?"

"Yes, I think so, Zachary."

"Good. Now, shortly ahead we're going to enter into a somewhat transforming state. I just want you to stay balanced within yourself, *centered* at the point of your greatest awareness. Just stay immediately close to me, and I'll help wherever it might be needed, though I think you'll be fine."

"Uh, what happens if I'm not fine?"

A stream of laughter cascades over to Peter in the form of rays of light. "Well, you won't cease to be or anything like that. Our movement would be slowed, that's all."

"Oh, okay. Thanks. Just checking."

Slowly, now, they move. The golden hue begins to diminish and in its place, there appears a luster of silver-white with some unique depth to it. It glows and reflects. Then it changes into an enchantingly brilliant blue-white.

Peter cannot help but comment. "Zachary, this is incredibly beautiful."

"Good, Pete. I'm glad you're happy with it because we have to stay here for a time."

"What?"

"Just a moment or two, and I'll answer your question."

Silently, Peter continues to follow Zachary's orb of expression in the form of light and then perceives Zachary coming to a state of rest. Peter does likewise.

"What is your state of expression, Peter? In other words, how are you?"

"I believe I'm fine. This was a marvelous experience. It seems, as I perceive at the moment, we are in the midst of a vast, if not endless, expression of color and light. I remember this from our earlier travels with Elizabeth and Rebecca, only this time it is of such magnificence, such splendor. Where are we? What is this?"

"This is, in essence, the outer limit of your expression at present. Another way of saying this to you is, were I to take you beyond this (presuming for the moment that I am capable of doing so, which is quite a presumption, I might add), it is probable that your consciousness would begin to fade and you would gradually fall into something similar to sleep in the Earth.

"That is because to go beyond here would be to subject you to influences beyond your grasp, beyond your comprehension, and therefore be so overwhelming to you that it would create a potential for disruption or imbalance. You see, Peter, within all of existence there is a gentle, loving expression of God's Law that grants each entity the fullness of their potential at any and all times. As one releases limitations upon themselves, they increase the potential of their movement in consciousness further and further.

"Where we are now you might consider to be roughly three full major realms above that of the Earth. Consequently, you could think that a limitless amount of expression is possible from here back 'down' to the Earth, giving you that as a form of reference."

"I believe I've grasped what you're explaining, in theory, Zack. But I still wonder why you brought me here."

"Good question. It's so that you would know your potential in this very moment, so that you could comprehend the immensity of existence by 'looking back' from the highest and best position that your level of spiritual acceptance will permit."

Looking in the direction from whence they came, Peter responds softly, "I see nothing. How can I 'look back over,' as you said, all of existence that is behind ... or whatever our present position is?"

"To do this, you must give up something."

"Give up something? Like what?"

"You must give up a certain quality within you that, while it is commendable and even a remarkable part of you who is progressing in other realms, it will be more of a burden than commendable in your future works. This does not mean you must abandon it or that you must assume an opposite position. That would be inadvisable. But you would do well to place that quality in an appropriate position of balance within you in order to accomplish what you have said you wish to do."

"You mean to be a willing worker?"

"Yes, that's correct."

"Well, help me to find that thing, whatever it is, and I'll do my best."

"I know you will, and I knew that would be your answer. So I would like you now to see if you can find within yourself some aspect that seems, in some way, inappropriate for where you are. Will you do that for me for a time?"

"Sure. How should I look for it?"

"However you are guided. You must follow your guidance in this work. And you must learn to do this more and more in those times ahead."

"Very well, Zachary. Excuse me a moment. I feel that I should go within now."

(As we observe Peter, his cloak—in other words, the outer periphery of his expression—takes on a more energized

appearance and quality. We can tell from our own experience in such things that Peter is exploring his nature thoroughly, bit by bit, in utter, stark honesty. He is striving to know himself, all the pluses and minuses as you would call them, to the greatest degree possible within him.

Now and then we can see differing luminosity here or there, which we know to be indicative of self-realizations, awareness, acceptance of past experiences, habits, attitudes, and all that sort.

Gradually, the outer sphere of Peter's countenance stabilizes and becomes consistent as "Peter" once again.)

"Well, Zachary, that was quite an experience. I seem to intuit that it was made possible by our position in this realm."

"Yes, that's true, Pete. You couldn't have actually been able to do that with such completeness in a realm where influences other than the highest and best were present. You would simply be too vulnerable. Certainly, we could have collectively—myself and Rebecca, Elizabeth, Hope, Paul and the others—protected you while so doing, if there was a need, just as we have done in the past. And you and I will protect others in times ahead as they seek to do this in the Earth and other realms.

"But you, in your direction and pathway as a worker on the Master's path, must have the right of complete individual freedom, unaffected by any other potential force, including myself, to make these discoveries in and of yourself. This is why none of the others accompanied us. If you will notice, I have maintained some distance and a condition of being 'closed down' so as to avoid any potential interference. So, have you made any discoveries that you wish to discuss?"

"I believe so. The one singular point is that my own humility somehow or other seems to be the heaviest of all of my aspects. Maybe humility is the wrong word for describing this, but it has to do with a quality of considering myself less than equal or worthy to such works as I presume lie ahead, and certainly to being associated with the Master, the Christ, in that way."

"That's it, Pete! You must strive for a state of understanding where you realize that you and the Master are brothers. Were you in a female body in the Earth in your last incarnation, perhaps we would be calling you sisters. But since there is no real male-female issue and no sense of polarity in this matter, for the Christ is complete, you can think of yourself as being a part of and even an extension of the Christ Spirit. Now before you can counter that with any comment, consider this: He has said this to you, has He not?"

"Yes, He did."

"Then if you doubt me, do you doubt Him, as well?"

"No, I don't, Zachary. It's just that I feel that He and you are being overly kind ... that I'm *truly* not worthy."

"Well, if you weren't worthy, He certainly wouldn't tell you that you are."

"I believe you, and I know that to be truth. So I must learn, then, to place my own feeling of lack of worthiness into a position of balance where I don't fall too much to one side or the other. So doing, I can function truly as an extension of the Christ, claiming my heritage from God, the Father, just like the Christ, without becoming 'personalized' in that."

"Excellent! That's a good discovery. Because you've made it by yourself, you will grow, even as we are speaking and in all things that we are doing, to move to a state of balance and harmony in that realization. Now I wish to accomplish one other thing while we're here, and I am confident that it will meet with your approval and joy."

Without a pause for any further comment from Peter, Zachary moves off and Peter follows. Abruptly, all of the color and light seem to infuse into an expression and one abrupt change after another, until finally, Zachary comes to a stop, and Peter with him.

"Take a form, Peter, just for convenience."

Dutifully, Peter focuses upon his own being and expresses himself in a way similar to that of his expression in his Garden.

"Good." Peter notes that Zachary has done the same. "Now, follow me."

They move into a vast continuum of color and light that is like flying into a beautiful white cloud in the Earth. Suddenly, it disperses and they come to what Peter thinks could very well be his Garden Realm or the realm where the hospital was that they left not long ago.

"Have we gone back down, Zachary?"

Turning to Peter, Zachary smiles and shakes his head. "No, not at all. I've only asked you for this expression for a sense of continuity. Any form could be used here, but this one will give you some grasp of that continuity and several other aspects for the order in your logical thinking process."

There is lush greenery, beauty everywhere, resplendent with color, flowers, and plants. Peter can hear sounds of laughter that is almost like singing. He marvels at it. "Goodness, this sounds almost child-like here."

Zachary continues to move, with Peter beside him, until they come to a group of entities gathered together, concentrating on something they are doing. "Excuse me," interrupts Zachary. "But we've come to look for a friend of ours."

One of the heads in the small circle before them pops up. Peter instantly recognizes Bobby!

"Mr. Peter, I see you have visited me as you promised. How wonderful. And Mr. Zachary, how good to see you again. I did mention your name to many here and, as you said, I was well received and joyfully provided for. Though I must add, Mr. Zachary, I suspect I would have been anyway."

Peter marvels at the melodious sound of laughter that spills forth from Bobby.

Zachary laughs. "Well, Bobby, I see you have fully regained your awareness."

"Oh, yes, Mr. Zachary, and thank you for your bit of ... *medication* in the Healing Realm. You, as well, Mr. Peter," laughing at his own comment, "though I suppose I needn't call you Misters any longer."

Still somewhat surprised by this event, Peter walks around the periphery of the group, which causes them to spew forth more melodious laughter. *Enchanting*, Peter thinks to himself. *Utterly enchanting.*

Bobby walks over to Peter. "Except ye be as these little children, ye cannot enter the kingdom of my Father. Right, Peter?"

"Uh, yes, it is so. But may I ask you, Bobby, your friends here ... they appear almost child-like, as well. Is this a realm of children? Or how would you define this?"

"I would not attempt to define it but merely to share it. Obviously, you are here because you are capable of being here, and that speaks for itself. And Zachary, I am so joyful to see you again." He moves over to Zachary and the two embrace mightily.

Then Bobby turns back to Peter. "You have chosen to join us, then, Peter, in our work with Him. I am most pleased, and we welcome you. Should there ever be that which we can contribute in service to any works that you are about, I trust you would call upon us, and we will be immediately at your side and at your service in our Brother's Name."

Peter realizes that the "Brother" is the Christ and now understands the importance of Zachary's work with him. Because of it, he is able to accept Bobby's comment. "And I am, equally, ever at *your* service, in our Brother's Name."

"Well, then, we must meet here often and in other works. Remember that, journeying in joyous spontaneity and the golden truth of child-like essence, helps make all things possible. For instance, the imagination and creativity that are found so prevalently in the youth of the Earth can be carried forth into the creativity of our Father's highest works. These are wondrous blessings and great treasures that we must somehow find the means to share, and with other realms and other entities. Do you not agree?"

Peter smiles and nods.

"Well, I know we will join our works together in the future, but I also am aware of the call to you at this moment from your colleague Paul. So, Peter, I will embrace you with the blessings I am permitted to give, that you might carry these with you wherever you dwell and in whatever works you might be about."

Bobby embraces Peter and then Zachary.

In the next moment, Bobby turns into a brilliant sphere, radiating spires of light from the central core of his being, and Peter notes that all of Bobby's group have done the same. Next, they come together in one immensely beautiful great sphere, many times over its brilliance.

"We shall look for you in future activities, Peter and Zachary, and hope that you will look for us."

There is a sound and an expression of light. The great sphere is gone, and the surrounding light previously present closes in once again.

Peter and Zachary re-express themselves as forms of light, and Zachary leads the way as they move. Peter feels their movement demarcated by the energy changes of various realms of expressions, until they are standing before Paul, Hope, Rebecca and Elizabeth, once again.

Paul is speaking. "So, in a state of rest, Zeb and the others will care for him." He turns to greet Peter and Zachary. "Welcome back. Now, on to other works. Are you ready?"

"Ready," answers Peter along with all the others.

So shall conclude, leaving you to consider your own works in a similar light.

Editor's Note:

For those of you who are also using the study guides accompanying the Peter Chronicles, you already know that there was a group following those Al Miner/Lama Sing readings. In 1986 this group, who called themselves the "Voyagers", began working together with the Lama Sing group on projects: channeled readings on given topics. Lama Sing would open the project, and the members could send in questions about the topic and anything Lama Sing had given. Al would then present these questions to the Lama Sing group. The readings would then be transcribed, and Al would mail these Q&A readings to each project member.

At this juncture in the "Peter Project", Lama Sing began the reading with the following message to the Voyagers, and now to you since your interest has brought you to this point.

A MESSAGE FROM THE LAMA SING GROUP

AUGUST 1, 1992

The relationship between Peter and his colleagues and the Voyager group grows in its strength and effectiveness with the passage of each Earth day. Why? How? It grows because you have opened yourselves to that as a potential, a possibility. Therefore, you have given permission, a license, if you will, that your spiritual self and these souls who serve, quest, and seek in God's Name, might, as appropriate, enjoin themselves into oneness to bring forth the realization of your eternal and unlimited natures.

In this, then, many works can be done, for where two or more are gathered, there do we find the strength, the emergence of a spiritual force, that gains in its power and potency by the addition of each one pledged to serve.

The following might be the thoughts that we encourage and that have been the intent in the question presented by the Channel as an overview of the Peter Works to date and perhaps intensified more recently:

The activities and works that you might consider now are those that you know in your heart need doing. Look for those aspects within you that are in need of change. What are they? They are those things that limit you, those that take from you in this or that small way in any Earth day—in any single hour, minute, or moment—the gift of abundant joy that God continually offers to you. For above all else, you will know those who bear His signet by the joyful countenance and light that comes forth from the joy within them.

Look for those things, too, that tend to be burdensome. Are they yours or someone else's given to you inadvertently, equally accepted by you? Do not abandon cooperation, grace, long-suffering and such, but put these in an appropri-

ate place within you. The equality of self and the equality of all others is the point of demarcation from whence you might measure any aspect within yourself that is in question.

We believe that you will, before this [chapter] concludes, know or understand, at least in part, that even though there may be a lapse between projects, you will not, in truth, be apart. For your oneness with this group, and others that are not yet identified to you, is already in action to the degree that it has momentum and continuity. Were there to be no further works in the nature similar to those that have gone before, those works would continue on an individual and group basis.

For the present, we are encouraged to return to Peter and colleagues that we might convey to you several more points that have transpired and those that are about to.

We thank the Channel and each of you for your continued love and prayers for these works and all those souls who are gathered about same. We wish you to know that we continually reciprocate in kind, enacting God's Laws, that your good wishes, thoughts, and prayers are returned to you many-fold over.

CHAPTER 5

Simultaneous Expression

AUGUST 1, 1992

Since our last contact with Peter and the group, there have been a number of journeys and what could be considered works. Among these have been visits to realms that are quite adjacent to the Earth in terms of their consciousness, their affinity or interest. Sometime in the past, the Channel titled these realms the "Sea of Faces," perhaps appropriately so in many respects.

The purpose for Paul having taken the group, and specifically Peter, to these realms and levels of expression was to identify to him and equally so to Hope the various levels of "illusion" that souls can subject themselves to. The journeys demonstrated the intensity with which these souls can support that illusion—that sense of separateness and of finiteness.

Noteworthy here has been Peter's surprise at how difficult it has been to communicate with some of these entities. He met with remarkable resistance, at least by his judgment, to logic, reason, and truth. He has also re-experienced the value and purpose of what has been called the spiritual cloak, and many other aspects as are associated with its functions in events and works.

And so now we rejoin Peter and Zachary, Paul, Hope, Elizabeth, and Rebecca in mid-stream of a line of conversation.

"Paul, is it always this way in these realms? These entities so intensely determined to continue an existence that is like how they lived in the Earth in their previous life? So much so that one cannot use any logic, reason, or any other tools to bring them truth?"

"Well, Peter, not all of these specific realms—or sub-realms, as they might more appropriately be called—are exactly like this. But generally speaking, you have correctly assessed your experience. As we move a bit away from the Earth, you will find the intensity diminishes a little. Maybe I could explain it this way: In the sub-realms or levels of expression in what has been called by some the Sea of Faces, it is the redundancy. This boredom causes them to be a bit more receptive to reach a point where they are just a whit more open to reason, logic, and truth."

"Wow, this has been a remarkable experience for me. Thank you for bringing us here and for sharing this understanding. After having visited Bobby and his realm, this is a real eye-opener. What an opposite end of the spectrum. Sort of like moving from the top of the Empire State Building to the basement, or maybe I'd better make that the sub-basement."

"A good analogy, Pete," responds Zachary, "but it implies that there is but one such structure when, in fact, there are many. If you would consider that we might place an Empire State Building upon the top of the one, and then another on top of that, and again and again, you'd have a better picture. Do you get my meaning?"

Peter reflects for but a moment. "So the level of acceptance can replicate itself in each of what I've come to know as the major realms of expression?"

"That's right. And with each rise of conscious acceptance, there comes a new, I'll call it, layer of experiencing that has some of the same energies, challenges, and so forth, as in the previous layer. This familiarity sharpens the ability of the traveller, the soul in motion, as they progress through each level."

"It is not that each major realm of expression is so numerically defined or so graphically depicted," adds Paul, "but more like one seeing their thought moving further and further from limitation and closer and closer to an unlimited state of expression. These major realms are like stopovers where the soul can readjust, re-evaluate its understanding, moving through, in essence, seven foundational perspectives.

"I believe I am grasping this." Peter glances over at Hope, remembering that she is less experienced with such things. "Hope, how do you relate to all of this, since you have had no physical experience to bounce it off of?"

A flicker of warmth flashes from her. "While I have no experience to bounce this off of, Peter, I do have some degree of observation borne by my earlier experiences. As a result, I can align this logically into my knowledge that brings me a better understanding of what I was dealing with previously. And I pray it better equips me to deal with such matters in the 'future.' as in the serial experiencing you call time."

Peter is reflecting, attempting to absorb the thought-forms communicated to him as well as the verbal description.

"Peter," Elizabeth adds, "we have learned much here regarding how we might deal with potential commissions in the future. As we learned in Hope's realm, you and I have a mutual oneness that gives us a continual flow of consciousness. So, when you were off with Zachary some time back and then visited with Bobby, in all that, I was able to be with you yet still be with Paul and his work with Hope and Rebecca."

"Just a minute! I did feel your presence as I almost always do. But your comment about being in both places or in both expressions simultaneously intrigues me. I would like at some point," turning to Zachary and Paul, "to revisit this topic and experience this for myself."

Paul smiles an affirmation.

Zachary is looking down and moving about in a manner as though he has a concern. "And when would you like to do this, Pete?"

A bit surprised, Peter gives off a little rivulet of light.

Zachary chuckles aloud. "Ah, yes, just checking. Wanted to be sure it was still you in there."

At that, laughter comes forth from the entire group.

"Well, to one-up you, I believe I'm ready at this moment. I'm perfectly in balance and ready to experience being here," smiling at Elizabeth, "and somewhere else at the same time."

Zachary looks up with his whimsical grin. "No sooner said than done, Pete." Then he just gazes at Peter.

A few moments pass.

Peter is puzzled. "Well, Zack? What about it?"

"What about what?"

"When do we go to somewhere else as well as here?"

"How's that?" Zachary feigns a lack of understanding.

"Well, you know, I'm here, you're here, we're all here. How do we be somewhere else at the same time?"

"Do you think there must be a mode of travel? A button to push? Some sort of magic statement of words? Or perhaps some of this?" He raises one hand and spins a finger in the "air" after which there is the familiar jingle-jangle associated with Zachary. Then he simply waits for Peter's response.

Peter looks, bewildered, from Zachary to Paul, then to Hope and Rebecca, and finally to Elizabeth, who is smiling as are they all.

"If you don't mind my saying, Peter, Zachary is just attempting to help you realize what you already know."

He turns back to Zachary. "Sometimes, Zachary, all of this is so, well, thick. You know, like I never understand what it is you're trying to show me, and then all of a sudden you do some little thing or take me around the barn, as they say in the Earth, and there it is right in front of me. How is it that I have been to Hope's realm and been in such magnificent forms of expression and I am still, uh, you know," as he glances from one to the other, "so limited."

"Limitation, Peter, is always self-imposed."

"That's it? Limitation is always self-imposed? What am I

to make of that? I am imposing my own limitations?"

Zachary merely nods.

Peter turns to Paul, who smiles and nods as well, as do each of the others in succession. When his eyes come to rest on Elizabeth, he pleads. "Elizabeth, help! I don't understand." Her laughter is so melodious and so soothing that it immediately sweeps away any vestiges of frustration and leaves Peter utterly balanced. At that moment, she looks at him in a manner that means she is about to communicate something to him, and him alone, to the exclusion of all the others.

There is a transmission that follows of streams of light, changing in their color and pattern. Associated with those energies are sounds. In effect, these are all thought-forms.

In but a few moments, Peter smiles and turns back to Zachary. "I understand now. Thank you, Elizabeth. When I moved from the Angelic Realm back to the finite realms of expression, I did so by adopting what was familiar to me. So as I, in essence, re-clothed my consciousness in the familiarity I know as 'Peter,' I also inadvertently accepted the limitations I had associated with that 'Peter expression.' So you're saying, Zack, that it is these that prevent me from knowing that I am in more than one place at the same time?"

Zachary turns to Elizabeth. "Well done, as usual," which brings from her a soft smile.

Paul touches Peter on the cloak or shoulder. "You have grasped that quite well. I would like to continue with this for a time, but I would also like to point out to you something else that I know Zachary and the others are aware of. I direct you inwardly, so that you, too, might be aware of this."

"Very well, Paul." Immediately, Peter "shuts down." His cloak becomes brightly illuminated. Momentarily he reappears. "I hear a call. Is it a call to gather, to meet?"

"Precisely."

"And this is a call to gather in the Great Hall?"

Paul confirms Peter's perception.

"Shall I lead, Paul?" asks Zachary.

"Excellent. But I might suggest that you afford Peter just one additional little opportunity to experience something in line with his last question, that it is not left hanging." He turns to Peter. "Pete, just to show you that you are conscious in more expressions than this one here," he taps Peter on the cloak, "I would like you to now visualize your Garden."

Instantly, Peter has the memory, the image, the thought-form. In that same instant, he realizes that he and the entire group are standing on the little knoll of his Garden.

"What? Wait a minute! That's the fastest trip we've ever taken."

Zachary shakes his head with a little upturned grin on one side of his countenance. "No trip at all. Just movement of consciousness from one expression to another."

"What are you saying, Zack?"

"I'm answering your question about being conscious in more than one expression at a time."

"Well, I am only conscious of being here in the Garden."

"You are also conscious back here."

Peter, in much less than an instant, is now aware of them being back on the periphery of the Sea of Faces where the first portion of this conversation took place. The Garden Realm is entirely absent.

"See? You are here. You've never left."

"But if I am here and a moment ago I was there, all that I have done is move very swiftly."

"No, all that you have done is slowly shift your focus."

"Slowly? You call that slow?"

"Everything is relative. Isn't speed is a relative meas-urement?"

"Ah, yes, Zack, you're right."

"Well, in comparison to simultaneous consciousness, that was slow."

"Okay. May I have a moment or two longer, Paul? I'm

almost grasping this."

Smiling, Paul moves back a step or two indicating that they should continue.

Zachary turns back to Peter. "Which shall it be, Peter? The Garden or this realm?" gesturing outward with his arm.

"The Garden."

Immediately, they are on the knoll in the Garden.

"Now, how about going back, Pete?"

"Very well,"

Again they are immediately back in the dull grayness of the periphery of the Sea of Faces.

"Now mentally, Peter, reach out with one portion of your consciousness, as though you were looking in a mirror, and see the Garden."

Peter does not question but visualizes, as though he were looking at himself in a mirror, and sees the Garden. He turns back to Zachary, just to make certain that he is still where he is. Then, shifting his conscious perception back and forth from the visualized frame of a mirror, Peter finds himself awestruck at the immediacy of the Garden. He moves forward and leans as though trying to peer through the frame of an actual looking glass, though this has no glass in it.

This brings uproarious laughter from Zachary as well as all the others. The laughter subsides, but Peter continues, as though oblivious to the mirth enjoyed by his colleagues.

Zachary slips up to Peter's side and, mocking Peter lovingly, places his shoulder up against Peter's. "Give me a bit of room here, Pete. Let me have a look, too. Hey, I've got an idea. I'll just take hold of this side and enlarge this a bit." He pretends to grasp the periphery of the Garden scene and gives a stout pull backward.

Peter stumbles forward, as though about to fall through the imaginary looking glass frame, and the laughter breaks out again, as Zachary reaches out to grasp Peter, as though to keep him from falling. With a note of humor, he feigns a warning. "Careful, Pete, don't bump your shins on the bottom of that frame."

Peter, so engrossed in the whole affair, automatically looks down before glancing back up at Zachary and laughing, as the others join in. All are resplendent in loving joy and humor for a considerable time.

After awhile, Peter, still amazed at what has transpired, steps forward again and perceives himself and the group on the other side as a sort of imaginary, albeit shimmering vertical energy. He remembers seeing the heat rays rising off the asphalt highways in the Earth and thinks of the mirages in the deserts and on the seas. All these memories place this in a sense of appropriateness in his awareness.

Zachary is aware of Peter's thoughts. "You wouldn't need that, either, Pete. But for now, it's of no concern. You'll notice, as we're speaking, that your presence, our presence, in the Sea of Faces is fading. As it does, don't let that bother you. We have no more active purpose there at present, so we are, in a manner of speaking, shutting down or turning off our conscious participation in that realm of expression. You could, if you wished, at any time re-awaken it with a ... well, call it thought or a concentration of your awareness on it. As immediately as you can do this, you would be there. You'll ask me next, how does that work, right?"

"Right," grins Peter, boyishly.

"Well, I'll tell you. Wherever you have been, whatever you have been a part of—or in the case of a willing worker, wherever there is the consciousness of the Christ (which is to say, everywhere)—you have the potential of being there."

"Truly? Anywhere?"

"Yes, Peter. Anywhere."

"Any place?"

"Any place."

"Any realm?"

"Yes, any realm. What's the difference between a realm

and a place, anyway?"

"Well, you know, Zachary, I'm talking about a finite expression and a less than finite expression."

"Okay, Pete. Have it your way. A place is a place; it depends upon the perceiver, doesn't it?"

"I guess that's so."

"Well, let me add this to the kettle of fish you're stirring inside your consciousness," which invokes a bit of humor from the others again and even from Peter. "You not only can be in any 'place or realm' but you can be there at any time."

"Wait! What do you mean 'any time'?"

"Your time, that stuff you lived by in the Earth. You know ... today, tomorrow, yesterday, this year, next year, last year. Understand?" Grinning slightly, Zachary studies Peter.

"I get the picture. Unbelievable as that might seem, I think I understand. You're talking about the difference between limitation and being unlimited. True?"

"Good!"

Paul agrees. "Very good."

"So, let me see," muses Peter. "If I wanted to be at a certain place during a certain time, you could show me?"

Zachary is more serious now. "I could help you understand how to get there, but I can't do it for you. Once you reach that point, Pete, it's pretty much a matter of you as an individual rising to the point of being so unlimited as to be able to pass through those ... well, for the moment, let me call them barriers or, yes, perhaps limitations. You have drawn from your experiences, and the resulting memories are very much a part of the foundation of who and what you are at present. But your foundational self must be, forgive the term, rock-solid, or you won't be able to accomplish this."

"It sounds like an awesome new adventure."

"I suppose you could think of it in that way." Zachary turns to Paul who is shaking his head. "But as you'll note, Pete, Paul is encouraging us not to pursue this at this point, and I must admit I agree with him."

"Why?" asks Peter, turning to Paul. "Why would you suggest that I not pursue this now?"

Radiating immense love and compassion as he has often known Paul to do in an almost magical, healing way, Peter perceives Paul's answer. "Because, Peter, what you are discussing and considering is so vast, so expansive, and the potentials utterly innumerable, that I am guided inwardly, as I know you would be if you inquired within, to proceed orderly along those lines, in an appropriate state.

"It is not that you would be harmed or injured or any of that sort. You would simply find yourself unable to accomplish your desired intent, and this, in and of itself, would require that you methodically explore why. In that exploration, you would possibly expend considerable amounts of your consciousness and what you might refer to as time that we collectively believe you might apply far better in other areas. Curiously, as is always known here, as a result of doing that which is 'the highest and best,' you will always be given that which you seek.

"So, rather than mire yourself in some of the other possibilities, use the best that you have—the talents, the opportunities, the consciousness—for the highest and best possible now before you. And the other will be given. Make no mistake about this. When it is purposeful for you to discover these tools within yourself, they will simply be there. The effort will be minimal, if not non-existent, for you to do these and even more. We can perceive in your thoughts the possibility of moving backward in what you call time.

"Let me offer you an alternative: There is a Universal Consciousness upon which all experiences are recorded. It is referred to by some as the Akasha. Whether it's called the Akasha or the Hall of Records, where the individual records or books (as they are often thought of and visualized by some) is not as important as the essence of what is there. You can think of this as a vast library almost infinite in nature, where many willing workers will assist you in finding any information you have a desire to know, and that is rightfully appropriate for you to know as governed by Universal Law." Peter is visibly softened now, thanks to the grace and love of the energies with which Paul has conveyed these thoughts. "I would like very much to visit the Akasha or Hall of Records and to simply know of all this."

"Well, to a degree, this you have already done, Peter. You will recall—as we passed through the various expressions that you understood as colors, vibrations, and energies shortly after your departure from the Earth—you were shown many things, given much understanding. You were counseled and lovingly, gently, guided to understand how all that had transpired fits into the composite of your beingness or consciousness. Reach back and remember that. Do you recall?"

Peter is pleased, as he draws to the forefront of his awareness the complete and vivid memories of all that Paul has described. "Zachary, I believe that last exercise opened some doors for me! My memory, my awareness, is much clearer, much brighter."

"That's great." Zachary muffles a hint of humor as he turns to the side and looks off into the distance. Peter knows Zachary so well now that he himself chuckles a bit at his own comment.

Paul moves to Peter's side. "Peter, forgive me for interrupting, but if you will turn inward again, the call is before us, and we must move to the Great Hall."

Instantly, Peter is able to confirm Paul's statement, and they move gently, as though borne by some undulating, silky-like fabric that is carrying them to the entryway of the Great Hall.

Pausing, Peter turns to look back. The others pause with him. "How vast, how wondrous and beautiful God is. I am so thankful for, my friends, and having all of this from which I might learn. Oh, how I wish and pray that others might have this same good fortune as have I, and good friends such as you all, so loving, patient, and humorous ... " with which he winks one of Zachary's exaggerated winks at Zachary and receives like in kind. "I guess you know what's inside me at this moment. Still, I had made a note to myself that I wanted to stop you all and thank you," and he embraces each one.

All are visibly moved by Peter's expression of gratitude, and as he embraces each one, he becomes increasingly aware of something taking place, growing. When he reaches Zachary, who is last, he turns and looks up over his shoulder to Zachary, who is immediately behind him. "What is that? What is happening here, Zachary?"

"It's a prayer, Pete."

"A prayer?"

"Yes. A prayer."

"Who gave it?"

Zachary laughs softly. "Well, you did."

Turning, Peter faces Zachary. "I gave no prayer."

"Oh, but you did."

Peter glances at the others, who are all nodding. He reflects over the last few moments. "I only expressed my gratitude to God and all of you for ... Oh, I see. I guess that is a prayer, isn't it?"

Smiling with remarkable softness for his nature, Zachary explains. "It is, indeed. Prayer does not have to be the recitation of certain words designated to be a prayer. Your very actions that come from within the core of your being are prayerful expressions of existence. They are like living prayers. They are like being in a state of joyous prayer, and all here would say that you, Peter, exist in a state of joyous prayer."

All smile at Peter.

"Are you saying to me that I am a living prayer?"

"Yes, Peter, a joyous expression of living prayer."

"But I have faults, flaws, limitations. How could you say

that my existence is one of joyous living prayer?"

"It's you, Pete."

"That is so," adds Paul. "You focus with sincerity on yourself and all things, and this is a trait that is borne by the Spirit of our Brother, the Christ. The earnestness with which you approach all of your actions and deeds is carried in an essence of truth and loving compassion. Where can we find you, among our experiences together, as having faulted another? Where is there, in all that we have shared together, where you have criticized another? Has there been an instance where you have not been willing to give of yourself utterly for the need of another? You are truly living in a state of joyous prayer, and this is living the principles of the Christ. You may not completely know this in your finite knowledge, but it is within you as truth.

"Not to test you or challenge you, Peter," Paul continues, "but repeatedly we have brought you to events and situations that offered you the opportunity to challenge and test yourself. In each and every one of these, we have never found you to be wanting." Paul glances to the others and they affirm this as truth. "You always came forth with the spirit and essence of God's Law, and that, you see, is living in joyous prayer.

"So, while you might not think of your expressions of gratitude and your actions of kindness and sincerity as being prayer-like, they are the equal of any prayer you might recite from your memory in the Earth, and far, far more than that.

"What you just experienced, that Zachary identified as prayer, is how you can perceive prayer when you move a step beyond that veil of finiteness or limitation that had been a barrier around you. Your humorous experience with Zachary and the looking glass penetrated that. This is why, as you noted, you can now perceive many things far more clearly than ever before, not the least of which is the true essence of prayer, its energy, its substance, its expression in any realm or dimension. Do you see now, Peter?"

"I do. My, how veiled is our thinking when in the Earth. We think of the specific words as being so important that we lose sight of the meaning of what we are saying. I couldn't begin to estimate how many times I recited a certain prayer, and yet I don't know, except at this very moment, that I truly understood what it was that I was saying or attempting to send forth."

"That's quite alright," responds Paul. "For actually, you see, it is not the explicitness of one's mechanism of communicating with God, but rather, what's in the heart."

"How beautiful. So God's Law grants to all, through the … might I call it, limit of their consciousness, the same grace, whether they are knowledgeable or not. God can see what is in their heart, and the Law works perfectly in accordance with what is housed within them as their intent and purpose."

They all nod to Peter, smiling.

"I can also see, in this same moment, how so many over the history of the Earth have attempted to give the impression to others of their holiness. Yet it was in their heart where it was measured, not by any judge or jury or even by God but by they themselves. The result of that self-evaluation is what determined their limit of consciousness and expression."

"There is considerable accuracy in that," responds Zachary, "and I'm so joyful, Peter, that you have come to this realization so easily. Just look at how many barns we've saved ourselves from having to go around."

The laughter from that comment reverberates, as though embraced by the very Hall itself. In a few moments, Peter is aware that others have gathered, and are greeting them and sharing in the laughter, complimenting him and the group for their past works. Peter recognizes and embraces many former acquaintances in his journeys in these realms, and introduces Hope. This unfolds as there is a general movement into the Great Hall, where Peter now sees the magnificence of the grand table that he has come to hold dear in his heart. He notes other entities who seem somehow familiar to him, though he cannot consciously recall them. As he reflects and reaches back to remember specifically some he notes off in the distance, who meet his gaze with warm smiles and gestures of recognition, he feels himself being nudged.

"We'd best take our places and be ready, eh, Pete?"

"Oh, yes, of course, Zachary."

Peter and his colleagues are now gathered at the beautiful table, which sweeps off in its immense expanse to what seems to Peter to be unlimited in distance. There is then a shift of Peter's focus back to the area in front of them, as the beautiful glow begins to form. His anticipation rises to a heightened state as he awaits the presence of the One he loves so dearly, which he now knows is the Christ.

Suddenly, there before him is the image of this loving personage, smiling at him with such a radiance as to energize him in every single fiber of his being. He is warmed to the core. Peter perceives that He has moved to each one present and, likewise, greeted them, communicated with them, until the Master once again stands before him in His utter glory and raiment.

Now Peter perceives behind and above, to the right and left of the Master, wondrous orbs of incredibly beautiful light and color, sound and vibrancy, that seem to be hovering, as though legions of angels are surrounding and embracing the very presence of the Master.

Unexpectedly, Peter recognizes a familiarity to one of these spheres. Inside his being, he hears, *Greetings, Peter. I told you we'd meet again. It's me, of course! Bobby!* Peter is stunned, yet thrilled.

Next, he hears these communications from the Master Himself: *We have had much to rejoice in, Peter, and there are many more joyous works that we now offer to you and your dear companions here. I have already spoken with each of them, and now I would communicate to you directly, you and I in a state of oneness.*

I have heard and accepted your offer to become what you have called a willing worker. I rejoice in this, as does my Father, your Father, the Father of all. There are those of our brethren who are in various states of limited consciousness and joy. I wish to offer you, as I have your companions, a new commission, that these who are in such need might be served some of the joy and blessings that you now know so well. Will you share in this work with me and your brethren?

Peter's being is resplendent in the reflection of the Christ, which has been awakened within Peter, as well. His nature comes to the forefront of his consciousness and he responds: "O Lord, wherever You send me I shall go willingly and joyfully to do whatever work You deem me capable of doing. I do not know, Lord, how I have come to be sufficiently worthy to be in Your presence, much less to do any service, great or small, under the mantle of Your Name. But this I accept with joy to the fiber of my existence. This I pledge to the end of my consciousness (if such might exist). Yes, my Lord, I accept joyfully."

There is but a nod, and the Master reaches out to literally touch Peter in an embrace. Softly, gently, He leans forward, and there appears to be the simple touch by Him in what you would understand to be His forehead to Peter's.

From Peter come spires of brilliant white light with a soft hue of yellowish gold.

The Master moves back and turns, then, to bless each and every one. Not one is missed at the entire gathering. Then He moves to where Hope is seated, lovingly, adoringly, looking up at the Master. He reaches out to her, causing her to rise, and then turns to the group. *My dear brethren. This is one of our own who has come to help those who have gone before. I ask you, in your own nature, to greet this one who is called ... Hope.*

Hope's angelic light merges momentarily with that of the

Master's, before His light envelops Him, becomes a sphere, and is gone along with the accompanying spheres.

We shall now conclude for this gathering. In the next works, Peter and his colleagues will be upon a work directly in the service to the Christ.

For the present, we ask that the grace and blessings of our Father's wisdom ever surround and guide you.

CHAPTER 6

The New Commission

NOVEMBER 8, 1992

We turn now to those events in our last gathering and attempt to recapitulate what transpired during your "absence" (with a note of loving humor, for only the mind conscious of these meetings has been temporarily absent).

After Peter and his colleagues emerged from the Great Hall, they moved to the knoll in the Garden Realm, Peter's beloved place, where many discussions transpired. At first, the focus was to help Peter better understand how it could be possible that he could ever be worthy of such recognition, much less to be given a work directly by the Master. There were many activities and journeys, which involved visits to Wilbur's realm and to see Todd, and numerous other such events. There were times when the group was temporarily divided for purposes that were unique to Hope and to Rebecca. We shall lay those aside for the present. If you desire, they can be explored at another time.

The group joined up again in the Garden Realm. A discussion and some events transpired that are worthy of being related here because these directly relate to the work. They will provide you with some understanding that may be essential to help you grasp more fully what shall transpire thereafter, so we shall relate the events as best we can and, thereafter, carry on into what shall transpire.

We would like to remind you and to emphasize, once again, as we begin this new journey into Peter's works (as they are colloquially called), that in the commentaries we give through the Channel we shall attempt to be as clear as possible. In some instances, we will augment what occurs with brief commentary from our group in order to facilitate better understanding. In all cases, you are invited to participate at all levels of your being. We encourage you to explore individually and collectively, as much as you feel guided to so do, the works that are forthcoming.

Surrounded by the greenery, augmented by brilliant colors and hues that exceed the known color spectrum of Earth, we find our group gathered—Paul, Rebecca, Hope, Elizabeth, Peter, and, of course, Zachary—on the beautiful high knoll in Peter's Garden. All are seated upon the lush grass. The energy about the group is highly charged and vivid in its light and brilliance. The Great Hall is a short distance away to the right (from our perspective). To the left is the beautiful, undulating white mist as Peter has described it previously (which, in effect, could lead to anywhere). All have been laughing somewhat vigorously as they recounted some of their previous experiences in answer to one of Peter's many questions.

The laughter lingers as Paul turns to Peter with a smile. "It has been so wonderful to have participated with you in these adventures. Adventure is a good name for these experiences and for what lies before us, which might be considered not only by you and our group here but many others as well, to be the greatest adventure of all."

This brings a note of seriousness to Peter's countenance. Zachary, who is somewhat inclined upon the 'earth,' gently brushing the grass as is his nature, glances up to peer at Peter.

"I have, as you might surmise, many questions. When the Master spoke of those in need (or however He put it, I can't recall at the moment specifically), but when He spoke of those in need and our opportunity to share with them that which we know and the joy and warmth and so on that I and all of you have experienced ... " He looks about the group and receives warm affirmations from all, coming finally to rest his gaze upon Zachary, whose face is essentially blank.

But he receives a brief wink and knows this to be about all he's going to get from Zachary at this point. In other words, Zachary is encouraging him to proceed. Zachary continues to brush his hand across the greenery. Peter notices tiny little sparks and pops of light that seem to come from the blades of grass themselves with every stroke. Somewhat distracted by this, but still wanting his questions answered, Peter continues. "Why would He need my help? I can understand why He would welcome your help, for you are all, well, you know, seasoned veterans." Humor comes forth from the group. Peter shrugs his shoulders. "You know what I mean. I have only these limited experiences and more questions than I have knowledge. What could the Master possibly see in me that would make my participation worthy of any significance? And I'm not being humble here, just honest."

"Honesty ... always a good policy, Pete. Keep it up. You'll get far that way." Zachary steals a quick glance up at Peter and then back down. The grass is now sparkling and popping spheres of tiny lights with even more vigor.

Peter accepts Zachary's comment and looks to the others, realizing that Zachary is waiting for an appropriate point of receptivity on his part before he is going to comment or do some work which will undoubtedly teach him something. As those thoughts pass through Peter's mind, Zachary glances up again. "Very good, Pete. Very good, indeed."

Peter flushes, remembering that Zachary and he have an open line of communication. The flush appears as a pinkish coloration over his cloak. He turns to focus on Zachary again. "Well, you know these questions are important. If I'm going to do this work, I need to have these answers in order to be balanced within, to have understanding."

"Oh, sure Pete. I meant no offense, of course."

Again, Peter realizes Zachary intends no further comment, so he glances at the others.

Paul smiles. "All are worthy, Peter. In fact, all are called to His service. The individuals who open themselves to perceive and hear that call, and to know that it is ever present, will find themselves before the Master in some time, in some place, or as you would call it in the Earth, one day.

"It is not so much what you know or what you have as experience," continues Paul. "It's who and what you are. It could be the traveler on a pathway of searching who is only several steps along the Way, but who has found Truth and taken it within. Compare this to the traveler on that same path who has journeyed for centuries and has seen and heard Truth but has not been, for reasons known to them primarily, able to bring this within their being. It requires a certain level of acceptance, which means that other things that are very important to some must give way to this as a primary focus of intent and living." He pauses, studying Peter to see if he is absorbing this.

Peter realizes this and nods to Paul to confirm.

Paul adds, "Neither you nor we, our entire group here, Peter, shall be alone in this work. Quite to the contrary. We shall ever be in the presence of many other loving souls, each one who has some uniqueness in the individuality of their soul that they are willing to contribute to the work, that it can be as complete as possible. It is similar to each one contributing an ingredient to a formula to make it complete. So you bring the essence of your being, which we see as pure and open and receptive. You are a seeker, seeking in the spirit of Truth not for yourself alone, but for the potential that your growth might give to others."

Peter begins to speak, and Paul raises his hand to stop him. "I know what you are about to say, Peter, and I ask you not to express it but rather to simply listen to this: We can see you as you truly are. While you might not see yourself in the potential as we see you, we speak only truth to you. Therefore, do not think that the comments just given and those yet to come are given to flatter you, to entice you, or to deceive you. We hope you will agree that this is so."

Somewhat disarmed, Peter sputters, "Uh ... well, of course. I would never think that any of you here would tell me anything less than truth. I was just, uh, thinking, you know, that ... Well, here I am, you know, only here for a comparatively short time, and uh, that in itself is ... "

"Goodness, Peter, stop and think about what it is that you are trying to express. All those words are disturbing me here. And look at this. I'm going to have to start all over again. I can't get a spark out of a single blade. Those words have de-energized every blade under my hand!"

Laughter pours from the group, including Peter, for there are none in the group who have Peter's undying trust greater than Zachary and, of course, Paul. Peter welcomes Zachary's willingness to rejoin the activity and looks at him as though to invite him to say something ... anything.

A chuckle comes from Zachary, along with dancing melodious light, which Peter unconsciously follows as it fades off into the distance. "That's what I like about you, Pete. You are so real. You know, if I didn't know better, I would think you truly *are* real. But then, as we all know, reality is, uh ... well, it's sort of, uh ... neither here nor there. It's always somewhere else. And, uh ... well, let me think about that and, uh ... See what I mean, Pete?"

Peter laughs again. "I get the message, Zack!"

"Well, look, Pete. I'm not poking fun at you, but it's like this: We're about to embark on a very wholesome work, but it's not going to be just, as you call it in the Earth, a piece of cake. When you speak or when you act, take a moment to attune yourself to the *totality* of your being. Once you've done that, it would be very difficult for you to err or for you to fail to communicate well. True, Paul?"

Paul is still chuckling at Zachary's humor. "Well spoken, Zachary, indeed."

"But Zachary, you talk about real and reality. What is that anyway? I know you, and you wouldn't use terms and emphasize them unless there was a purpose, and I could see when you expressed that, that there was indeed emphasis."

"Excellent, Pete! It's good for you to perceive with all your faculties, not just that which is so common in the Earth but the inner self. When I speak of reality, I'm speaking of that which is conditionally effective for the individual. This conditional effectiveness has much to do with the works that are before us. You, when you were in the Earth, were conditionally effective as a man called Peter, were you not?"

"Well, I suppose I was reasonably so, Zachary."

"Come, come, now. You were Peter and, therefore, you were conditionally effective as Peter, because you were Peter. Right?"

"Hmm, I get what you're saying. Yes, I have to say I did a reasonably good job of being Peter." Humor pops and snaps all about the group. Even Hope radiates her gentle, rosy energies, which bounce off each one, and when they cascade into Peter, he is warmed and delighted to the core of his being. "Thanks, Hope. I needed that." She simply smiles.

Elizabeth chuckles. "We always need a bit of that, don't we, Peter?"

"Yes, I guess it's so." He turns to look at Hope. "Hope, you generate an essence, in the event you don't know it, that in the Earth—and I guess in many realms, if not all of them, I don't know yet—is similar to what we call true love. It's not a love bound by contract or promise. It's the love that comes from a person when they look at a flower or a newly hatched creature, something just born, new hope when they look into their children's eyes as they make a discovery. It's a glow of warmth many call love in the Earth, but I believe now that it is much more than this, and you have it. I would say (and correct me if I'm wrong) that you possess it at its primal level. It is an ecstatically joyful experience to encounter."

Hope is smiling. "What I am, Peter, is what God has given me. I have not learned, as many appear to have learned, that this should not be shared or given freely. I'm aware that by giving, I receive, and that the Source is unlimited. So it is natural for me to express this, as you call it, love, or glow, to those with whom I am sharing." Her eyes softly fixed on him, she notes he has understood, so she shifts her position back to observe the group.

"Rebecca," continues Peter. "I've often seen this essence in you, as well. I know you to be sort of family to Hope, and I know you two have been together for great periods of time. Yet somehow it's different. I don't know how to express it to you, but could you comment on that?"

Rebecca shows that she is pleased to be called upon. "That is a very astute observation on your part. I have attempted to blend this primal quality with many other essences I have come to understand as being of significant benefit to my purposes. And these, as I have gathered them through past experiences upon the active path, have become a part of my expression and are, therefore, evident in my cloak as they are in my consciousness. I can shift these aside, in a manner of speaking, and re-adopt the primal focus. Would you like to observe that, Peter?"

A bit surprised, Peter speaks without thinking. "Why yes. I would find that delightful, if you don't mind, Rebecca."

Rebecca glances at Hope, and Hope smiles and nods at her. Rebecca pauses for a moment, and instantly it becomes difficult to discern the outer periphery of either Hope or Rebecca individually, for they appear to be alike.

Peter is astounded. "Remarkable! You are almost as one light. Did I not know you each in the individual sense, I would think I am seeing two of the same before me."

Rebecca laughs softly. "That which is within—that is, the same as within Hope—is now evident. But you know our uniqueness, Peter, so you can yet perceive us as individuals.

Others who might not know our uniqueness in the personal sense would likely be unable to so do." Rebecca then returns her spiritual cloak to her previous countenance.

Peter marvels at how swiftly she is able to control this. "That was lovely, Rebecca, Hope. I thank you both." Turning to look around the group, Peter notices that Zachary is continuing to stroke the grass and once again the little popping bright spots of light are flashing. He cannot contain himself. "Zachary, why is it that you are always stroking the grass? No matter where we are, what we're doing, you always seem to fall back into that habit. Is there some point to it?"

Zachary never looks up. "Of course, Pete, why would I be doing this if it were pointless?"

"Well, I didn't mean that, Zachary. I meant, beyond just a pastime that brings you joy, is there some significance beyond that?"

"Sure, Pete, great significance. I am nourishing the grass, and the grass is nourishing me."

Studying Zachary, Peter knows there will be what he considers to be a punch line. "Okay, Zack. How is it that you are nourishing one another?"

Zachary straightens up, seats himself cross-legged with his hands on his knees. Smiling, he looks Peter in the eye and answers gently but directly. "You could say I am reminding myself that I am a part of the All." He pauses for effect and continues. "And the grass, which is also a part of the All, is responding in kind. After this connection is established between us, I commune with any other need I can contribute to. Conversely, should I ever have a need, the All will hasten to supply that to me. Got that?"

Peter reflects, remembering all the examples … the butterfly, the colors, the tinkling jingle-jangle sound so typical of Zachary as his humorous but wonderful trademark. "I believe so. But why do you have to stroke the grass to do that? Can you not simply do that?"

Zachary shrugs his shoulders and looks at the othe "Well, what do you all think? Do you think I should break the … *habit* and try some other method?" He feigns a look of expectancy, which brings a small bit of laughter from Peter and then from the others.

Paul looks down to keep from bursting into laughter. "I have every confidence in you, Zachary. I am certain you could, indeed, break the *habit* and certainly form some alternative connection to the All, should you so desire."

The others are smiling broadly, understanding Zachary's mischievous form of teaching as being most imminent.

Peter, too, is wisely aware of this forthcoming. "Okay, Zack. You can get to the point now."

Looking very innocent, Zachary shrugs his shoulders again. "Actually, Pete, there is nothing to it, except what you make of it. I find joy in making contact with every expression of creation. I suppose you could consider that a habit. Although, if I'm not in a realm that has an expression of creation in the form of grass, you might notice that I don't have any withdrawal symptoms."

Humor spews forth from all, including Peter.

Zachary continues. "The point, and coming right to it as you have requested, Peter, is simply this: One can attune themselves to the All no matter where they are if they look at that which is before them and reach into it to find the source of its creation. By so doing, just as you have learned when you go within, anyone can find the Golden Light, the Light of God. It is important for you to recognize this, Peter. I'm hoping you will keep this as a part of your consciousness, that you might be able to draw upon it in future events and experiences.

"I know there is great meaning in what you are offering here, Zachary, but I don't think I've fully grasped it. Can you help me?"

"Of course. I was hoping you would ask." Looking down

he points to Peter's hands. "Put them upon the grass."

Peter leans over and does so.

"Now, gently put your hands in motion upon the grass." Peter begins to move his hands in a slow, gently swirling motion. "Tell me when you can perceive something, or as you say in the Earth, when you feel something."

Suddenly Peter cries out, "I do feel something! It's like a tingling bit of energy that seems to be flowing into my hands. Oh! It's becoming much more pronounced now. And the more I focus on it, it's like a river of light passing up through my hands and into my being!"

"Precisely. You can stop now, Peter."

"I'm not so sure I want to."

"See what I mean? It is a joyous work. And by *work* I mean an activity of placing self into oneness with the essence of God in the expression of where you are in your consciousness. You can do the same in any realm, but you need to seek out that source of the All that is in that realm or expression in which you are focused. See?"

After a bit, Peter stops. There is a soft electrical-sounding popping as he moves his hands from the grass, as though it were energized, as though a part of him were expressed now in the grass and the grass had expressed itself proportionately within his own being.

Zachary helps Peter further understand. "It's the same as the essence from Hope, you just perceive it differently."

"It's a continual flow of energy," adds Paul. "Knowing of it and knowing that it is omnipresent in all, a willing worker one can do much with this awareness."

Peter nods with understanding. He turns to look at Elizabeth who is also nodding. "It's like the realms that you love so well, isn't it, Elizabeth?"

"Yes, Peter, it is. It is being at one with All That Is. When one knows they are unlimited and they move to a realm where their unlimited nature can express itself in accordance with God's Law," and she turns to nod at Hope, "then all is possible, and your uniqueness can express itself in an unlimited sense. This I find to be particularly joyful."

Zachary looks about the group. "I think it well, now, to be about our Father's works. So let us briefly review the commission before us."

All nod, and Peter eagerly straightens himself and comes to complete alertness.

Zachary, more serious than usual, rests his gaze on Peter. "Peter, the commission will involve the realms of the Earth."

This has an impact upon Peter, and he is silent.

"I suggest that we begin by journeying to the Earth itself and working from there to the other realms where some of the work the Master has offered us might truly begin to take form. Are we in agreement with that as a plan?"

He receives consent from all, although Peter is reserved, for he does not know what is coming.

"Peter, you will know in detail all the activities that lie ahead in just a few moments. But let me first emphasize that we continually be aware that we are one in this work. In other words, where one of us might be involved, all are present. Agreed?" They all nod and, again, Peter rather dutifully nods.

"Thus, I speak in the name of our Brother, the Christ, that as we have agreed to this commission, I lay this affirmation upon the altar of Truth in the presence of God and in accordance with His Law, and on behalf of all our group, it shall be so henceforth."

At this, all bow their heads.

After a moment or two, Zachary rises to his feet and claps his hands together mirthfully. "Well then, how about an outing, Pete? You know what they say, all work and no play makes one lazy ... or no, let's see, all play and no work makes one dull ... No, that's not it. Well, whatever it is, Pete, let's go."

Peter catches the inference to his continual references to

his time in the Earth. "That's, *idleness makes Jack a dull boy,* Zack."

"Oh, yes. It slipped my consciousness for a moment." Without a further word, Zachary motions to the others, turns and strides briskly towards the beautiful, white undulating mist, linking his arms with Peter's and Elizabeth's as the rest, each one, in turn, do the same. "A bit of a traveling song seems in order, eh wot Pete?" Zachary bursts forth a sound of resplendent brilliance, startling Peter with its beauty, depth, timber, and tone. Zachary glances at Peter and winks.

Peter understands and attempts to emulate Zachary. To his own surprise, he finds the music coming from himself to be equally beautiful to Zachary's.

Zachary pauses his singing. "Well done, Pete! Obviously, you've had a lot of musical training." He chuckles and resumes his song. This continues for their journey until, finally, the group comes to a stop. They gather in a small circle, and Zachary says softly to Peter, "Mind your cloak now, Peter, we are about to enter the Earth."

Peter is taken aback. "The Earth? The real Earth?"

"Well, everything is subjective, isn't it, Pete. So it's as real as they can make it. They're doing their best to forget about the rest of reality, so I suppose you could call this their subjective reality and the collective mind-consciousness of their agreed upon reality, which is thereafter the premise upon which their realm exists."

"What?"

"You know. It's what they believe, so it's what they get."

"Oh, I see."

Peter's comment brings laughter from the group.

"Now, Pete, we are about to move into what you call the *very real* Earth," teasing Peter a bit.

"Okay, Zack. I get the point."

With not another word, keeping a connection to Peter, Zachary begins to move slowly forward.

Peter notes that he is now flanked by Rebecca on his right, Elizabeth on his left, and Hope immediately behind. Paul has moved to be at Zachary's side. In this formation they move forward until they are in the atmosphere of the Earth, soaring.

Peter marvels. "Oh, my! This is something I always dreamed of doing when I was in the Earth. I am ... flying!"

Soft chuckles come from Zachary up ahead of Peter. "Tell me, Pete, what is it that you presume you have been doing in all the other realms?"

Somewhat embarrassed, Peter replies. "Oh, yes. Silly of me to think of this as being different."

"No, not at all. That was simply a teaching. Things tend to be relative to one's reference points. Here you are in the Earth and that is a familiar reference point. Earthly laws are mandated here, but you are not of the Earth at this point. You are in a non-physical body, so you are in harmony with the Universal Law and not a subject of this realm's finite law."

All the while they are continually moving.

Peter notes now that they have descended rapidly, soaring perhaps several hundred feet above the Earth. He notices the dark thickness of the atmosphere. He had forgotten what pollution was and he sort of shivers as he passes through it.

"Not to worry, Peter," Paul reminds him. "None of the expression in this realm can have impact on you because of your cloak. Many other things, too, but perhaps it's sufficient for you to focus upon the fact that your cloak is impenetrable by expressions here in this realm. Only you can open yourself to receive anything from here. See?"

"Thank you for the reminder. It's just so unpleasant. I had forgotten that it existed."

Below them now is a city and all of its environs. The group slows its movement over what Peter perceives to be a rather dreary portion of a city he remembers as a slum.

"Peter, come forward here, if you will."

Peter moves up beside Zachary. The group is hovering some distance above a group of irregular-shaped buildings.

"I would like you to focus over here." Peter looks in that area. "Now, remember the grass, Peter. Remember the grass." Peter recalls his experience with the grass. Instantly, in a sense of duality of consciousness, he is back on the knoll.

"Now, in your consciousness, stroke the grass."

As Peter does, suddenly he can perceive, in the direction that Zachary is indicating, the very dim outline of a cylindrical light, as though some sort of searchlight were focusing down from up in the clouds onto some indeterminate location in the streets of the city ahead of them.

"Good. You can perceive it then."

"Yes. What is it I am seeing?"

"It is the life-force connection of a person yet in body in the Earth. But when you see it in this form, know that there is the probability that that person is soon to leave their body."

"What?"

"Paul, will you help Peter understand?"

Paul turns to Peter. "Remember when I first joined you. Do you recall us traveling? Go within and retrieve that."

Peter responds quickly and finds to his delight that he is able to immediately locate the event and re-experience it. "I have it, Paul. It's the shaft of light you and I moved in when I was departing the Earth."

"Right. Now look over there again to what you are perceiving and draw the correlation between the two."

"I see. Yes, Zachary, I understand now."

"Good. Let's move closer."

The group begins to move until they are perhaps a few hundred feet above the highest building. Directly in front of them is the outer periphery of the dim life-force connection.

"My goodness, Paul. I don't recall anything like this during my movement with you."

Paul nods and Peter discerns a sense of sadness from

him. "What is it, Paul? What is it, here?"

Zachary answers for Paul. "It's not so much that Paul is sad, Peter. It's that he sees here the absence of the hope, the vision, the absence of the Light. This person is so unreceptive that there is no path for the Light to flow to him. The way things are now, only at the point of his release from the body would you perceive the brilliance that you would expect from this Light as it attempts to bring hope to the person. And only this one can determine whether or not it is to be accepted."

"Why are we here, then?"

"To help. This is where it begins."

"What begins?"

"The commission, Peter."

"You mean, wherever that dim gray light ends up down there in that city, that's our commission?" Peter feels a heaviness as he considers all this and wonders deep within his consciousness how he can be worthy of such a work.

Zachary obviously knows these thoughts. "Do not move before yourself to anticipate that which is not present. Do remember to keep yourself connected with the All. It is always present and will supply you with anything that the circumstances in which you exist might lack. Understand?"

Peter nods, still transfixed on the weak, gray-white light extending into the dismal layer of concrete and smog below.

"Ready?" Zachary calls to the group.

An affirmation is given from all and finally from Peter. "I think so, Zachary, though I don't know what to expect."

"Expect a work no greater or lesser than any other. Just different. All the tools you have gained apply here, as well as in any other realm though of course, we are in this realm and, therefore, we must honor it and honor God's Law. Now, let us move to the person."

Ever so quickly, Peter perceives his group in the midst of debris. Rubbish everywhere. Paper bags. Containers. Rotten food. Cans. Large boxes. Automobile tires.

"Where are we, Zachary? A city dump?"

"Nope. Just a city street."

Peter looks up and down the street in dismay at the refuse. In a corner alcove where several structures come together, it is piled haphazardly. He hears a moan. "What was that?" Zachary looks at Peter with deliberateness as though to say, *Remember the Oneness, Peter. Be Complete.*

Though Zachary speaks no words, Peter understands. He follows Zachary's gaze as it moves to embrace a person who lies upon the refuse in the center of a dull, gray-white light, the focus of this one's dim tunnel of light.

"Oh-h, my! He is so young."

"About sixteen years, I'd guess," responds Zachary.

"I'll check." Paul's cloak becomes translucent for a split second. "Sixteen and three-quarters, plus several days."

"Over here, Pete," directs Zachary. "Look at these markings on the arm."

Peter studies the person with seriousness, nods and shakes his head. "Narcotics. It was so widespread when I left. It's shocking to be this close to someone using this. Is there nothing we can do to save him?"

"Save him from what?"

Looking at Zachary carefully, Peter realizes Zachary is serious, lovingly so. "I see. If we were to save him from dying, we would only assure him of further pain and suffering here. Then what are we to do here?"

"We'll do the best that we can and aid those who are to serve him."

Peter hears a low moan from the person again, which seems to rattle about within him, like a clanking inside a hollow well. A chill passes through Peter.

"He's leaving," explains Paul.

Rebecca reaches out in her consciousness. "Where are they?"

"Patience," Zachary responds. "They'll be here."

At that moment, two spheres of light appear off to either side of the dim gray shaft.

"See?" Zachary smiles and addresses the spheres. "Greetings."

"Welcome," Peter discerns from the spheres. "We were told that you would be here to assist in this. Thank you."

There is a pause as the two spheres move to the dim gray light, the young man's life force coming from his midsection. Peter marvels as they merge with it and it begins to glow.

"Beautiful, isn't it, Pete?"

"It really is, Zachary."

Peter continues to observe. Suddenly, previously dim gray light has become brilliant and pure, a radiant shaft. Within that radiant shaft, that tunnel of light, the two entities can be seen on either side of the now glowing sphere of light, and they begin to rise slowly up within the tunnel. Slowly. Slowly.

Peter realizes that he and Zachary and the others are following the movement of the three spheres of light within the tunnel but on its periphery. He is transfixed upon the tunnel and its occupants, remembering vividly the joy, relief, and wonder of Paul's presence at his own passing. "Will he pass through the same experiences we did?"

Paul turns to Peter. "I do not believe so, for he has not, at this point in his consciousness, prepared himself. What is about to occur here will be utterly different than your experience, and it is, in part at least, why we are present."

Whoomph! There is a sound, as though some muffled explosion or some force has hit the group. Again. And again.

"What *is* that?"

"That, Peter, is part of our work. You will now begin to see souls who are bound to the Earth for various reasons."

It is here that we shall begin our next work, dear friends.

CHAPTER 7

A Soul Is Freed

DECEMBER 6, 1992

As we rejoin you in this work, we wish to offer this open-
ing comment: We encourage you to seek out those means by
which you can joyfully disseminate your own spirit in every
thought, word, and action of your day's events. For you can
never discern how meaningful these, as seeds of hope and
joyfulness, can be in the hearts and minds of those with whom
you shall interact. We believe that what lies ahead will pro-
vide graphic illustration of this.

We now return to our group and, specifically, Peter, the
whoomph having continued for some time.

Peter is obviously impacted by the unfolding events of
the departing person's journey. "What is happening
here?" he asks without directing his questions to any
particular member of the group. "What are these sounds I'm
detecting? Where are they coming from? And what is their
purpose?"

Zachary responds in a calm, soothing tone. "These are
souls who are *inhabiting*, so to say, realms that are adjacent to
the Earth. To anticipate some of your questions, as they will
no doubt immediately come forth from you, Peter, they are in
these 'realms of consciousness' because of desires that still
linger on in their consciousness that directly involve the
Earth. These desires can be many-fold and can deal with
many different types of what you would call addiction, but
may also involve attitudes, emotions, habits and the like, that
have very little to do outwardly with what is collectively em-

braced by the term *addiction*. Is that much clear?"

"Yes, I understand that. You are saying that these entities are creating this sort of percussion sound. This is the best way I can describe it, though I feel the impact all throughout me. And they actually stay here at this … *level?*"

Zachary simply nods, waiting for Peter's consciousness to digest the information and for the subsequent questions that are no doubt about to be asked.

"So, I know you said it was caused by addiction and that sort, but can they not, uh, you know, see or understand that they have no physical body any longer and that they have no means of, well, interacting with the addictive nature that pre-occupied them when in the Earth? I mean, how can you enjoy (if there is such a thing) a narcotic if you have no physical body in which to take it or inject it? Are there some means by which they can do this that I'm not aware of here, Zachary? Something you haven't told me of that enables physical habits or events to be transferred into the non-physical body?"

"Their bodies are not physical, that is certain, though many of them won't acknowledge that or at least not to the point that it will do them any real good, if you know what I mean. The *something* that you ask about is present to a degree, though very subtle. It is like this: They can't partake in the physical sense of any desire that is carnal, but they can associate near and about those who are in physical body and interact with the energy or vibrations of the thoughts and emotions that result from those in physical body fulfilling the habits that these discarnate entities still desire. Understand?"

Peter attempts to not only absorb the communication but to reach out and embrace Zachary, as he has been shown in past, to glean the utmost amount of information possible. "I believe I understand this much and correct me wherever I might be misunderstanding—you're saying that these non-physical entities, whose bodies no longer exist in the physical sense, try to be close to people in physical body who, in the example of this one now departing, might be a drug addict. That through that person's habits these discarnate entities can gain some semblance of the effect of what they remember as getting high in the Earth?"

"That's close enough, Peter. To carry it one step further, when some of those who are incarnate get so high that they are unconscious, these discarnate entities move in and out of their physical body sort of like virtual merry-go-rounds. They literally struggle with one another for the opportunity to dwell in the same time and space as the now high drug addict in order to absorb the greatest effect from that addict's 'high'."

Peter is impacted heavily by this information.

"Don't be concerned," Zachary advises.

Paul adds, "Yes, Peter, all things are in their appropriate order in terms of the progression of each soul. To the limit of their willingness and ability to accept, it is continually offered to them. Which brings us back to our commission here."

Peter's attention turns again to the continual impact of energy taking place around them. "Are these entities, then, causing this sound and impact? If so, why? What is it they are striving to do?"

"There are certain energies," Paul continues, "that radiate from entities that have to do with thoughts, emotions, habits, and all that sort. Just as you have learned to discern from the cloak of others what their spiritual nature is like, so can these entities detect from the emanations of another entity what that one's attitudes and emotions are like. The entities are coming just as insects might be attracted to a flower in the Earth. Remember that?"

Peter haphazardly nods, still deep in contemplation.

"Just as in that example, these entities are more or less flying blindly merely by their sensory perception of their addiction or habit as remembered from the Earth."

"Do you mean to say, Paul, that they are actually crashing into this light, this tunnel?"

"Not only into the tunnel, Peter, but into our group and, in fact, into you."

"Me? I have no addiction nor have I had ever any such urging."

"I know.

"I know you know that, Paul. I meant that as a question. Why me, if I have none of the emanations, why would they crash into me?"

"It is your proximity to their goal."

"Your proximity," adds Zachary, "to the target of their destination or desire. That, at least partly, is why we're here."

"Well, what do we do, Zachary? What can do to help? Are the entities in the tunnel of light and their newly departed … *ward*, I guess I'd call it, in danger here?"

"No, not in danger. Remember, these entities are eternal as are, you. There can be no danger in the literal sense … limitation, yes, and perhaps a number of other aspects that you haven't been shown to any depth as yet. I would loosely call these aspects the limitations of self. Remember that this young fellow is now completing a brief, comparatively speaking, lifetime in the Earth, and much of its duration was spent under the influence of alcohol and narcotics."

Paul affirms Zachary's comments, for Paul, you will remember, had previously observed the Akasha and the records for this one.

"Well, then, what do they hope to attain? If they can't harm him, what can they do to him?"

"Most of these new arrivals do not intend to *do* anything to him," explains Zachary. "They are attracted by vibrations that are similar in nature. You could say they're attracted by the same frequency as is the level of their previous addiction. Not necessarily to the fellow himself, although there are several here who have been, in your Earthly colloquial term, hanging around this young fellow for quite a period, fulfilling as best they can their remnants of carnal desire."

"Wow! That's unbelievable! To think I might have been walking by people when I was in the Earth who had others around them and didn't have the faintest idea."

All in the group chuckle softly at this and Peter suddenly realizes what he just said applies to him as well. "You're telling me that one or more of you *were* present with me when I was in the Earth?"

"Absolutely, " responds Zachary. "Many times. Paul was with you more often than not. I frequently. Elizabeth more often than not. And so forth. Others as well, to be sure."

"Even though sometimes I seemed to feel something like a presence, I didn't consider it to any depth. It just ... "

Suddenly the sound and the energy become very strong.

"We'll pick this up later, Pete. Some of this fellow's friends are here, and they can possibly have a strong influence on him because of their intimate knowledge of him."

"What do we do, Zachary?"

"We actually do nothing, but we are allowed to be in harmony with the intent and purpose of this soul. It is to be determined now by the two loving entities who are with him in his tunnel the level of spiritual acceptance that can be gained here. That will guide what we can or cannot do. For now, as they continue to move, let us continue to move adjacent to the tunnel, parallel to them while on the outside of the tunnel."

Immediately, the group is as one entity surrounding the tunnel, creating a luminous band that moves with the inner three spheres as they struggle to ascend upwards.

Some measure of what you would call time passes, and Peter inquires, "Why is there such a labor here? I can clearly discern the amount of effort taking place. Paul, are they passing through the colors as we did?"

"They are trying to but having a difficult time of it. They can't get through the first basic levels. If you focus and tune in, which it is acceptable for you to do, you can observe what is taking place inside the tunnel. It may be of value to you, Peter. I will join you, to be certain that your questions are answered immediately and ensure no possible disruption to their activities. Ready?"

Nodding rather automatically, Peter signals his readiness. Instantly, he feels his consciousness inside the majesty of the tunnel's luminosity and the flow of light in it. He can perceive in every aspect of the physical senses, and much more, the wonder of what is being offered to this soul. It is incredibly beautiful, and it reminds him of the Master Himself.

Paul picks up on Peter's awareness. "It *is* the Master, in a manner of speaking. The Master's Spirit is here to welcome this soul, should it choose the highest and best he is willing to accept."

"You mean *he* must determine to what level of expression he can go?"

"Exactly. His passage through the colors and the counsel that he is being given—he is not aware of the counsel, but it will continue to be given until he will know it—are a part of that process. Currently, he is laboring to pass through the most primal levels of the colors. Do you recall those?"

Immediately, Peter cascades, in his consciousness, through the collage of colors, the banding, the sensations, the feelings, the essences, the sounds, the warmth, associated with each. "I understand where he's at. Goodness, he is so heavily burdened. He seems to have much within him and certainly upon his cloak that matches these very low levels."

"Good observation, Peter. The matching of colors in his cloak to the colors of these lower levels in the spectrum of consciousness we are examining are a part of the process at issue here at the moment. Allow yourself to perceive more. Observe his cloak carefully."

As Peter's consciousness focuses on the young man, the center sphere of light and the cloaking luminosity around it, he notes the predominant darker, heavier colors. But he marvels at the occasional glimpse of tiny resplendent blue and gold, soft pastel pink, azure colors, emerald colors that seem to pierce through the cloak, as fingers of light would pierce through the circumference of a shade or a spherical globe over a much more luminescent inner light.

"Now that you have seen this, look at smaller portions of light on the cloak. Watch those carefully, particularly near the upper left from where you are."

Peter notices a baby blue color in a regular pattern upon the upper left portion of the entity's cloak. As quickly as he perceives it, he notes light moving from the sphere of light on the left of the entity into that blue, matching that blue for every particle of its blue-ness, and he can see a pulsing movement now of a bit more luminescence of the blue. Then he perceives another portion of the cloak that has a yellow-gold mottling or opening, and the sphere of light on the right matches that yellow-gold and amplifies it just a whit.

So it goes that every one of the small openings on the cloak (that are really small splotches of color and light) are matched and met with a slight amplification by the two spheres, the entities to the right and left of this young man.

"Amazing! What is it that they are doing exactly, Paul? My impression is it is like they are feeding these colors or matching them with slightly greater color or energy."

"That is an excellent assessment, for that is, indeed, what they are doing. They are encouraging him to remember the goodness, the happiness, the hope. They are striving to enrich the spiritual side, the positive side that has for so long been overshadowed by the habits perpetuated while in the Earth and by his abandonment of all hope, joy, and love at an early age. But let us now rejoin our group, Peter. I believe you have seen what is sufficient for the present here."

Without a moment's hesitation, Peter feels as though Paul has gently but assertively moved him from within the tunnel back to his previous position as a part of the band of light surrounding the tunnel.

"Well, what do you think now?" asks Zachary.

"I believe I understand. They are trying to awaken the healthier qualities in him. They are drawing on spiritual essences in order to provide a continual flow to the memory, that he can break free of the limitations and habits that so burdened him while he was in the Earth."

"Good. In fact, that's excellent, Pete. Now, let's turn our attention to these entities on the outside of the tunnel.

Peter follows Zachary's suggestion and scans the vast darkness that is all about. Some several moments pass and Peter whispers, "Zachary? Paul? I see nothing."

Neither replies to Peter. He continues to scan the seemingly eternal darkness surrounding them.

Suddenly, in every aspect of Peter's sensory perception, he feels another impact and immediately discerns a face.

"See that?"

"Yes, Zack, I see it. Right in front of my nose, if you don't mind. What now?

"Just continue to observe."

The face intrigues Peter. It has a strange, alluring quality to it. Even though he can discern the similar heaviness of color and energy as in the darker portions of the young man's cloak, he is somewhat taken by the essence emanating to him from the face.

Some additional brief moments pass and Zachary comments softly, "Mystical, in a way, isn't it, Peter? Almost tempting, wouldn't you say?"

"Yes, Zachary, strangely enchanting. Almost transfixing, although I'm certainly aware that it is of less than a spiritual essence."

"Excellent!"

"Yes, very good," Paul adds.

Rebecca, Hope, and Elizabeth offer similar notes of encouragement.

Peter suddenly realizes that they have all been silent during the whole of these experiences. He turns to Elizabeth, who is at his side. "Elizabeth, and you, Hope and Rebecca, I hope I've not been rude. I had forgotten your presence, and I dominated all of the communication here."

Hope's gentleness restores Peter. "You have done remarkably well in seeking the information that I, myself, would have sought, Peter. Please continue, knowing that your questions are as my questions. Be my words and extend your experiences as though they were my own."

Peter is deeply touched by this flow of love. "Nothing but the highest and best ever comes from you, Hope. You are truly an angel."

Only a soft pinkish glow comes to Peter. No other comment is given by Hope.

"Elizabeth, what do you make of this? Have you experienced such as this in past?"

She nods. "But not in the breadth and depth as what we are now experiencing. Only in passing, so to say."

All this while the entity's face has remained immediately before Peter.

Peter suddenly realizes this. "Goodness, you all! I'm beginning to feel uncomfortable here. This entity is just staring at me ... seems to be sort of imploring me to do something."

"Well, Pete, what do you discern that something might be?" questions Zachary.

Peter focuses on the face again. "Why ... I believe it's ... to go with her!"

"Do you have any perception of why it is that she wishes you to accompany her?"

"I have no idea, Zachary, and now that I hear you mention *her* back to me, I wonder how it is that I associated the face, which has no body that I can perceive, with the feminine. The more I observe it, the more difficult it is for me to discern whether, in fact, it is male or female."

"Continue to perceive, Peter."

Peter opens himself sufficiently to perceive, yet remembering, keeps his cloak snugly intact. "It is a she, I believe. I'm almost certain of it ... but I can't be sure."

"No matter, I only suggested your continued perception for your own understanding and development, and for the experience it will give you in those times ahead. See if you can communicate with her, Peter. That should prove of value to you in some respects."

Hesitantly, Peter stammers. "Uh, forgive me, dear, uh, lady, but may I ask why you are here?"

Nothing.

No response.

Peter turns to Zachary. "You know, I don't think she can hear me. For that matter, I'm beginning to wonder if she can even perceive that I'm here. I thought she was staring at me but now I think she is staring through me, like I'm just in the way." Peter seems almost relieved to realize that.

Zachary chuckles softly. "Well done. And it is appropriate, to some degree, to feel relief, for as you can tell, there is a peculiar charm associated with her. True?"

"Yes, there is. Strange. Something I seem to recall from the Earth, but I can't quite put my finger on it. But if not me, who is she focusing on? Oh-h! The entity in the tunnel! I can't believe I didn't realize that. But Zachary, why can she not perceive our presence?"

"In a manner of speaking, she does perceive it (if, in fact, the entity is a she) and is somewhat displeased because we are blocking her from reaching her objective. Tell you what, Pete, if the rest of the group will agree, we'll move into some experiences now that should prove invaluable to you for your understanding."

After a moment of affirmation from the others, Zachary turns to Paul. "Paul, you re aware of my plan, yes?"

"Indeed, and it is a good one. Proceed. I think this would

be good for all here, and certainly help lay some cornerstones for the commission ahead."

Zachary turns to the somewhat puzzled Peter. "Listen carefully to what I'm going to say to you and try to follow not only the communication but the thought-forms I'll give you as I do so. ... Think of the colors, the levels of consciousness, that the person in the sphere is dealing with at this moment." He motions to the spheres who are now laboriously moving upwards, and Peter can perceive them clearly. "Good. Now turn back to the face in front of you and place those energies, the colors, the associated vibrations, in front of you."

"What?"

"Remember, now. Take the thought, not only the communication. Take the thought of the color, the emotion and energies, that this entity in the tunnel is dealing with, and place them in front of you."

"I understood what you said, Zachary, and I have the thought-form. But how do I place that in front of me?"

"Bring to your consciousness the All, Peter. It is not only the All of joy and light. It is the All of existence. All things are a part of God. Whether they are understood by some as not being light and therefore misused is irrelevant. They are, nonetheless, a part of God."

Peter allows this consciousness to flow through him, and he tries, again and again, to manifest the thought-form in front of himself. Suddenly, there it is—the dark, thick, almost mud-like browns and darker hues, not so much unpleasant but just thick and heavy. He is startled that they are now immediately in front of him.

With equal amazement, he now sees the completeness of the entity before him. She is utterly charming, a very young feminine entity, or so it would seem, probably about the same age as the young man in the tunnel of light. "Goodness, she is quite beautiful by Earthly terms. But there is all this heaviness about her, something I can't define, that seems to be emanating from her."

"Good." Almost as though Zachary is a great distance away, he speaks slowly and deliberately to Peter. "Communicate with her, Peter, if you can."

Peter turns back to the lovely, teenage entity before him and, not knowing precisely what to say, begins to speak. "Hello there, young ... "

"Get out of my way!"

"What?"

"You heard me. Get out of my way. You're blocking my way!"

"Uh, sorry. I didn't mean to interfere with whatever you are about."

"Are you one of those?"

"I beg your pardon?"

"You know what I mean ... one of those."

"Who?"

"Don't play games with me! I recognize you as one of those."

Peter can feel a softness on his right side and realizes that Elizabeth is now positioned firmly beside him.

"Oh, I see. Two of you, huh? I suppose you and your girlfriend intend to take this one, is that it?"

Elizabeth does not speak. Peter begins to realize that he must somehow attune to the consciousness of the entity. Feeling inside himself a growing, golden glow, he is gaining a knowing that this must be a part of the commission.

He can discern Zachary, but at a great distance. He is reminded of his experience, his and Elizabeth's, with Hope, as the fallen angel, and at that moment he feels a radiant, pinkish warmth, and he knows Hope is with him, too. Renewed by this companionship of those he loves dearly, Peter turns to the young female entity before him, who is directly challenging him. "I don't intent to take anything from you but to simply ask you what it is that you are doing."

"Are you kidding? You know very well what I am doing. You *are* one of those. I can tell. I can see some of the light slipping out from inside of you."

Startled, Peter quickly looks to his cloak, but he cannot discern any openings. "What light do you perceive?"

"Don't kid me. I can always tell when one of those is present. Why don't you just admit it and get out of the way? You know you can't stop me."

Peter is flustered now, and he feels an almost sickening heaviness, some sort of overwhelming sensory perception. It's a combination of all the unpleasant odors from the Earth, unpleasant sights and sounds, pain and sorrow, hatred and anger and anguish. But stronger than all that, he feels the golden light pulsing within and the pinkish orb of Hope's love and, of course, the presence of Elizabeth at his side. He summons his inner strength. "I suppose you could say I am one of *those*, though I don't know entirely what you mean by that term."

"Well, you're not from here, that's for sure."

"No, I'm not, but I would be pleased to help you, if you would allow me."

"You can help me by getting out of my way ... Now! That's what you can do."

Peter is in a state of bewilderment, yet bolstered strongly by that within him. "Are you seeking to somehow or other join yourself with this newly departed person?"

"I don't have to answer your questions. Now get out of the way, or I'll just go right through you."

A warmth radiates from Peter's upper consciousness and down throughout his being. Then he hears himself communicating, softly and in a strange, warming sort of way to this demanding young woman before him. "I welcome you to pass through me, but you should know that, as you do, you must pass through the light. It is, truly, the light that you are seeking and the light that you shall ultimately find. But if you seek after this soul who is striving to reach the highest point of his potential, you will only limit yourself through those desires and possibly limit him, and this will only compound your own burden all the more."

"If I've heard that once, I've heard it a thousand times!" The young woman seems to be changing right before Peter as he continues to observe her.

Very good, urges Elizabeth silently. *Do continue.*

"Then, not, then pass into the light, here? Do you fear it? You sound as though you are fearless. What could you ever fear from the light?"

"Look here, I'm not afraid! I happen to like my way of life here, and I know enough to know I have a right to stay here. And the more companions I can get to stay here with me, the stronger my way of life becomes. You and I both know that's what I'm after here."

Immediately, to his amazement, Peter feels and hears his response. It is with a profound depth and breadth. He knows he is the instrument of all that is taking place, of its initiation, yet he feels as though he is the observer. "Your way of life is not something I seek to threaten. I only seek to ensure that this newly departed soul has his right of free will, his right of choice. And that you and others like you do not coerce or enchant by applying your influences to this one's recent weaknesses or habits and thereby attract him to your way of *life*, as you call it. But again, I welcome you to pass through me, knowing that as you do, you shall enter the light."

"Well, what if I do pass through you? What will you do about it?"

"Nothing."

"Well, then, that's just what I'm going to do. I'm going to get that one and bring him into this realm. He'll like it here, and he'll help strengthen the power that we have."

In the blink of an eye, as you'd call it in the Earth, the entity surges forward. Peter is immediately strengthened by the presence of Elizabeth, and a pinkish light flows into every aspect of Peter's being, which he knows is from Hope. The gold essence that was once contained and centralized within a certain portion of him becomes an all-encompassing sphere around his consciousness at the exact moment that the entity crashes headlong into Peter.

Steady, now, he hears from Zachary.

Yes, adds Paul. *Just be at ease. Remember, there is nothing that can have any impact upon you unless you wish it to be so. Remember the All, Peter.*

Peter seems strangely, almost magically, enchanted by the event. *Can she, you know, actually pass through me, Zachary?*

No, not through you, Peter, but through the light. She has entered and is now in the light. You are also in the light, so to a point of order here, she and you are both in the light.

I must admit to being a bit unnerved here. I feel sort of invaded. At that moment he realizes Hope's entire presence is one with his own, and before him is Elizabeth, smiling softly. *I remember. I remember. I'm okay now. But, gosh, how quickly and how profoundly the familiar emotions and habits of the Earth can flood back! How swiftly things can become nearly overwhelming and how powerful they are.*

Exactly, he hears from Zachary, *and that is the essence with which entities in these realms work. They know these things. They've learned them. They more or less feed upon them. They live them, and they strive to multiply them. See?*

I sure do.

Good. Turn back to the entity now—the young woman (as you perceived her).

Okay, Zachary, I'll do my best. Peter attempts to locate the young woman in the midst of the light. He is warmed and comforted by the presence of the light and, even after all these experiences, he finds it to be breathtakingly beautiful.

As he searches to find the identity of the entity in the

light, he is stunned to find an aged-appearing male entity, stooped over, hunched and withered. *Where is the young woman, Zack?*

This is the same entity, Peter. One and the same.

But this is ...

The entity's comments interrupt Zachary and Peter's communication. "See, I told you. I told you I could enter this light! Here I am. What do you intend to do about it now?"

Peter looks at the withered-looking entity and is flooded with empathy for him. "I intend to do nothing but to welcome you, to encourage you to shed the darkness and replace it with light and joy, to cast off limitation and come with us into those realms of light and hope."

The aged entity has become visibly shaken by the impact of the light and by the failure of Peter to challenge or threaten him. His response, while still defiant, is weakened. "And what if I did? What if I did go with you? I wouldn't be happy there, wherever it is that you all come from. You're such do-gooders, always striving to disrupt a fellow's happiness."

"Are you *truly* happy here? Do you even remember what happiness is? How long have you been here?"

The entity is now obviously releasing some of his guard. He looks at Peter intently. "You won't force me to go with you, will you? I mean, I don't think you can anyway."

Peter simply shakes his head. "I have no wish to make you do anything."

"Well, okay then, I'll take you at your word. I know you folks live by your word more than anything else."

"I would say that is so," continuing to reassure the entity.

"Well, I've been here a week or two, or ... " becoming a little flustered, "maybe a couple of months or ... who knows? It all sort of runs together here, you know."

Peter can hear Paul. *He has been here two hundred and seventeen years, Peter.*

What?

Two-hundred-seventeen Earth years or the equivalent. Tell him.

Peter turns his attention back to the entity, who is even more stooped over now, shaken by the experience. Obviously to Peter, some burden of memories seems to be causing the portrayed image of his physical countenance to be more and more weighted down. "If you will forgive me, sir, it has been more than two hundred Earth years."

"*What?*"

"Two-hundred-seventeen, to be precise."

"I don't believe you."

"Why would I lie, sir?"

"Well, it's ... maybe it's just a trick."

"Not at all. Do you remember when you came?"

"What difference does that make? I'm here, and this is where I belong, and that's what there is, nothing more, nothing less. This is my lot. I did it to myself, and now I'm here. I can handle it. I just like company, that's all. It seems the more company I have, the stronger we all feel, and we get to share it. It has something to do with the structure of things, I suspect. I don't understand it, except that God picks favorites."

"You believe in God??"

"Well, yes, who doesn't? I mean how else could existence be? It had to start somewhere, didn't it? But it's a not a very nice God. He picks favorites. Some have this, and some have that, and others have nothing, and what I had was all taken away from me. I suppose someone's going to tell me now that it's my own fault, but it was taken, nonetheless."

"Why was it taken?"

"That's none of your business! I think I'll leave now. I don't need that fellow, anyway. I have plenty of others here." Half turned, the withered male entity glances back over his shoulder to see if Peter is going to do anything.

Peter, now fully expressed in a physical form, at least to the perception of the entity, simply shrugs his shoulders and states softly, "It's your choice, of course."

The entity makes a small movement away from Peter, as though he were about to turn back into the darkness, and stops. He turns again and looks at Peter. "Do you know anything about God? I mean, have you seen Him or have you any other experiences than this?"

Gently, Peter responds. "Yes, I have had numerous experiences other than this, and I believe I have indeed seen some aspects of God, if you would call it that. I have certainly seen the Master, the Christ."

This impacts the entity somewhat, and he softens a bit. Peter notes this, and he hears from Zachary, *Good, Peter, good. Just follow what you are guided to say and do.*

The entity responds, with a growing gentleness. "You know, I believe I saw Him once, too, a long time ago. In fact, it was so far back I can only barely remember."

"Probably two hundred and seventeen years ago, sir."

"Do you think it could really have been that long?" the old man asks of Peter.

"I suspect so, but it needn't continue."

The old man softens even more. "Do you have a name?"

"Yes, I am called by my friends ... " and with a note of reservation, instead of Peter, he states, "I'm called Pete."

"Oh. I thought you were maybe one of those angels. You know, you could have been Saint Peter, himself. I've heard they come and go through these ... you call them realms, don't you?"

"Yes, we do, and you needn't be concerned." Peter chuckles softly. "I don't think I'm Saint Peter."

"Well, at least you folks have a sense of humor. I wondered about that over the past weeks or ... I guess they were years. Who knows? Everything seems to run together. You know how that is."

Peter shakes his head no and answers still very gently. "I'm sorry, sir. No, I don't. Everything is new and exciting and joyful. It seems to me that only here, where you have chosen to stay, would it all seem to be the same over and over again."

"Wait a minute! I didn't choose to be here, what's your name … Pete. You know very well that this is where I was sent. This is where I was put because I was, well, not the best I could be in the Earth."

"Do you think that it is God who has mandated that this is where you shall be?"

The old man straightens himself in wonder at Peter's question, then shrugs and waves his arms about. "Why else would I be here if it weren't for this being my lot? I'm a sinner. I have wronged others, I have stolen, I have misused, and I have been unfaithful to those who loved me most. I suppose that's why everything was taken from me, my family, my happiness, my wealth, my position. And this is it," turning to look back to the darkness, "this is what I've deserved."

"If you can recognize those things as not having been the highest and best for you, then that can free you."

"What do you mean, *free me?*

"Exactly that. When you realize what your limitations are and realize that they are or were yours, then you must also realize that it is your thoughts and memories of these that burden you, not that God decided to punish you."

The old man, obviously agitated at Peter's remarks, begins pacing back and forth, mumbling and uttering little comments. Peter answers these as adroitly as he can without threatening the entity.

Finally, this long discourse unfolds to the point where the old man suddenly turns and stands defiantly in front of Peter. "If what you say is so, then prove it!"

"I should be pleased to prove it, sir, if you are willing."

Stepping back as though he had been struck a blow, the entity straightens up and places his hands on his hips.

It is at this moment that Peter realizes that, through the

course of all of the interchange between them, the entity has grown younger and younger. His body is no longer withered. In fact, he looks like a man would probably look in the Earth who is in his early to mid-forties, and he looks quite well.

"Sir, I would call your attention to the fact that you are no longer stooped and withered and are now much younger."

"The dickens, you say!" The entity extends his hands and arms. He gasps as he looks down at them. He touches his face all about, and then he realizes that he is standing erect. "How did you do that? It's trickery!"

"No, it's your own action of accepting, of looking at yourself in an attitude of truth and openness."

The entity studies Peter carefully for an indeterminate amount of time. Finally, in a much softer voice, he states, "You are speaking truthfully, aren't you? In fact, I seem to remember that none of you can do anything less. You can't tell me lies or falsehoods, can you? I mean, you are not allowed to do that, are you?"

Peter smiles and shakes his head.

"Can you prove it to me? Can you prove to me that I need not stay here, that God has not banished me to this … " turning to gaze at his realm of existence, "this horror?"

Peter answers with a warmth and encouragement that reaches out to embrace the entity. "Yes, we can."

At this point, Elizabeth becomes visible at Peter's side.

The man gasps. "She is beautiful! Are you the Holy Mother?"

Elizabeth, smiling, shakes her head. "No sir, I am not. I am no different than yourself."

"Oh, but you are! You are so radiant! You are one with God, aren't you?"

"You, too, sir, are one with God, if you would allow yourself to be."

The man stands before them, mouth agape. Suddenly, he throws himself upon Elizabeth and Peter, or what would be their bodies, and bursts out sobbing. "Save me, please save me. I do not wish to dwell in darkness one moment longer. My heart yearns for oneness again with God."

There is the bursting forth of spheres of light, the sounds of incredible beauty as the celestial hosts proclaim in joyfulness this—the retrieval of one lost soul.

We are through here for the present. May the grace and blessings of our Father's wisdom and joy ever be with you.

CHAPTER 8

An Amazing Appearance

DECEMBER 6, 1992

As the one soul was freed from darkness and turned toward the Light of God, the light that billowed forth, cascading and radiating, so awe-inspired Peter that he was spellbound. To him, it was as though the very fabric of heaven had opened itself to the darkness and was pouring light and jubilation into every recess of its being. On and on, went the collage of beauty and celebration until he was so filled with joy that he believed there was no more that he could absorb.

As we rejoin the group and Peter, his consciousness has settled, and he is remembering what has just transpired.

Before him, where there once was a teenaged young woman, limited and clearly bound by some carnal desires, there is now an aged, withered, stooped man, his façade torn asunder by his entry into the light as he challenged Peter. Now standing before Peter is the true nature and potential of this soul. Even though the entity, as an aspect of the soul, has not grasped it yet, Peter can perceive his brilliance and is awestruck by the beauty standing in the very spot where only moments ago was a contrary, argumentative, limited entity of weariness.

"I am free! I am saved!" On and on he exclaims.

Peter, marveling at all this, now looks about and perceives the presence, not only of his own group, but many other entities of light, and more and more coming. He turns to Zachary, who is now radiating his own joy and love as are all here. "Zachary, this seems unbelievable, yet I know it's true because I experienced every part of it. Is this our commission? Have we once again been blessed with success?"

Zachary is nearly overwhelmed with warmth and loving admiration for Peter. "It is, indeed, our commission, though only the first step of it. But it is far greater than we had anticipated, so successful that all who have been a part of this have come here to celebrate."

Looking about at the continually growing collage of entities, their unique individuality pouring down on and all around them, Peter asks, "All of these entities helped?"

"Every one. They were all a part of the work. Now, perhaps you can see that you are never alone and that you are always in good company."

After a time, Peter turns to Elizabeth. "Oh-h," he says softly, "thank you, Elizabeth, for your help and support."

She is smiling, equally radiant as all the others. "It is one work, and we are one, Peter. I would have it no other way, as I know you yourself would seek the same."

Now the loving radiance of Hope comes before Peter. The rosy essence, which is always present, seems even greater now. "Peter, thank you for the opportunity to be a part of all this. I wish to express to you how much understanding I have gained. There is not a doubt or question of the worthiness of this path and of the validity of continuing on no matter what, and to be ready to help one's brethren until the moment when they are prepared, and have chosen, to return to the Light.

"I can see, in what you call the past, that it was my will for my dear friend to break free of limitation and return to the realms of the Angelic Host. Because it was my will and not his, I limited that progression, equally to his own choice of limitation. In these past few experiences, I have learned from my brethren the equivalent of observing many incarnations, and I have chosen to return to follow the one I followed before. I shall do so in the sense of never being absent from your side, Peter, but rather in the knowing that you and I shall ever be one. Where one is and dwells in consciousness, the other is also present."

Peter is swept with emotion. The thought of being without Hope—her warm, loving presence, the consistency of her soul's illumination—momentarily saddens him. Yet that same moment, he understands that Hope has pledged to ever be with him and is asking that he do the same.

Peter looks lovingly at Hope. "We have already made such a pledge. Zachary stated it on our behalf, and we all affirmed it in silent prayer. Just as I pledged in that experience, I now re-affirm that pledge to you, Hope, that you only have to call and I shall answer. That where you choose to be or serve, so as the Father permits, my presence will be at your side, as well."

"Thank you, Peter. I now take my leave. Rebecca chooses to travel with me as a companion in our mutual works, much in the manner she has observed Paul and Zachary. We shall attempt to emulate their good works, their teachings, and their spiritual oneness with the Master, the Christ, the Way." She turns to acknowledge the others. "We are all ever one. Until we next meet, I leave my love with you throughout eternity."

There are looks of loving exchange between Hope and Peter and with each of the other group members. Rebecca moves to Hope's side and radiates an exchange of communication similar to Hope's. There is almost an explosion of rosy light and, immediately, Hope and Rebecca are gone.

In the momentary emptiness, Peter feels, his consciousness reels from the series of concurrent events. A part of him, he can feel, is going with Hope and Rebecca, yet inwardly he feels strangely stronger, more resolute in his commitment of service to the Master.

He is brought back to the consciousness of the group by Elizabeth's warm touch on his side and then by the presence of Paul immediately before him.

Paul's gentle gaze seems to fill the void of Hope's absence. "This has been a multifaceted work, Peter, some aspects of which could not be revealed to you for reasons perhaps which are now quite apparent to you. The strong bond between you and Hope, and you as well, Elizabeth, was and is such that what you know, Hope knows. Therefore, in participating in this experience, you have not helped just this entity who is before you now to break free from darkness, but you contributed to placing an angel back in our Father's heaven, who is now in direct service to our Brother, the Christ. A great and glorious accomplishment has been made here, but the commission has just begun."

Paul turns to tell all present, of which there are many now gathered, that this is the first step of the commission, with many more remaining.

Peter perceives that there is great meaning to what Paul is saying. He directs his consciousness to the entity before him who has only recently departed from two-hundred-seventeen years of self-imposed darkness. He can only imagine the heaviness that has been removed from the entity. He observes this one who is now rejoicing before him, unaware of what has taken place between all these entities of Peter's group nor of the departure of Hope and so forth. Peter realizes that he must turn his focus back to this one, for he knows that this is the work at hand and that Paul is correct, there is more, much more, to be done. He assembles himself to be able to project an image perceivable by this recently released entity so that he might communicate with him.

"How can I ever thank you, Pete? Already I feel so wonderful, so free. God *is* great and forgiving. If He can forgive me, He surely must forgive all souls."

"What you say is true, my friend, and I believe this with all my being. But the things that you have done are not so extraordinary. They are not great wrongs. And the more you can realize these as circumstances and events that are opportunities for your growth, for your advancement spiritually to accept your unlimited nature, then the greater can your accomplishments and your works be."

"Works? What works would I ever do? I am a sinner, and only God's grace has released me."

"You have released yourself. God's grace is for all souls and is ever present. It is only we, in our lack of recognition of our own worthiness, who prevent the grace from manifesting itself."

Well done, Peter, Zachary offers from the side. *But do continue.*

Peter recognizes in Zachary's message some essence of importance to continue on, and he does so without question. Not knowing specifically how to proceed, he simply questions the entity. "How do you feel now?"

"I feel wonderful, and I am joyful we are ascending."

Suddenly remembering the tunnel and the three entities within it, Peter notes that the progression has accelerated dramatically. As he studies the one within the tunnel, in between the two greater spheres of light, he can see that the cloak of light over this one is much brighter now. Then he hears a moan. He turns abruptly to face the entity he has just participated in freeing and recognizes the presence of growing sadness. He can see tinges of coloration seeping down over his cloak. Peter becomes concerned and quickly moves forward to touch him.

No. No, Peter! he receives from Zachary. *Don't do what you think you should do in the sense of the physical. Do what you know to do in the sense of your eternal self.*

Stopping abruptly, Peter turns to Zachary. *What are you saying? He's in trouble. Something is going wrong. Are you saying I shouldn't reach out a hand to help my brother?*

No, Peter, Zachary answers. *I am simply reminding you that you are a part of the All, and that you are not alone in this work. And to remember what he is dealing with now. He must meet it, to see it all for what it is. In your own experiences with Paul in passing through the colors, recall that some of them were heavier than others.*

Reflecting but an instant, Peter does remember, and a realization comes to him as he looks to Paul, whose countenance is fixed lovingly upon him. Peter turns to the entity, whose grief has increased, evident in the streaks of darker, mixed, mottled colors cascading over his cloak.

He is moaning loudly now. "Oh, what have I done? What have I done? Look at him. I've contributed to this. Oh, God, I am not worthy to be delivered unto Thee. Forgive me. How great has been my wrong to another soul."

Peter feels a pull, a strong sensation at the midpoint of his own awareness. The entity is actually trying to break free from the light. He is trying to move back into a different level of darkness.

Peter thrusts his consciousness out into that darkness, and while he finds it much lighter than the darkness in which the entity had previously dwelled, it is a realm heavily saturated with what he would recognize as remorse, as regret. He shudders within, as he contemplates the possibility of this one dwelling for even a moment in this new realm of agony, of self-imposed guilt and remorse.

Quickly he collects himself and calls out to the entity, "Good sir, why do you lament so? May I assist you?"

"No, no, no, Pete. You can't! I realize how much grievous harm I have caused that young lad over there."

Turning to see where the entity is gesturing, Peter knows it is the dull, mottled-colored cloak of the young lad who has just departed the Earth. He turns back to the grieving entity. "But sir, you have dwelled in your previous realm of darkness and limitation for many, many years. How could you have wronged this lad? He was but a youth in the just previous incarnation; only sixteen-plus Earth years duration."

"It was me and others like me, but me heavily. I influenced him. The more he used narcotics, the more I influenced him to use them in greater abundance and frequency. I obtained my sustenance to my own needs through him. Oh, I am worse than I had thought before, for not only have I wronged others while walking upon the Earth, I have wronged them from here. Thank you, Peter, for your kindness, but you have misjudged me. I am not in the least worthy of God's grace."

Peter can feel the searing pull of energy present as the entity begins a struggle to break free from the light. "But wait. Wait, sir! Is there need for haste? Could you not pause a moment in the light? It may help you to understand and perhaps even to forgive yourself."

Abruptly the entity stops and turns, again full-on facing Peter. "How *dare* you, Peter. How dare you suggest that I could possibly be forgiven!"

The countenance is once again of the young teenaged woman he first met as the apparition of this entity or soul. It actually causes Peter to smile. It is like seeing someone who has broken a habit in the Earth, only to pop back into it for a moment or two. The recognition of the return of that habit is sufficient cause for humor to both and all involved.

Peter's warm smile has that impact upon the entity. He feels his humor grow into laughter, and he attempts to contain it, fearing that he will offend the entity. But he entity reciprocates, surprising Peter, and their laughter grows and grows. After a time, they both pause and look at one another.

"It's that quality, Pete—or perhaps I should call you Peter, for you are like an angel in my eyes. But in truth, even though your good cheer warms me beyond my understanding, I have nonetheless severely wronged that young lad over there. I am no doubt the reason he is laboring so hard at this very moment."

Peter hears Zachary softly. *Pete. Hey, Pete. Ask him if he would like to be forgiven. Just ask him that.*

Nodding, Peter continues to look at the entity. "Would you like to be forgiven? Would you be willing to try that?"

"What? How could there be forgiveness to such a degree for such a grievous, wanton wrong."

"No harm in asking is there?"

"Well, who do we ask?"

Peter, following his inner guidance, turns to look at the entity in the dull cloak or sphere in the tunnel of the light. Turning back to the entity before him, Peter surprises himself by stating, "Why don't we ask *him*?"

The entity's bewilderment and startled reaction to Peter's suggestion are self-evident. Peter now notes the incredulous emanation of energies pouring from the entity.

"Look at him. He's not even conscious. Still probably in a narcotic stupor, one that I no doubt contributed to heavily." And looking down, the entity says remorsefully, "Probably helped to cause his death."

"There's nothing like truth, is there, dear friend."

"What? What's that you say, Pete?"

"Nothing like truth to free one's spirit, is there?"

Gazing intently at Peter, the entity realizes that Peter is offering him something very profound. "Truth, you say? Who ever can look at themselves in an attitude of truth? Oh, I suppose you folks can, but after all, you're angels and all that sort of thing, standing at the right hand of God."

"What?"

"I know you for what you are: Beings of Light. Light workers, we call you. We can always see a bit of the glow of light around you somehow, not visibly you know, for you keep those things over you. But we can tell when one of you is present. Things are different somehow."

"Well, I suppose you could call us angels," and Peter chuckles a bit, hoping this will ease the entity's intensity. "But on the other side of the coin, then, if we are angels, what are you?"

The entity is listening intently to Peter, sensing within himself a great opportunity. Not truly wanting to return to the darkness, but feeling this is his just reward, a struggle takes place within him.

"Look, you're struggling. Don't do this. Let me offer you again this opportunity. Let 's just ask this young lad for his forgiveness. The worst thing that can happen is that he denies it to you, and then you can feel justified in your guilt if you want to."

The softness and sincerity of Peter's comments are recognized by the entity, and he responds to Peter's invitation with a communication that is barely understandable it is so weak. "Well, Pete or Peter, I suppose if you think it is an acceptable thing to do, nothing is to be lost in trying." Pausing for a moment, he continues, "But wait. We wouldn't duress him or burden him in any way, would we? I would rather languor in my own guilt than cause that young lad one moment's more anguish."

Having said that, the entity's own light grows. It startles him. "What was that?"

"It's the truth I just told you about. There is nothing like truth, God's Truth, and you are experiencing it."

"I feel lighter somehow."

"No doubt, because your first thought was for the young lad and not yourself, and because you were willing to endure more darkness rather than risk darkness for him."

As Peter turns he can see, to his own amazement, that the center sphere, which is the life consciousness of the young lad, is also brighter. "Look!" exclaims Peter. "Look at him! Your sadness was his sadness. And when you accepted responsibility and thought of him first, you lightened yourself *and* him. It's possible that by asking for his forgiveness you might not only bring more light for yourself but more light for him."

"Do you really think so? I mean really? You're not just

saying that to coerce me into this for some reason known only to you?"

"Not at all. You said it yourself, we don't have that capacity, do we?" Peter's smile, almost to the point of a bit of laughter again, warms the entity.

"No, that's true. You don't. Never seen one of you who ever resorted to trickery or subterfuge or anything like that."

"How about it then?"

"Don't leave me. Don't leave me alone, will you, Pete? I mean, stay with me. Help me. He may be angry with me, and he has a right to. Would you please?"

"Sure I will. But come. Let us ask if we can enter."

As they turn to face the tunnel of light, a strange thing happens. The three spheres of light—the young lad and the two guides—seem to transform themselves into visible figures of entities. On the right and left are beings of great beauty and peace, love emanates from them, and in the center is the young lad entity who seems half asleep.

The entity from the darkness peers, transfixed at the young lad. Peter hears him say, "That's him. That's him. Oh, Lord, forgive me. What wrong, what harm, I have caused him."

At that moment, the young lad's eyes blink, flutter, and open. As he glances around, a smile comes across his face. The entity from the darkness is stunned, and Peter watches silently, spellbound at the unfolding events.

The young lad turns to look at the beings to the right and left of him. "I knew you would be here. I had always felt it. Sometimes I longed for death just to be free of the darkness there, the heaviness, the sadness. I guess, wrong as it was, I wished for death and participated more and more in my habits just to be free."

Nothing is spoken or communicated by the two beings within the tunnel, but warmth and that which is needed by the young lad are given. A peacefulness comes over him, and he turns to gaze in the direction of Peter and the entity who recently emerged from the darkness.

"Oh, Lord. Good God! He sees me! He'll know me. I know he'll hate me. He'll hate me right back down into that darkness, and he has a right to."

Moans come from the entity that reverberate down into the finite essences of Peter's being. Peter reels from the remorse and sadness that seem to impact the entirety of the environs in which they are. He can feel within himself a reemergence of the golden glow, the Christ Light. He remembers the Hall of Wisdom. He remembers his own Garden. And he remembers Zachary's teachings, and Paul's support and love.

As he recalls these things, he remembers the All. In his consciousness he reaches out, just as before, and touches the grass in his Garden realm. Instantaneously, Peter feels renewed. He reaches out to the entity before him, pausing for a moment to glance at Zachary who is smiling and nodding, and realizes that it is acceptable to contact the entity in the direct sense. "Take my hand."

"What?"

"Take my hand, if you please."

"I cannot touch one of you. I am not worthy."

The steadiness of Peter's gaze and love reassures the entity. Finally, slowly, deliberately, he reaches out and makes contact with Peter, thinking that it is hand to hand, but Peter knows that it is much more than this. "Oh, thank you, Pete. Thank you so much. I can face him now."

Turning to look at the young lad again, both Peter and the entity are in wonder of the growing beauty of him. Without further encouragement, and to his wonder and joy, the entity with whom he is in contact pulls Peter forward until they come directly before the young lad within the tunnel of light. Peter looks back to see Zachary smiling just outside the periphery of the tunnel. The beings to the right and left of the young lad are radiant to the full extent of Peter's conscious-ness to perceive such a potential. After reviewing these things, he turns to focus his gaze upon the young lad and marvels at his youth and vitality, his beauty.

Then he hears, "Please, can you forgive me? I knew not what I did. Now I know that my influence upon you grievous-ly wronged you. I seek no atonement in the sense of expect-ing you to grant me license for what I did. I ask only that you would find in your heart the ability to understand. My own limitation and need were so great that they blinded me to your rights. I have trespassed against you. Please forgive me."

Peter, studying the young lad whose beauty has now reached awesome proportion, marvels as he sees the young lad step forward from his position between the two beautiful-ly radiant spheres of light, just dimly transposed upon which there is the outline of an image in each. Peter is stunned utter-ly to his core when his consciousness returns to the young lad, and he observes the following:

"Rise, my brother. For even before your first thought or intent did I forgive you. In any moment of doubt or darkness, I gave to you only love. This I give to you now for all to be-hold. I forgive you your trespasses and give to you that of my Father's eternal Love."

Peter is reeling with the knowing that here, before him, is the Master! How can it be? He turns to look at his compan-ions who are now gathered close by. Then he turns to see the entity from the darkness looking up into the loving gaze of the Master Himself.

"Lord, how can it be that a sinner such as I would ever be worthy to be in your presence? That you should come for-ward for one who is as lowly as I, who has not, in one mo-ment of consciousness in the Earth, sought for the needs of others but only for myself. How can I believe it is You? How can it be possible?"

The Master places a hand upon each shoulder. What is

communicated then between the entity and the Christ is not clearly known to Peter and perhaps to none gathered here. But Peter can perceive the glow growing around the entity and the communication that continues between them.

Then the Master turns to look steadily upon Peter and the others of the group and Peter hears within himself, *"This has been, my brethren, a good work. Do continue on, and I shall ever be with you."*

In that moment, the Master turns into the brilliance of the light so familiar to Peter now. The spheres to His right and left, Peter now recognizes, as the angelic host. Instantly, they are gone.

The entity stands aglow with a light shimmering about him, head bowed, looking down. Then he turns to Peter. "I cannot express to you my thanks. These events have freed me from some of my own misunderstanding, portions of which I know now were imposed upon me by the actions and deeds of others in other lifetimes. While I could have chosen to throw these off and call upon my greater light within, I did not.

"I also understand from the Master that I followed that path for a purpose, and I have pledged to the Christ that I would choose to serve in some capacity. He said you would know the best place where others who might not be fully awakened or might be in need often go for care and love and rest. Will you take me there now, Peter?"

Peter pauses a moment to attempt to understand. He cannot comprehend that the Christ would have him do such a work. Then he is aware of the presence again of Elizabeth, Paul, and a soft communication from Zachary. "The Hospital Realm, Peter. That's the ticket. Just what he needs. How's that feel to you?"

Peter turns to the entity. "Very well, I will take you to such a realm of expression where you can accomplish many good works in the Master's name and in your own good service for the enrichment of your own spirit and joy."

The entity is delighted. "Thank you, Pete. I shall ever be in your debt."

"Oh no, we're together in this. Willing workers together. And let me introduce you to my friends." Peter introduces Paul, Zachary, and Elizabeth. "I've learned much from these friends that I'll share with you what I am permitted and capable of as we travel. Let me start by telling you about Zachary here. He has some unique talents. One of them is delightful modes of travel. Zachary, would you take over and guide us to the realm of this entity's service? By the way, sir, might we know your name?"

The entity smiles at Peter. "I am simply known as Jack."

"Very well, Jack, let's be about this journey."

Zachary, in his inimitable style, comes to the forefront. "Okay Jack, let me just adjust your cloak a bit here. Wouldn't want it to be with any lint or such." He moves about brushing Jack, as though dusting him off.

Peter stifles his humor, remembering how so often Zachary did the same for him. As he perceives Zachary cloaking Jack with a cloak made from his own essence, Zachary steps forward to stand in front of Jack, one hand on each shoulder. "Let's see how you look here now." The energy pouring from Zachary surrounds Jack. Nodding and smiling, he links an arm up around Jack's shoulder and motions for Peter to do the same.

Peter leans in to Jack. "Careful now, get ready for this. He may not have the best voice around, but he has a large repertoire of songs."

Zachary's laughter billows forth, and he follows that with an exuberant song.

Jack, somewhat taken aback by all of this, hesitates for only a surprisingly brief moment and then joins in, to Peter's delight.

After a journey of joyfulness within the beautiful white mist, they arrive at the Hospital Realm and are met immediately by old friends and colleagues familiar to Peter and all, the entities Chen and Edol. Exuberance is exchanged between them all and introductions are made. Peter assures Jack that he is in good company and promises to visit him often. He thanks Chen and Edol who radiantly beam their understanding and gratitude for this opportunity to serve.

The group moves off a bit, and Elizabeth suggests that they move into a formless state and re-orient their individual and group awareness.

After a short while, they are upon Peter's favorite knoll in the Garden Realm, gathered casually about.

Peter is speaking to Zachary and the others about the specifics of the events. "It was difficult for me to believe the transformation from the rather appealing, teenaged young female entity and suddenly there I was looking at this aged, almost crippled man. What was the mechanism there, Zachary? Was that a mask of some sort that Jack used for that purpose? What can you tell me about that?"

Zachary is stretched out in a semi-inclined position, stroking the grass with one hand, which Peter notes with a smile. "In those realms, Pete, it is possible for the entities there to understand the strengths and weaknesses of those who are in physical body in the Earth. In their understanding, they realize what to avoid and what to focus on. Here was a case where the entity we came to know as Jack was focusing on the then teenaged entity in the Earth and realized that his strongest possibility of attracting himself to that entity was as a female of equal or approximate age. That's about the extent of it, Pete. It was used as a ploy of sorts, as you surmised."

"You mean they have the ability to change their projected image?"

"Certainly. To the extent that they have knowledge of power and knowledge of thought-forms and all that sort, they are capable of functioning within same, at least some of them. Others sort of flow with those essences, not truly understanding what's taking place but just being a part of the path of least resistance. Is that understandable?"

"I think I understand what you are driving at. But let me ask you something very intriguing to me. I saw the teenaged entity on the pile of refuse in the Earth. Later, that turned out to be the Master, right?"

They all nod.

"Why is it that I didn't know it was the Master when I saw Him?"

Zachary now sits upright, legs crossed, and leans on his knees with his elbows. "I suppose had He wanted you to know it was He, or felt that there was purpose in so doing, He would have."

"Well, was He, the Master, in the Earth for sixteen years? Or, what happened? I mean I can't conceive of the Master moving into the Earth ... you know, being in a physical body for sixteen years just to help Jack, not that Jack isn't worth helping, I understand that. But how could such a thing be? How did all that take place? What was involved there?"

Glancing over to Paul, Zachary pauses for a moment waiting to see if Paul will comment. Paul nods and turns to Peter. "You are considering the Master from finiteness and from the perspective of Earth consciousness. Here, particularly in the Hall of Wisdom, you have seen the Master in forms or expressions of unlimited nature. True?"

Peter, listening intently, nods.

"Well, then, consider for a moment that, no matter where the Master would dwell or express Himself, He is still the Master and therefore unlimited. Would you also accept this?"

Again, Peter agrees.

"Then the answer to your question is that the entity in the Earth was and is the Master, the Christ, and ... "

"Wait a minute, forgive me for interrupting. You mean that the Master was a, well, uh, you know ... "

"You mean an addict, Peter?"

"Yes. Are you saying the Master was addicted to narcotics for sixteen years? All leading up to the breaking free of Jack?"

With a gentle smile and looking at Peter carefully, Paul continues. "Think about it. Jack was in that realm of darkness two hundred seventeen Earth years. Is it so much to give sixteen years to free a soul who has suffered such agony, even though self-imposed, but been in darkness for such a time?"

"Well no, I suppose, if I were to look at it that way. But what of His other duties? You know, maybe not duties, but what of His other works?"

"You have seen how you can be here in the Garden Realm and elsewhere at the same time," interjects Zachary.

"Yes."

"Well consider for a moment that the Master can do the same and much more."

"So you're saying, if I understand you correctly, the Master was in the Earth for sixteen Earth years and that the Master was elsewhere for all those years at the same time?"

"I'm not only saying that to you, Peter, but the Master proved it."

"I guess I thought that the Master just appeared and that young lad went somewhere else.

"I suppose that could have been so, but the information we have before us clearly indicates that that is not so."

"I can't imagine, Zachary, that the Master would endure sixteen years of a limited focus in the Earth, subjecting himself to narcotic addition and all the pains and agonies of it just for—and he's a wonderful person, and his soul is beautiful—but for *Jack*."

Zachary becomes more serious. "You are not keeping this in good perspective, Peter. You are not using the completeness of your Consciousness. Your closer proximity to the Earth has brought you back to a more finite, focused, and limited, field of perspective and understanding."

"Yes, I suppose that's so, but I need to grasp this."

"Very well then, let's go grasp it."

"What?"

"You know, another outing."

"So soon?"

"What has time got to do with it, Pete?"

Peter recognizes the humor. "You're right, nothing like an outing." He rises, as do Paul and Elizabeth.

"The best place to learn to understand this would logically be the Earth. If the Master can endure it, as He obviously has, then no doubt we can as well. True?"

"Well, I suppose so, Zackary, but what are we getting into this time?"

"The continuation of the commission, of course, Pete. What else?"

Before Peter can comment, he feels himself swept up and then moving with the group, with Zachary's melodious song cascading before them.

Somewhere within himself, Peter knows that what lies ahead will be not only revealing, but challenging to him to the depth and core of his Consciousness.

As our group begins to move, we shall conclude here for the present, returning to find our group in their next work when next we meet.

CHAPTER 9

Station Earth

JANUARY 31, 1993

Our group is in motion as we rejoin them, Jack particularly delighting in the experience of formlessness and the lack of definition that limits. We find them almost tarrying, as they share in the oneness, laughing and simply knowing joy.

As this continues, a sort of blending is taking place, so much so that an observer might think that there is but one entity, one beautiful sphere of light, moving through the universe, creating a wonderful collage of sound and color and a radiance of light.

The group begins to slow as it reaches a closer proximity to the Earth. They are moving into a space that is brightly illuminated. As they reach the periphery of this great light, the group slows, and each of the entities can be distinguished as an individual much more clearly.

Peter is speaking. "These experiences of formlessness are always such a delight. I feel as though I have regained a considerable degree of energy. You know, like recharging one's batteries, as the term goes in the Earth."

All in the group smile as Peter turns his attention to what is in front of them. The group has been drifting slowly towards the edge of the light. "This looks familiar, but I can't quite grasp it."

"Then go inward," Zachary jokes, "find it and grasp it."

Peter chuckles a moment and then follows Zachary's suggestion. As he turns inward, his outer periphery takes on a beautiful golden-colored glow. Only moments later he "re-emerges" and the countenance is individualized as Peter. "I have it, Zack!"

"Wonderful, Pete. Perhaps you'd like to share with the rest of us what 'it' is."

All in the group smile, for indeed they know what it is, but as is Zachary's nature, with humor he calls this forth from Peter.

"What I discern from my inner reflection is that this is a control center similar to those we've seen in past."

"Very good, Peter," comments Paul.

Elizabeth nods and smiles, as does Zachary.

Turning his attention back to the great sphere of light in front of them, which they are now slowly entering, Peter is joyful as he recognizes within it his old friend, Zeb.

"Hello, Peter! Welcome." Zeb rushes forward as a great wave upon some sort of celestial ocean, crashing into Peter, embracing him mightily. "Our compliments, Pete, on a job well done. Some here wondered for a moment or two if that fellow Jack would get the best of you. I knew he wouldn't, of course. I told them that it simply couldn't be."

Zachary chuckles. "That was a sure bet, Zeb."

"Well, Zack, come on over here. Let's give you an embrace, too." Without waiting for Zachary to go over, Zeb cascades into Zachary, then into Paul, and of course into Elizabeth. Something similar to fountains of mixed color and light spews from the collisions. Peter makes a note in his consciousness to ask about what the mechanism of such an interaction, but he notices that it feels so wonderful even standing off to the side that, for now, he will simply revel in it.

Zeb moves off and waves the others to follow. "Come along here. I have some things to share with you. I'm told to give you a hand here, so to say, in the continuation of the commission."

"So you'll be working with us in this, Zeb?" asks Peter.

Zeb turns halfway and comments over his shoulder. *(That's only a descriptive term for your understanding—*

remember this in all such descriptions, see?) "Of course, Pete. You wouldn't think we'd miss out on such a joyful work."

"Oh, that's wonderful, Zeb. It makes me feel so good to know you're a part of it."

"Good. Now come over here and let's take a look at some of your earlier questions in the Garden and other thoughts you had."

Peter is shocked. "You ... you know of those?"

"Certainly. It's all a part of the commission."

"It is?"

"Of course. It's the Law. Zack? Paul? You haven't explained that to him yet?"

Paul and Zachary smile at one another, and Zachary responds. "Yes, Zeb, we've explained that to him. He hasn't formalized that understanding completely yet, but he will soon enough."

"Right-o, Zack. Well then, let's take a look here, Pete, and see what we've got."

Peter, looking around and seeing the lustrous expanse of white, appearing like white clouds in the sky of Earth but with more of a fluffy spun substance like cotton candy, only radiantly white. He decides he has no true comparison from his Earthly experiences with which to describe this, and he makes another note to inquire about this later, as well.

"Now, if you'll look over here, we'll see what's going on." He motions Peter and the others to come forward and stand very close to him.

"Where am I to look, Zeb? It's beautiful, but I see nothing but the white."

"Yes, the life essence. We've focused the creative flow of God at this point to create a sort of oasis that we call the Control Center, and the result always ends up looking like this. But yes, very beautiful."

"Indeed it is. But did you say life essence?"

"Yes, you know, the Spirit of God fashioned in a pristine primordial (formed, yet unformed) envelopment. In this, we can function in our own individuality while leaving the surrounding realms adjacent to us intact. As such, we can migrate this Control Center to suit the works before us and have no disruptive effect upon those whose 'time and space,' as you call it in the Earth, might be in that same position. Got it?"

Peter, though still with many questions, nods, simultaneously digesting that information.

"Now, if you will, look over here." Zeb gestures with a small counter-clockwise circular motion.

"Cleaning the windshield, are you, Zeb?" asks Zachary with a bit of his humor.

"I suppose that actually wouldn't be an inaccurate description, Zack."

Peter, looking from one to the other, doesn't know quite what to make of this, but caught up by the obvious love between these two friends, simply relaxes and observes.

Immediately where Zeb made the small circular motion, the white becomes clear as it gradually spreads larger and larger. Peter understands, then, why Zachary made the comment he did, for it appears every bit as though he is looking through an immense window. Before him is a vast expanse, which he recognizes to be the Earth.

"A beautiful sight, isn't it?"

Peter is taken aback in what seems to him to be an awkwardly long pause. "That is incredible, Zeb. You must tell me how you did that at some point when appropriate."

As though he himself is pleased at Peter's own pleasure, Zeb turns and smiles. "I'd be honored to, Pete. All you have to do is ask. But for now, take a look here. You had asked in the Garden about the Master's works on behalf of our friend Jack. Before us are several of the continents of the Earth. Can you make them out?"

"Yes. I can see very clearly. This is amazing."

"Well, all things are possible when one aligns themselves with God." He turns to look at Peter, who simply nods and smiles. Zeb goes on. "Now if you will observe, I will attempt to show you here only a few of the locations on the Earth where the Master is involved in service and support of individuals and groups. Understood?"

Peter's consciousness is racing at this point. Almost robotically, he responds. "I understood, with the qualification that I get to ask questions later. Okay?"

All laugh heartily. "It would be my privilege. Now, let's take a look at this portion of Europe. If you observe, you will see several involvements."

Again, Zeb raises his hand and makes a slow counterclockwise motion. Small spots of beautiful light begin to appear here, there, over here, and again and again.

"Goodness! Are you telling me that all of those spots of light are individuals where the Master is personally involved?"

"Yes, but these are only the direct involvements in the sense that you phrased your question earlier with your colleagues. This is where He is personally, as you called it, a part of the life experience and helping, serving. Now if you will continue to observe, you will see something else. I would be happy to accept your questions on that or anything else." Again his hand rises with the small circular pattern.

Suddenly Peter can see lines of light leap forward, so it seems, to make contact with those dots of light on this small portion of Eastern Europe. The lights are resplendent, and Peter recognizes quite clearly the coloration and essence so familiar to him from the Great One in the Hall of Wisdom, in the Hall of Light, in his Garden. "That is remarkable!"

"Keep watching."

As Peter does, very intently, he feels a touch on his left side. He glances over to see Zachary smiling at him, and he realizes that he has begun to lean so far forward so that he is actually drifting.

"You don't have to strain to perceive this, Pete. If you want a closer look, then take one or ask Zeb to help, but don't fall out of the Control Center straining yourself."

All laugh again, good-naturedly, as Peter realizes that he had moved forward as though leaning over a balcony railing to get a better look at a performance on a stage below.

"Need a closer look, Pete?" asks Zeb. "Here, let me give you a hand." Again, the circular motion and everything seems to have been magnified, which keeps increasing and increasing. "Tell me when it's to your pleasure, Pete."

"Yes, yes!" exclaims Peter. "This is fine."

At this, Zeb again motions with his hand, and the magnification immediately stops, as all laugh, including Peter.

The laughter subsides and Zeb continues. "To anticipate your questions, Peter, if you'll notice around the primary golden-white light, which of course you recognize as the Master's own essence, you are seeing parallel lights moving along the primary, I'll call it, river of light. These other bands of light accompanying the Master's are the essences of those who are serving with the Master to help those individual souls. In some cases they are the person's guides, in other cases, they are those who serve continually with the Master."

Peter's mouth is agape. "What a beautiful sight. It is incredible to think that this was in place when I was in the Earth. Was it?"

"Yes, ever in place."

"So what I am seeing is common?"

"Very common, though this activity has increased somewhat significantly in the last several Earth years, Pete, and we are told to anticipate that it will continue to increase. Therefore, we are expanding the Control Center here and increasing, what might be called in the Earth, our staff." Commenting to the side, "That's quite humorous don't you think,

Zack?"

Zachary nods vigorously and chuckles to himself, and little rivulets of light bounce off of him as he does. "Anyone we know, Zeb, to be the new staff?"

"Thought you'd never ask, Zachary. Peter, you'll be delighted to meet an old acquaintance later, for someone called Wilbur has recently volunteered to join us here."

"What?"

"Oh, sorry. You didn't hear my communication?"

"No, no, Zeb. I was just surprised. I thought Wilbur was, well you know, a worker in the Crystal Realm."

"He was and is."

"Well, is he going to be here, you know, full time? Or just for a short time? And when is he coming? Will I get to see him? Will any of the others from the Crystal Workers' Realm be with him? Will he be bringing crystals here?"

Before Peter can continue, the group bursts out laughing.

Zeb winks good-naturedly at Zachary. "Not all things have changed, have they, Zack?"

"Not at all. Peter is just as he was—unique, and wonderfully so. His inquisitive side is, as they say in the Earth, always in high gear."

Peter laughs aloud at that.

"Well, let's see. Would you like me to answer those serially as you asked them? You know ... Yes. Yes. Yes. No. Yes. Or would you like to have them more fully answered?"

"The latter, if you don't mind, Zeb.

"Well, he's elected to move on to be sort of a bridge to those who will remain in the Crystal Workers' Realm, which I should add here is progressing nicely, thanks to their continued involvement in service to the Master. Once he arrives here, there may be one or more with him. It's doubtful he will actually have crystals here, but one never knows. You will get to see him, and he'll stay here for as long as he wishes. We do hope that's a wonderfully long stay, for we are very fond of him, as well."

"Oh, how wonderful. I have wanted to see him again. This will make it an even more wondrous opportunity. You know, like having your cake and eating it, as we say in the Earth."

Of course, humor follows this, including a counter comment to Peter that *as we say in the Earth* no longer applies.

Then Zeb shifts the focus back to the immense opening in the mist. Peter can see a broad view of the Earth. "Now let's take a look from another perspective of consciousness, if you don't mind."

Without waiting for a response, Zeb motions with his hand.

Peter follows Zeb's direction and begins to see small spheres of light that seem to be floating up from the Earth. He remembers his previous experience of watching those who are now his friends as they departed from the Earth. "Are those souls departing the Earth?"

"Yes," nods Zeb.

As Peter continues to watch in wonder, he sees that some of the spheres of light are drifting slowly while others are moving more rapidly. He can make out accompanying spheres around the periphery of the main sphere and remembers the process with the young lad who was accompanied by two other spheres of light.

"Keep watching."

Now Peter can see beautiful lights moving extremely rapidly to the Earth, like rockets. These become superimposed on the other spheres moving at varying speeds and varying numbers of spheres of light in each group. As Peter watches in awe, it seems to him that some of these spheres of light rocketing toward the Earth are so close that he looks to his right and left to see if they are actually passing through the Control Center.

Zeb is aware of this thought. "They could be, Peter. But

since we are in the field or life essence of God, we are unknown to their consciousness. They wouldn't be aware that we were here.

"Now let's adjust our perspective." Zeb again motions with his hand, and gradually Peter's perception of the spheres rising from the Earth upwards fades away. He can perceive more sharply, now, the wondrous luminosity of the spheres who are moving towards the Earth.

"Take a closer look at some of these." Once again, Zeb motions, and it is as though some of the spheres are in slow motion. Peter realizes that they are ringed by beautiful lights all around the circumference of each sphere. The luminosity of these lights in some cases "takes Peter's breath" away *(to give you a descriptive term of his reaction)*. As he continues to observe, he feels a wonderful essence within himself and his cloak takes on a rosy glow. "Wait a minute! I know that essence. That's Hope's, or should I say it's an essence associated with entities such as Hope from the Angelic Realm."

Zeb smiles at Peter. "Well done."

"You mean those *are*, as I would call it, angels accompanying these souls to the Earth?"

"In many cases. Those of the angelic host who have joined in service to the Christ in God's Name love that work. They love the sort of magical quality that is a part of the emergence of a soul into a new incarnation, and they will often remain for various lengths of Earth time in close proximity to the soul as it engages this new physical expression. So it is with that wondrous illumination that a newborn baby emerges to take on the new opportunity of growth and exploration in the Earth. "

"That is utterly beautiful. And you know, it's familiar to me, because when I saw my children for the first time I felt as though I was blessed or was in the presence of angels."

All nod or smile, understanding.

Zeb now directs Peter's attention to a singular sphere of

light moving towards the Earth. "Take a look at this one. I think you'll find it interesting."

Peter follows Zeb's direction again. He attunes himself to the sphere and begins to perceive the essence. First, he notes a large luminous sphere primarily white or sort of a silver-blue mixed with white as the primary sphere. "That is such a beautiful combination of colors." Around this primary sphere, he perceives four that are very much like the essence that comes forth from the angel Hope. He notices that there are several other orbs of light, some of which are moving at a distance in front of the primary sphere, as though they are moving as an advance guard for someone of importance in the Earth who might be on a journey there.

Tuning and expanding his consciousness even further, unaware that he is being aided in this by Zeb and the others in his group, Peter discerns, off some considerable distance, all around this greater sphere are yet other lights, each in their own way beautiful, resplendent in their glory. "Is this one who is heading towards the Earth unique? I know all souls are special, but, you know, is all this intended for some unique or special work in the Earth? Or of high spiritual stature or something?"

"I suppose you could say so, from the perspective of the Earth, and I suppose that collectively speaking you could consider this unique, though it does happen quite frequently. There are many things to consider, and we can get into those when it's appropriate. But as Zachary is always the first to remind you, the best way for you to find out about these things is to be a part of them."

Once again, Peter is caught off guard by such a suggestion. "Are you saying we should join with that group?" pointing to the cluster of lights now moving in what Peter considers to be slow motion. *(The motion has not actually changed one whit; it is Peter's perception and Zeb's ability from the Control Center to manipulate Peter's cognition of time).*

"Yes. What do you say, Zachary? Our friend's limitations seem to have momentarily gotten the better of his curiosity again."

"Give him a moment or two, and he'll be all for it."

Peter looks from one to the other and glances at Elizabeth and Paul who are standing quietly by the side. "By all means. Knowing we wouldn't be disrupting anything or violating any of our Father's Laws, or you wouldn't suggest this, yes. It seems a remarkable opportunity."

"As a matter of fact, Peter, this is a part of (as you would call it) the plan."

"Plan? What plan, Zeb?"

"Well, perhaps that's a misnomer. It's a part of the opportunities presented to you and to all in the commission given to you by the Master Himself."

"Wonderful! Then let's get to it."

"I was hoping you would say that. I'd have been very surprised if you didn't. Have a nice trip, then." Zeb turns and motions with his hand toward the group, as he did towards the beautiful white mist.

At once, Peter feels his own motion. Looking around, he sees Paul, Zachary, and Elizabeth very near to him. Not very far off, he can see the other spheres of light and immediately before him, the beautiful large sphere of light is now moving rapidly towards the Earth.

"May we communicate?" Peter asks Zachary.

"You may indeed, Peter. If you will notice we are within our own sphere of consciousness here, and in essence, we shall be perceived by the others as one sphere of uniqueness among the many."

"You mean the others can see us?"

"Perceive us, yes, for they haven't physical eyes, you know." A bit of laughter occurs.

Then Peter turns his attention to the sphere in front of them, wondering at its beautiful luminosity. The purity emanating from it is so majestic that, were Peter capable, he would weep at the beauty of this individual moving towards the Earth. Because of their position immediately behind the great sphere, He feels the full impact of its radiance and is so moved and awestruck that he is unable to communicate for some indeterminate period.

After a bit, Zachary nudges him. "It's a wonderful essence, isn't it, Pete."

This breaks Peter's concentration, and he shifts his focus to his colleagues. Observing their loving smiles, he realizes that, from each of them, there is a similar essence as from the great sphere but that it is blended somehow into the uniqueness of their own being. As he looks from each of them back to the sphere before them, he understands that the difference here is that the sphere they are following is a simple, pure combination of these multiple expressions, with no specific individuality to them. He turns back to the group to share this discovery with them.

This time Elizabeth responds. "Parallels, Peter. In a sense, it has to do with parallel essences. In each of us, you will find that we have taken those things that have been meaningful as individual expressions of God, as you discovered with Hope and Rebecca, and we have forged them, shaped them, into that which we are fond of, that which we find comfortable and joyful. So this becomes our essence, and therefore that is how we are perceived. Similarly, would you find our uniqueness present in our cloak as a collage of essences, color, sound, and all such descriptive terms in the Earth. The entity we are following here is expressing primary essences associated with God—not individualized, but pure and unobstructed."

"If you search inwardly," Paul adds, "as Elizabeth has described this to you, you will find that you are capable of defining each of these individualized essences within you. Once defined, you can use that realization and definition in accordance with your own objectives, your own goal or purpose, to develop yourself towards any work that you may have elected to accept in our Father's Name."

Peter reflects on all of this and then turns his attention back to the sphere they are following. "Then I could conclude from what you are expressing to me that this entity in front of us somehow or other is not as individualized as we are? Or that they are capable of being an individual entity and yet express each and all of these essences in their purest form?"

"Actually, Pete," responds Zachary, "both are correct."

"Truly?" Peter turns back to gaze in wonder at the sphere of light and then turns about. "Wait a minute. I know by now that whenever things like this occur, they're not just chance. They always offer me remarkable insights and discoveries. As I relate this to my earlier queries and Zeb's awareness of my questions of you, and your suggestion, Zachary, to quickly have another outing ... can this be ... " Turning to look back at the sphere, Peter answers his own question. "We're following the Master, aren't we?"

Paul smiles. "Well done, Peter."

Elizabeth and Zachary simply smile.

(We shall attempt to describe as specifically as we can the events that follow, but we ask your understanding that much of this communication is without descriptive terms.)

"Greetings and welcome, my brother Peter and dear friends. It is a joy to have you with me in this work and in this journey. You are, of course, encouraged to assist in any aspects of what is to transpire as you are guided from within by our Father. I lovingly encourage you to follow that above all else. As I seek to enter the Earth, in the image of that which is acceptable by that of our brethren in their realm, you will know of my presence and of those things that are potentials for you from time to time by way of those who are now mov-

ing with us. I call your attention to them and ask that they acknowledge themselves to you now."

At this point, there is a communication beyond description that takes place between Peter and his group and many of the other spheres of light in motion parallel to the Master. One of these, to Peter's amazement, he recognizes as the entity he calls Bobby. This warms Peter's inner awareness. He then hears these final words from the Master:

"Remember, Peter, that you are never alone. Even as I go to be a part of this answer to a prayer in the Earth, I am never any the less with you. We are all one. And in those things we do in our Father's Name, thereafter we become all the more aware of our oneness. If there is the need, I shall be with you, and you shall know of my presence. I must continue now. My love and blessings remain with you and your group, each one, always."

At that moment, this beautiful sphere moves with unbelievable speed and all of the accompanying spheres with it, until Peter sees that the sphere, along with what could be called His entourage of companion souls, seems to become utterly absorbed by the Earth in a burst of light that then remains as a constant glow.

Peter and the group now have slowed to what could be considered an almost complete stop. He is spellbound by the experience and looks toward the Earth in wonder. The group gathers close by him, aware of his intense inward movement of energy, his great effort to assimilate the immensity of the event that is transpiring.

He turns to the group. "I never dreamed when I questioned you in the Garden that this is how you would explain this to me. It is nearly overwhelming as I strive to correlate this with what I remember from the Earth. You know, we did our thing there with prayer and services on holidays and Sundays and other days, and I tried to often be prayerful for the things I had, and even for some of the things I didn't have when I saw others in dire straights.

"But to think that I have just witnessed the Master return to the Earth, I cannot seem to be able to grasp that. I mean, many religions taught that someday the Master will return. I had always believed, as the ministers and priests had encouraged us to, that this would be, in effect, the end time. And that He would appear perhaps on a great cloud of light and, you know, do miracles and be surrounded by angels and all that sort of thing."

"Well, Peter," Paul comments, "your description varies quite a bit from what you have just seen and experienced, wouldn't you say?"

Peter reflects on this for a moment. "Yes, I guess you're right. The obvious question for me to ask you, then, is this the end time for the Earth?"

Paul answers lovingly. "For some it is, Peter; for others, perhaps not. Since there is in the answer to a prayer the presence of the highest and best, then so might there be the awakening in those who are about to depart that the true heaven exists not like a mansion in the kingdom of our Father but that it exists powerfully in the hearts and minds of those who believe. And also that it is, indeed, capable of being expressed in finiteness."

Turning to look with Peter at the constant glowing sphere of light now upon the Earth, Paul continues. "We are unlimited, Peter. The Master is offering you that realization gently and with love. This privilege we have had—of being present during His movement to do a work in the Earth—could be thought of as a rare blessing.

"But I hasten to add that it is not rare in the sense that we should consider ourselves to be singled out for being special, but that it is a rare blessing that we—and you specifically, Peter—are offered a work by the Master and that you accepted it without concern for what might happen at your expense. You questioned not any hazards, any potential loss, or anything of that sort. You freely, willingly, completely, offered yourself in service to the Christ. The rarity of this is that you were willing to so do immediately, without reservation. Any others willing to so do would certainly be granted this and other opportunities, as are we."

Peter nods, obviously feeling more balanced. "Is He a child in the Earth at this moment? Has He manifested a form of a certain age and gender to do a specific work? Can we know if He will remain for a long time or if this is but a momentary sojourn?"

"We can do more than know the answers to that, Peter. We can join Him if you so wish."

"You mean, be present to observe and perceive what is going on?"

"Yes, those things we can do, but we can do more than that. We can join the Master in this experience."

Peter focuses intensely on Paul. "I am striving to comprehend this thought-form you are giving me. Am I to understand that you are suggesting that we can be literally one with the Master as He has this experience?"

"Yes, that is what I am telling you, Peter."

"I could not sustain what would be required to be in harmony with the Master more than a half a dozen steps! The Master is so pure and so without flaw or limitation. How could I be in that essence without detracting from Him?"

"It is that quality of selflessness that enables you to do just that," responds Zachary supporting Paul.

"Indeed," continues Elizabeth. "Those are the qualities the Master sees in you that bring forth His great joy and love of your presence. You must know, though, that these things are easily met by the Master. Your presence, our presence, in a state of oneness, are welcomed."

"Forgive me, my friends. I know you speak truth. But I must have some time to balance with this. I have too many questions, too much that is uncertain within me. Could we pause for a time? Is this an opportunity that is presented only in this moment and will be gone if we do not accept it?"

"Not at all." Paul answers. "We can join the Master when we, when you, so wish."

"That's good. I just need time. This is an invitation of the highest order I would think. Like, in the Earth, being called to the White House for a personal meeting at a moment's notice. One would want to check their clothes, get a haircut, you know, make sure they're putting forth their best presence."

Zachary reassures Peter. "You don't have to worry any further. We understand completely. How about this ... Zeb's Control Center is just a thought away, and that would be a good place to *take a break* (as you call it in the Earth). Would that work for you?"

"Oh, yes. Thank you."

The group is immediately in the envelopment of the Control Center.

"Had a good trip, did you?" Zeb is but a short distance away, standing with several entities.

"Yes, indeed, a real barnburner, as they say in the Earth," laughs Zachary.

Zeb produces the image of slapping his thigh and laughing profusely. "You can rest over there, as I tend to several things I must be about. But if you need anything, call, and I or one of the others will be with you immediately. Have a good respite, Peter. See you shortly." He waves and moves off briskly with the entities at his right and left.

"Busy chap, that Zeb. Imagine trying to observe and sustain some sort of coordination over all those lines of light. Looks like so much spaghetti, to me, Pete."

"It does to me, too. That's one thing I thought of when I first saw it."

Zachary is masterfully chatting with Peter, and it is having on obvious affect on him, relaxing rapidly by the moment.

"Quite a bit to chew, wouldn't you say, Pete?"

"What's that, Zack?"

"What he means," Paul interjects, "is that it is quite a lot to have all happen in a short span of consciousness, or time."

"Yes. I guess it overwhelmed me, contemplating moving into a state of oneness with the Master in whatever He is doing there in the Earth. That just seemed a bit too much. I mean, I can accept the other accolades that have been presented, even though I must admit I still don't feel quite worthy of them, but to have the opportunity to be one with the Master in a work He is about … that is just inconceivable."

Zachary responds. "I think this would be a good point to explore, Peter. While it is one of your finer qualities, this selflessness, do remember that we had some previous experiences where it is important for each entity to claim their heritage and their uniqueness and their own rights.

"You can't be *wimpy*, as they call it in the Earth, and still be the willing worker at the forefront of God's service that you said you wanted to be. You must know you're going to be challenged repeatedly. With challenges such as Jack gave us it's important to know and remember your own heritage, to have some sense of balance between selflessness and the courage and conviction and yes, even the sense of Self—a consciousness, a command of your own power—as an expression of God. So, let's go into that a bit, okay, Peter?"

"I think that's a good idea, Zack."

At this point, dear friends, we are required to conclude. Our prayers are with you, all of you, in every moment.

CHAPTER 10

The Law of Self

APRIL 2, 1993

As we resume, Zachary is speaking with Peter about some things he had explained and demonstrated to Peter in the past that have to do with discovering the beauty of one's individuality and the Law of Self.

The Law of Self recognizes that each entity is a part of all others, and therefore, when one attends to the needs of self, are they not actually caring for some part that is shared by all others? If we are truly to come together in a completeness, as is foretold, then does not our impending oneness imply the importance, the stewardship, one has over self? It is the gift to be ultimately given to God, of course, but also to all Soul-Consciousness. See?

Zachary is casually pacing about, looking nonchalant and a bit removed from the immediate activities. Peter is speaking to Paul and Elizabeth, translated into words from thought-forms something like this:

"To consider actually being in a state of oneness with the Master is beyond awesome. It is nearly inconceivable to me even as I consider it from my total being."

Paul simply nods, as does Elizabeth. Zachary is walking slowly around the periphery of the trio, looking down, his hands behind his back.

Peter continues. "What if I were to do something I would regret. I know you said that the Master can counterbalance any actions I might inadvertently commit ... " He pauses to invite, almost anxiously, commentary from his colleagues. He looks to Elizabeth, whose face is glowing, and can perceive radiating encouragement from her, but somehow it is not enough. Elizabeth does sense this but simply continues to maintain her continual flow of kindness and support.

Peter then turns to Paul and is met by Paul's unwavering, reliable gaze. After what seems to be a prolonged period, he glances over to see Zachary still strolling about, now casually looking up and about, and off to the side and here and there, as though he is on a bit of a holiday, pausing just to relax.

Paul speaks, drawing Peter's attention. "As it has been shared with you and demonstrated to you, a certain degree of self-appreciation is important. After all, we are created in a uniqueness that is special to God. His love fashioned our uniqueness to ultimately be a part of the completeness of all existence. As one accepts the responsibility for the maintenance of self, one would do well to simultaneously accept and recognize God's intent of blessing to self.

"So, like a good gardener, they tend to their ward, preventing the blight of negative thought, fear, and doubt from damaging the tender seedlings as they are taking their nourishment and converting it in order to grow. Similarly, one would take experience and convert that into knowledge, and by combining it with all their past knowledge and experiences, they gradually learn how to apply and control the flow that shall ultimately become wisdom. Wisdom is an essence of God and us, being an expression of God, are constantly being offered it. The most profound and, perhaps I could call it, classic way to wisdom is through experience. That, after all, is what you are being offered, Peter. Do you understand?"

Peter has been listening intently and has indeed absorbed what Paul has given, for it is similar to what he has been given repeatedly in numerous circumstances and situations. But even so, a part of him feels incomplete with this understanding. "Not in any sense meant argumentatively, but how can I know when I am ready to accept such a position that I have just been offered? I know that many entities dwell in different levels of consciousness and that because of their choice it becomes their reality. What is my reality and is it of sufficient, uh, purity that I should dwell in such close proximity to the Master when He is about a work of the magnitude as has been defined to us?"

Paul simply gazes at Peter with that look of his, unwavering yet always with gentleness and understanding. It never fails to make Peter feel good.

Glancing around, he locates Zachary some distance away, looking up, studying a massive collage of colors on the whiteness of the Control Center that seem to be focused above Zachary's head. Peter is transfixed upon Zachary until, again, he hears Paul's voice calling back his attention.

"It is a question paradoxical in nature to be sure, Peter. You cannot know your potential until you exercise it. You can't know how much you are capable of achieving until you reach for an achievement that is just beyond the periphery of your current accomplishments. True?"

Peter reflects a bit and a hint of light dances around on his cloak. "Yes, I resonate with that. I know that to be true. Even so, where does one draw the line between reaching for growth and reaching in a sense that is foolhardy? It's like someone attempting to become an opera singer just because they sound good in the shower, and if you remember my earlier comment, even my dog couldn't stand my singing."

Humor ripples through the group and Zachary casts an exaggerated wink over his shoulder at Peter.

Moving towards Zachary a bit, Peter calls out. "Zachary, what are you doing over there? Don't you have any thoughts that could help here?"

Hands behind his back, still looking up, Zachary continues studying the colors that are inter-playing on the whiteness of the Control Center. "I am helping, Peter. I'm doing the very best I can. After all, in your own words, that's all one should be expected to do."

A brief pause, and laughter pours from Peter as the others join in, for Zachary always seems to reflect Peter's own thoughts back to him so beautifully and profoundly that it is virtually impossible for Peter not to find humor in his own statements of limitation. After the laughter subsides, Peter responds. "Okay, Zack. I know you're up to something."

Zachary again turns to glance over his shoulder, hands still clasped behind his back and states softly yet steadfastly, "I'm completely serious, Peter. I don't know why you find that so humorous, though I have been told that I have a knack for humor."

A little more laughter comes from the group at Zachary's obvious intent to lighten the intensity that Peter seems to feel. Turning away from Peter, looking up, he raises his arm motioning for Peter to come and join him. Somewhat obediently yet also eagerly, Peter moves to stand beside Zachary. Paul and Elizabeth follow.

"For example, Pete, take this color up here. What do you make of it? I've been noticing it. Did you see it? It started appearing not that long ago. Look around. Do you see the presence of any color anywhere else on the Control Center?"

Peter turns to study the expanse of the Control Center that is visible to him at present and realizes that Zachary is correct. This comparatively small location of a collage of color is singularly present.

"What do you make of this, Pete? Think it could be an invasion of some sort? After all, the Control Center is, you know …. what's it called? Can't think of your word. But entities from the Earth certainly couldn't pass through that without detecting something being present."

Focusing more intently on the colorful collage, Peter again remembers his own initial experience with Paul in passing through the colors. "You're right, Zack. That would have some effect on them, just as my passage through the colors had on me."

"Well, what are we going to do about it? Someone needs to clean it up. Get it out of there. Let's go see if we can find out where it's coming from." Reaching out, he grasps Peter's hand before Peter can comment, moves off and circles the area of colors. After going full circle around the orb of varying colors, they are back where they started. "That settles that. It's not coming from outside. No danger of an invasion."

Paul and Elizabeth laugh quietly in the background.

"Well, you didn't really think there would be an invasion, did you, Zachary? Uh, I mean, is that possible?"

Zachary shrugs lightheartedly but with a wink. "Who can say, Pete? Strange things happen now and then. I just wanted to make sure. But now that we have eliminated external sources, what do you suppose that concentration could be, after all?" He then turns to look at Peter deliberately, awaiting a response.

Studying the colors, Peter moves here and there a bit to get different perspectives. "I don't know that I can answer that, Zachary. It must have some point of origin. From what I've learned, I know now that something like this would not be present unless there was an originating source. You know, like the butterfly, my purple flowers, and … " Peter pauses mid-sentence and, were it to be physically expressed, his mouth drops open. He stares dumbfounded at the colors. "Zachary, are you showing me this because *I* am the source?"

Zachary turns to focus intently on the collage and speaks to Peter off to the side. "Well, what do you think, Pete? As I study the colors, they do seem to remind me a bit of you. But it's probably your opinion that's going to matter the most here, don't you think?"

"Why is that? Can't you or Zeb or Paul or Elizabeth do something to dissipate that and bring back the uniformity here in the Control Center?"

"You mean, destroy it?"

"Well no, I don't mean destroy it, but well, whatever is

necessary to re-balance the Control Center."

"Yes, I suppose so." Zachary lets his gaze wander around the Control Center. "This is an important place, you know, and the integrity of it should be kept uppermost."

Peter now perceives the approach of their friend Zeb from off to the side. "Greetings, friends. Sorry for the prolonged delay. Glad to be back with you. How are things going? Wait a minute. What's that? You're examining Peter and his limitations?"

"What?" Peter exclaims.

"You know, your limitations—your doubt, your fear. That's quite a collection of color. How are you approaching all this?"

Startled at Zeb's directness, Peter looks to Zachary.

"He's doing well, Zeb. But this will make for a merrier work, having you present."

"Oh, good, I really do enjoy these kinds of works. I don't get that many here, you know. So, let's see … " Stepping between Zachary and Peter, Zeb moves to reach his finger out to place it firmly on a vibrant blotch of red. "Now this here, let's see … Peter, you've got a mixture here of something that probably was in one of your childhood periods in a previous life. Oh, I see that it was reactivated in the just previous life, and you're still carrying fragments of that around with you. How's that? Pretty good?"

Peter, in a daze by all of this, manages to nod.

"And over here, this green. Look how it blends with the blue. Oh-h, the spiritual side of you is muted by this, and here you've got a beautiful opportunity for spiritual growth. See how these energies, as they are expressed as color for you, are clearly trying to tell you this? There's strong support for spiritual growth, yet they can't seem to function together. You have this dull area here, down the middle," and he gestures to it with his finger. "The trick seems to be to simply sort out this little area right here, and that will be just the ticket to moderate some of these memories that are lingering as flotsam and jetsam. No offense intended, Pete." Zeb turns to smile at Peter.

Observing Zeb's forthright honesty and loving warmth, Peter ponders how anyone could ever have less than a high regard for Zeb.

Zeb pauses for just a moment. "Well, thank you, Peter. What a lovely thought."

Peter quickly gets over his embarrassment that Zeb heard this. "Well, I do mean that, Zeb. But I really do want to get what you're telling me here. How is it that you are determining all that you have from this simple projection and blending of a collection of colors?"

"Nothing to it, Pete. If you'll come over here, I'll show you just how. It's all in the wrist and finger."

Zachary, a few steps away, is laughing. "I'm taking notes here, Zeb. Do give us your trade secrets."

Zeb laughs and vigorously bobs his head up and down before turning back to the colors. "Here, Peter, give me your finger to put on this." Without waiting for an answer, he grasps what would be the projection of Peter's thought in the form of a finger and swiftly plunges it into the boundary between the blue and the green where they overlap and form a sort of dull band.

"Wow, Zeb! That has a very strong effect on me."

"How so?"

"Well, I feel joyful and hesitant both at the same time. Like a bird who wishes to fly but can't let go of the branch it's sitting on because of its fear that it might plummet to the ground when it tries."

"Excellent. Right on the money, as you say it in the Earth. Now, try this over here." Zeb continues with each color and color blending, and Peter realizes he is making immense discoveries about himself.

After a time, Zeb and Peter turn back to the remainder of

the group, Peter obviously now in a much more balanced state. "What an amazing experience. I hope that at some point we will have the opportunity to explore this in more depth."

Zachary tilts his head. "Why wait, Pete? You have that opportunity waiting for you right now."

"Really? You mean I might experience this is the sort of thing, uh, down there?" He points in the general direction of which he presumes the Earth would be were Zeb to open a window once again.

"Yes. That and many more wonderful things that I have no doubt will pique your curiosity no end." Zachary chuckles.

"So," Zeb continues, "the problem here as I see it, Peter, is the old pitfall of unworthiness. Is that so?"

Slightly embarrassed, Peter looks down and then quickly back into Zeb's eyes. "I must say, Zeb, there's nothing wishy-washy with you. Right to the point, gently but directly."

"I hope my manner of communication is not disturbing to you. If it is, do tell me. But with all the activities I've become involved in here, this manner of approach in situations like this is almost mandated."

Peter nods. "I can only imagine, beyond what you've already shared with us, that this must be so. Do you have a suggestion for me that I can digest and accept?"

"Well, sure. Nothing to it. Why don't you go and join the Master and observe? If you feel okay about becoming one with Him in the more literal sense, then do so. And if you don't, I have no doubt there will be good benefits from the experience, nonetheless. Wouldn't you agree?" Zeb turns to Zachary, Paul, and Elizabeth.

Paul answers. "That is an excellent and workable solution. What do you say, Peter?"

Elizabeth transmits her warm, supportive, energy, and from Zachary, he gets the traditional wink and smile.

"I think you're right, Zeb," nods Peter. "Thank you. If it's acceptable that I not make a more conclusive decision at this point, I would like that very much. I feel very comfortable with that now, and as you say, Zeb, who knows, once I am exposed to whatever is going to transpire."

"Well then, excuse me a moment, and I'll give you a focal point here. Not that you need it, but you might enjoy it." All watch as Zeb raises his hand. The soft swirling motion causes the transparency to occur again in the whiteness around them and there before the group once again is the resplendent beauty of the Earth.

"Oh, it is so beautiful. Thank you, Zeb. I'll be certain to give you a full report."

Smiling as he walks away, Zeb casts a wave to Peter. "Not at all necessary, Peter, for this is the Control Center, remember? I'll know as you know." A wonderful laughter comes from Zeb, a final wave, and he strides towards a new group of entities that Peter realizes has just appeared off to the other side.

"Well, then, Pete, a bit of traveling music, don't you think?" Zachary raises his hand and swirls it, and there comes the tinkling, bell-like sound associated with Zachary.

"Oh, that's always such a nice touch, Zack. We haven't heard that in some time."

With that, Peter and the others join together and off they go, in a heightened state of joyful anticipation.

(As they journey, we will follow Zeb for a moment to where he has moved, for reasons that will be evident later.)

Zeb is now standing immediately before the new group. "Welcome, my friends. You are here to serve in the commission?"

Essences similar to smiles and nods come from them. Each has unique beauty, yet together they form a wondrous completeness that seems to just go together. It is like seeing a brilliant rainbow. Each of the separate colors is explicitly displayed in their individual bands, but there are those essences that unify it into the complete expression of the rainbow itself, and if any one of these colors were absent, the observer would feel the rainbow was incomplete. So it is with this group.

"You have made your preparations, I see, so let us move over here. I would like to acquaint you with some of my colleagues so that you will know them from this point forward."

They all move toward yet another group of entities that seems to be simply standing all along the whiteness, doing nothing but standing. This is, of course, misleading in the sense that "doing" has nothing to do with physical, material, or mechanical activity, but is a spiritual work.

All the entities in the newly arrived group are joyfully exchanging thought-forms and consciousness with the colleagues of Zeb, while he simply moves back a bit to observe. After a while, he returns to his previous position where he can more or less oversee all the activity taking place.

(Now we turn back to Peter and the group.)

As they are approaching the Earth, their movement becomes slower, and they are now moving at a very gentle speed.

"I thought it would be wise to move slowly at this point, Peter, so that you would have the opportunity to make some observations and to exercise just a bit."

"Exercise what, Zachary?"

There is, at this remark, a bit of laughter along with some lights and sparks and beautiful sounds all resonating within the sphere of light in which the group is traveling.

"Well, exercise whatever suits you, Peter, but why pass up this opportunity. Look about you. Reach out and perceive. It's always good to know the path one is following. You can't ever tell when you'll need to find that same path again."

Puzzled but with a great deal of faith in Zachary and an intuition that there are lessons to be learned, Peter eagerly attempts to do as Zachary suggests.

"And mind you, Peter," adds Paul, "you needn't force anything. Actually, it's the opposite. It's opening self. Not concentrating on something outside of self but relaxing and opening self."

"Yes, I remember, Paul. Thank you for reminding me."

"I might also suggest," Elizabeth comments, "that since you were so interested in the colors that Zeb was showing you, perhaps you might try to perceive if any are present."

"Excellent idea, Elizabeth. Let me open myself." Peter extends his focus and gets the unique feeling of being extended out from himself. He thinks of ways to define this: *Hollow*, he thinks. *Open, as though I were looking inside a great hall or a cylinder. No. The tunnel! That's it!*

Turning to look at the others, they nod an affirmation. He opens himself and simultaneously feels his consciousness moving along this tunnel, and perceives colors. Most of them lack luminescence. Most of them are darker, heavier, denser colors. A few are lighter than the others, but essentially the feeling is of darkness and heaviness.

Peter asks his colleagues what this represents and asks if these could be correlated with his experience in his own tunnel of light, since he is moving through the colors in reverse to that which he originally experienced—in other words, now he is moving through the colors back toward the Earth.

Paul confirms that this is the case. Then Zachary suggests that Peter reaches out again, as they are in continual movement, not only in the physical sense as you would know it in the Earth, but also moving through realms or levels of spiritual awareness and spiritual acceptance.

After Peter realigns himself and opens. For a few moments, he essentially perceives nothing very distinguishable. The denser colors are gone, and there seems to be a translucent opaqueness to what he is observing.

Zachary explains. "This is a kind of carrying medium that can support varying forms of thought and attitude that are quite relevant to the Earth. In other words, you might call this the supportive envelopment of the Earth itself."

"How curious," comments Peter.

"Do keep your consciousness open now, Peter," Paul advises. "As we approach the Earth, we also approach closer and closer to its consciousness and thought."

Keeping open and relaxed, Peter observes. After a few more moments, he notices some types of subtle forms that they are passing by, most of these distant, not very dense, greatly scattered in their positions and number. Recounting this to his companions, they simply encourage him to keep open. A few more moments go by, and he comments more and more about the shapes or forms, some irregular, some having a certain uniformity and continuity, others that seem to be far more resilient than the earlier forms, and here and there some are much more active. "What are these occasional active forms that I am perceiving? I can tell that these are becoming more frequent and more active as we approach the Earth."

"Keep alert and keep an open focus, Peter, and you will find your own answer."

Following this encouragement from Paul, Peter's perception increases in its sharpness. He uses those exercises, moving within and claiming his own uniqueness and unifying his consciousness with the more unlimited aspects of self that are within him. So doing, he is now capable of reaching out and almost touching or experiencing some of these irregular and more active forms.

With a start, he returns to his consciousness, taken aback, almost shocked. "What was that? I found no familiarity, no sense of any of the harmony that I'm so used to. In fact, it was an experience I can only relate to from my just previous life in the Earth."

"Precisely," comments Paul, "because that is what it is. Turn again and look, before we are completely past it, and observe."

Again, Peter follows Paul's suggestion, and as he, more cautiously now, reaches out to perceive one of the forms, he is startled to see that it begins to manifest itself into a familiar shape. "Why, that's an entity! I mean, you know, a person!"

"The former is more accurate, Peter," answers Paul softly. "It is an entity. We are entering and passing through what has become called by some in the Earth the Sea of Faces. You might want to simply keep your perception open from this point forward, but not reach out and experience anymore. Not that there would be harm in so doing, but we really don't have a right to disturb these entities, unless of course, we are invited by them to engage with them in interaction or conversation. Most of them will be utterly unaware of our presence and passing. Here and there you will find some who will recognize our presence but only dimly."

Peter turns his attention again outwardly and observes more and more of these forms. They are becoming more visible and clearly distinguishable as entities. He is in wonder, as well as dismay, at some of the expressions he is experiencing. "Those poor souls. So many of them. Why are they here and what are they doing? Are they like our friend Jack? Are they limited by their own lack of sight or by their desires? Or some of both of those things?"

"Yes, Peter," Zachary replies softly. "You'll find a situation that will conform to all your explanations and more. Think of almost any situation you can from the Earth that might limit someone and you'll find it here, and hundreds of variations on that single theme alone."

"Oh, my … " Peter now casts his gaze all about them as they pass by them in this, the Sea of Faces.

"Pay particular attention, now, to what's just ahead,"

Paul directs. "This might surprise you."

Peter does so and observes more of the same until, finally, he notices that the dark, heavy color seems to be changing. It is lighter and lighter. It is still thick, syrupy, heavy-like, but the colors and hues much brighter.

Suddenly, he sees more forms, yet these are very different than the ones just observed. Some of these, he can detect, seem to be aware of the group's passing. Some attempt to communicate or reach out to the group and their sphere as they pass by, but they do not seem to have the ability to accomplish this.

Knowing Peter's curiosity about this, Paul explains. "Many of these entities are just the same as those we've just perceived, and you might think it odd that they are even closer to the Earth than those who are obviously much more heavily limited. But consider this: These entities are still, in a manner of speaking, tied to the Earth or bound to it in the sense that their goals, their personal intent and purpose, are still heavily involved with the Earth. These entities here do not intend to do harm as you would call it. Rather, their ultimate intent is good, at least by the definition of goodness in the Earth."

"Can you explain further what you are saying, Paul?"

"Certainly. What is present in some of these entities is such an overwhelming feeling to do good that they are actually narrowed by that desire. In some cases, the entity's understanding of doing good is rigidly structured, strongly ordered, and dynamically expectant in the sense that, to them, there can be only one way of accomplishing this and only one end result. They allow no latitude in their good work, and consequently they have allowed no latitude for themselves. Does that make it clearer?"

"Yes, very much so."

The group continues explaining to Peter the various aspects of the levels of consciousness or spiritual acceptance that they are passing through as they continue their journey to the Earth.

"Are each of these levels of spiritual acceptance specifically positioned, in the physical sense, in proximity to the Earth?"

"In the sense of three-dimensional finiteness, no, Peter," responds Paul. "In the sense of spiritual finiteness and levels of thought, mind, and thought-form expression, yes."

Peter nods, continuing to study what they are passing by.

Now they begin to approach very close to the Earth.

"Very well, Peter. Here we are back in the Earth, in its atmosphere and all its three-dimensional thing," Zachary says lightheartedly, obviously intended to relax Peter.

Their movement is towards the position where Peter perceived the Master as having entered.

Peter is now observing other activities outside the group. "It seems much different now. I don't detect that opaqueness any longer. It's quite clear, familiar yet I can't quite recall it."

"You will," offers Zachary. "Of that, I have no doubt. But just relax and continue to observe. There are some good things to discover here."

After a time, Peter notes a much brighter light off in the distance. "That light ... it appears to be moving towards us. And there's another and another and another. Are these entities who can perceive us, Zachary?"

"Yes and no. They're not fully conscious, but they can perceive us."

"What do you mean, not fully conscious?"

"At this moment, they are in a sleep state. What you are perceiving is what they call the astral body."

"No kidding! I always thought that was just so much malarkey. You mean there really is an astral form?"

"Well, call it whatever you like. Astral is as good as any term, don't you think?"

"I don't know enough to respond to that, Zachary," turning back to look at the very pleasant light forms that are in motion. "Do they know we're here?"

"Yes, they know of the light we have."

"Some of these," interjects Paul, "you may even be recognizable, if you will concentrate just a bit inwardly."

Peter reflects. "I have a sense of something, but it's very distant. Should I try harder or relax more or what?"

"Don't concern about it," Zachary offers. "You'll have that discovery and more. We will engage in activities with entities in the astral body in experiences ahead."

"You mean, people who are sleeping are going to somehow or other interact with us?"

"Most assuredly, and perhaps on occasion, entities in other states of rest. Not all factors are under our control, for those who are the owners of these astral bodies have something to say about it all, you know."

A little humor passes among the group, including Peter. "Yes, I suppose that would only be right. This is very intriguing, though." Suddenly, Peter is aware of very brilliant light forms, and he recognizes immediately that they are no different than their own. "Look! Look over here. There are others."

"Yes," answers Zachary. "Indeed there are."

"Who are they? Are they sleeping, too?"

"No. These entities are wide awake in all respects, spiritually, as well as what you'd call mentally, Peter."

"Well, where are they from and what's their intent? Are they going to work with us?"

"I should hope so. These are entities who are in service here in the Earth as guides. You remember, Peter, those who are here serving with people who are in physical incarnation."

"Oh yes, like the entities who journeyed up with Jack."

Here, as the group settles down, Paul explains to Peter that these brilliant light forms are not necessarily present to guide someone who is about to depart the Earth. They are here to work with Peter and the group in the commission.

That commission will involve not only the works of the Master, the Christ, but will also interact with others in the Earth in physical body whose spiritual level of acceptance is sufficient enough to participate.

CHAPTER 11

Winds of Light

MAY 13, 1993

It is our humble and prayerful intent to take you literally into those effects and influences that are a part of these times of change and to bring forward, with as much clarity as we can, the understanding of how you might better deal with these. Then, as you make further discoveries, that you would claim the tool of wisdom, for it can, not only make the way passable for you through the effects and influences of the times but joyfully so.

The key will be, indeed, to seek out and to claim joy. For the test of any work to determine if it is the Father's or less than same is to ask: Is this truly a joyous work? If so, then it is the Father's work.

What is joy, then, the question might follow. Is it the individualized perspective of one's own perception of the attainment of certain goals, accomplishments, or material things? Is it a state of existence? The presence of abundance sufficient as to allay any need? Is that joy?

Could joy be called knowing the eternal nature of one's own soul and, therefore, seeing the present as one step along an eternal path, that the timeless opportunities that lie before each soul ever offer the blessing of joy?

Or lastly, can it be said that there is a common essence in the term joy which, when summarized regarding any individual definition of that term, would be discovered as a common ingredient for all?

It is perhaps the quest for the latter that might be thought of as uppermost in this and future works. Not so as to cause anyone to fall into a path that is rigid, structured, and limited.

But conversely, and perhaps strangely to some, that path is entirely the opposite: It is free-flowing, unencumbered, utterly unlimited, and as unique as the one who follows it.

How can it be a path if it is as described, for does not a path have definition? Here is a good entrée for us to return to Peter and his colleagues and their present and forthcoming activities. For there is a path, and it does have definition, but in its definition is the unlimited essence of God. Therefore, it has as its parameters eternity and timeless qualities, which are only subtly known by most in the Earth.

The brilliant lights continue to approach Peter and his colleagues with greater and greater rapidity. Peter, observing in wonder and admiration of the unique beauty and brilliance in each of these, turns eagerly to his colleagues. "Oh! Look how each is so beautiful, yet the next and the next have differences that are equally so beautiful! Words cannot describe the magnificence of what I am perceiving."

The number of those approaching seems immense but is only about fifteen or sixteen entities. Of these, three are at the forefront of the group and are the first to arrive before Peter and his colleagues, who are now more or less suspended at what you might think of as the outer atmosphere of the Earth, though that is only for your understanding.

Greetings take place between these entities and Paul, Zachary, and Elizabeth. Peter is somewhat tagging along, for he is yet a bit hesitant, being unfamiliar with the proceedings and cautious about his activity so as not to be inappropriate (according to his own assessment).

After the greetings, Paul speaks referencing Peter. "As you see, friends, Peter is moving along extremely well. The Master invited him to participate in works in the Earth. In his admirable quality of selflessness, he has somewhat reluctantly decided to participate and to contribute what he can."

One of the three entities with whom the group has been

---

communicating comes forward, perceived by Peter in a form that is physical for purposes of reference and communication, for this will make for greater clarity and understanding for him. He admires the gentle countenance of one before him, noting that he appears to be somewhat outside of the familiar, as though he has not come from the Earth in recent times.

The entity speaks to Peter. "I would like to welcome you, Peter, on behalf of myself and my colleagues." He turns to gesture to those with him, all of whom are now gathered around Peter and his little group. Each of them in one way or another affirms their spokesperson's comments, and Peter smiles and acknowledges them in return.

"We have heard much of your works and of progression, Peter, and we consider it truly a joy and a blessing to be a part of your continued quest. In these works now being offered to us all we know you will find much to gladden you and, as well, that you will surely have many questions about what shall follow.

"We will, at all times, attempt to support your inquiries and to provide you with that which is needed in any works that might lie before us. We all understand that you do not comprehend specifically what I am referring at this point, but all will become clear to you as we progress. We would also like to indicate that in situations that lie ahead there will be some immediacy involved, since we will be dealing with what is called in the Earth real time or serial time. Because we are here in the expression of the Earth, we shall, of course, be obliged to abide by God's Law, which we call Universal Law, and that is to function in harmony with those we are attempting to serve.

"But all of this, as I stated, will become clear to you as we proceed. So, that having been said, do you have questions, Peter, that you would like to ask us before we proceed? If so, please do so at this point."

Peter is somewhat glowing and vibrating in an intensity

of effort to absorb and comprehend all that is being offered to him. Of course all present are aware of this.

Zachary leans in to Peter. "Easy does it, Pete. Don't short a circuit. Just relax and flow with it. Know what I mean?"

Peter, glancing at Zachary, receives that exaggerated wink, which of course warms Peter, and he spontaneously relaxes.

"Much better, Pete."

Paul and Elizabeth also move to Peter.

"Peter," explains Paul, "this is a wonderful opportunity that lies before us, many-faceted and marvelous in many respects, which you will surely discover."

"Indeed," continues Elizabeth. "And as in the past, Peter, if ever you are in need, I will contribute all I can to help you remain balanced."

Recalling the precious experiences shared between Elizabeth and himself, Peter smiles warmly at her.

"Well then, Pete," Zachary bends over and peers up into Peter's eyes, "how about it? Are you ready for an outing?"

This causes another reaction in Peter's cloak.

Zachary reaches out casually to tend to Peter. "Hmm, let me see here. Might be good if we were to adjust your cloak a bit and clean it off a bit here and there."

Warmed within beyond measure by Zachary's simple yet compassionate gesture, Peter realizes yet again how Zachary is ever present to contribute whatever might be needed by him. They turn to the spokesperson of the group, letting Paul speak to the entity. "You are, of course, aware of the activities and events we have reviewed with Zeb?"

"Yes, and we are prepared to follow any one of these courses of activity that you feel is appropriate for Peter's present state of consciousness."

Paul responds. "Agreed, then."

A loving warmth emanates in sequence from the entities. He feels it to the core. They are focusing on him and seem to be contributing some essence that surrounds and meets within him, then passes through, as winds of light that leave behind only joy. They position themselves on the outer periphery, and the entire entourage begins to slowly move.

Peter notices that the movement is steady, without effort. The flow of light continues. It brings such a joy within the center of him. He marvels at this. It is as though the beautiful wind they are sending purifies him before any doubt can take root, or any seed of fear can become a part of the mantle of his being.

He detects the group coming to a pause. The spokesperson turns to the group. "We are at the periphery of the thought-form surrounding the Earth. Do you wish to identify any specifics to Peter or shall we proceed?"

A gentle, loving wisdom emanates from Paul. "Peter, surrounding the Earth is a sort of massive structure that has no tangible essence when viewed by a person in the Earth unless that person has conditioned him or her self to be able to perceive in the unlimited sense. So the normal person does not realize that this massive ocean of thought is engulfing them. Do you comprehend?"

Peter only half-heartedly nods, for he understands what has been communicated to him, but he does not understand the full nature of its meaning.

Elizabeth explains further. "It is similar, Peter, to the realms of expression where entities of like-thinking, like-levels of acceptance, actually create their own reality."

"Are you saying that this is a reality created by all of the people in the Earth?"

"Exactly so, Peter. Whether or not any person is knowingly contributing to the massive sea of thought has no real direct relevance, until they wish to do something that is beyond the parameters of the thought-form that is the prevailing force in the Earth."

"Could you give me an example of that?"

"Surely. It is like this. When a person has allowed their life to more or less drift, and they do what is expected of them, and suddenly one day they awaken and decide that they no longer wish to be controlled or directed by forces outside themselves, they wish to claim control of their own life, at that point they are facing the struggle to break free of the expected, to break free of the habit or the mold or the influence of mass-mind thought."

Peter contemplates this thought-form Elizabeth has given it to him.

Zachary offers more. "Consider it this way, Pete. Some people in the Earth excel and others don't. The measure of excellence in the Earth is by generalized standards, isn't it?" Peter simply nods. "Well, who sets the standards by which one measures excellence?"

Reflecting for a moment, Peter responds. "Well, I guess they're not actually set, Zachary, as you perhaps well know, but are just more or less implied. Everyone just knows them. You try to do the best you can in a certain field or at a certain work so that you can excel. The excellence is measured by accomplishment, probably more often than not measured by material gain."

"Well then, that's a mold, isn't it?"

"I suppose so, but I don't know that anyone intentionally contributes to it."

 "Everyone contributes to it if they follow it. The contribution is in the doing, in the conforming. The exception is the one who breaks free from those expectations and establishes their own. That's what Elizabeth was explaining to you."

"I understand now. So then, we are at the periphery of the mass-mind thought of the Earth. Correct?"

"Yes," answers the spokesperson.

"By that, can I conclude that it does have certain boundaries and certain limiting fields of reference?"

"You are correct, Peter, and perhaps you will find some

conforming, contributes to the pattern

comfort in that realization, for in order to sustain itself, mass-mind thought must occupy time and space close to a source that is generating the essence for its existence. Were we to grasp a large mass of this essence, which you will perceive before you in a moment or two, and take it elsewhere, let's say back towards Zeb in the Control Center, you would find that before you could arrive at the Control Center, it would be gone. It would have simply dissipated, as though, particle by particle, it just ceased to be. See?"

Peter nods, and the spokesperson continues. "Well then, let us move into the *Thoughtform Earth*, as I shall call it, and you can let us know what you perceive." Without waiting for a response from Peter, the entire group moves easily, swiftly, as though at the command of the spokesperson of the group.

"May I inquire of you as we are moving, is this group the sum total of the guides in the Earth?"

Smiling by way of a radiance of light emanating from his being, the spokesperson responds. "Not at all, Peter. There are many such as us in the Earth. This too, you shall discover in those times ahead. But for now, let us pause," at which point the group instantly comes to a halt. "If you will, Peter, we would like you to experience the essence of the thought-form 'Earth', or 'mass-mind thought' as it is often referred to in the Earth."

"By whom is it so referred?"

"Many. There are those in the Earth who are awakened, those with whom you have worked in the past and who have been working with you and your group for quite some time. These are but an example of those. There are many others, fortunately. But if you will, extend your consciousness beyond the periphery of our group to experience the essence of mass-mind thought."

To Peter's amazement, the spokesperson seems to somehow associate himself with Peter, as though he had enjoined himself, similar to the linking of arms between Peter, Paul,

Zachary, Elizabeth and the others previously.

To his great pleasure now, he can sense the presence of Zachary, Paul, and Elizabeth at equidistant points around him. Moving easily now, Peter detects the periphery of the ring of guides around their group's position, and the effect is as though a window of translucent light is opened. Peter and this small cluster of companions move into what he perceives as a substantial essence of swirling colors and all sorts of muted and subtle and over-toned forms of energy, some of which he cannot completely understand, others of which strike familiar chords of memory within. He pauses a short distance from the periphery of the group of guides.

The spokesperson questions Peter. "What do you experience and recall from this mass-mind thought, Peter?"

"I feel the memories of experiences in the Earth. I can hear sounds of laughter. I can hear sorrow, crying, sobs. I hear shouts of anger and words of condemnation. All these emotional arrays and disarrays are as a discordant symphony of extremes, flows of struggling energies and emotions."

"Very good. Now let your consciousness relax a bit and see what else you might detect."

Attempting to follow the spokesperson's suggestion, he turns inward and claims his inner peace. As he does, he feels the essences of this mass of thought like it had its own force, like it was of one mind and one will. "Fascinating! It is as though this is one entity, one massive intent. It is as though it has direction, purpose, and goals."

"Good. Just a few more moments and see if there is anything else you perceive."

Peter continues to claim his inner peace. He still perceives the presence of his companions nearby, yet unobtrusively. The closest in proximity is Elizabeth with a rosy energy flowing to him inwardly, not encompassing him but allowing him to be open. Perceiving *[in the Earth realm you would call it intensely, but it is the reverse of this here]*, he opens himself to be as passive as he knows how. He becomes aware of occasional rivulets of light, some greater, some lesser, some brilliant but widely dispersed. Some are very isolated.

Before he can turn to relate this, the spokesperson comments. "Very good. That is sufficient. Let us return to the group."

"You knew what I experienced?"

"Yes, of course. Not in the sense that I would invade your experience but that I might support it. I was with you, as were and are all of the group here ... and others."

"Curious. I was aware of Paul and Zachary and Elizabeth, but I was not aware of your presence. How is that so?"

"We are guides in the Earth. Our way is to be present yet not to interfere or get in front of those we are serving with."

"Serving *with*?"

"Oh, yes. For as one in the Earth whom we are serving with might gain, then so do we all gain, as well."

"Fascinating. Is this so in all realms?"

Peter's small group affirms this with smiles and nods.

"So, you have said that I have progressed. This means that you as well have progressed?"

"Yes, of course, Pete," answers Zachary. "We told you that at various times before."

Pausing to reflect, Peter realizes this. "I guess you have, but I never understood it in this way before. So the progression of one that is being served is a progression for the one who serves?"

Now it is Paul who responds. "That is God's Law, and it is a blessing that is returned. As one gives, so does one receive."

"Of course. I've heard that a thousand times if I've heard it once. But let me tell you, in the Earth, the actual understanding is often long in coming."

Humor breaks forth from the group and is echoed by the guides who identify with this in that they know all too well the interaction that Peter is referring to in the Earth.

The spokesperson continues. "Now, not to cut you short here, Peter, but we would like to take you to some of those with whom we are serving in the Earth, that you might have further comprehension of what lies before us."

"Oh, this is exciting. I would like to meet them."

Zachary chuckles a bit along with Elizabeth and Paul.

The spokesperson explains. "To an extent, that will be one-sided, Peter. For even among those who are *awakened* (if I might call it such), it is difficult to accomplish a formal introduction. Do you understand?"

Half understanding, Peter nods, thinking to himself that time will answer many of his questions.

"We shall now begin our journey."

At this point, the entire entourage begins to move almost imperceptibly, but by referencing the outer periphery of the group, Peter can distinguish what he surmises to be a motion towards the Earth itself.

"That is correct, Peter. We are moving towards the Earth and to the North American continent. Since this is a region of particular familiarity to you, it will serve to exemplify much of what we are attempting to convey to you here."

In a moment or two, the group pauses as though from an unspoken signal from the spokesperson. "If you will turn your consciousness now to North America, we would like to show you some of what we believe will be interesting and important points, and the latter comment is somewhat of a play on words, as you will see in a moment or two."

Turning to focus in the direction indicated, Peter perceives the outline of the greater portion of the North American continent. It causes a rush of memories and familiar essences. He notes with interest and some curiosity the region of his previous existence in the Earth, in the Northeastern portion.

As he does, the spokesperson guides him. "Allow your

consciousness to move along the eastern coastal area. Good. Now sweep westward with your consciousness, and as you do, open yourself as much as possible once again. We will preserve your integrity and deal with mass-mind thought while you are in that open state, so there is no need for concern or reservation on your part."

These comments from the spokesperson answer unspoken questions within Peter, and he is immediately at ease. With remarkable swiftness, Peter suddenly perceives an array of patterns seemingly super-imposed upon the surface or topographical outline of the North American continent.

Here and there, there are areas apparently following the geographic terrain, but in some cases not so. Some are very much darker than the surrounding areas, and occasionally, he can detect small shafts of light or spires of light or something of that sort. In some areas, he notes that the light seems to be concentrated, as though many smaller lights have come together, forming a much larger area of brilliant light, this super-imposed atop a background of muted shades of varying darkness. It is as though, he recalls, flying at high altitude over rural and then populated areas at night in an airliner.

"Very good." The spokesperson continues, "And now, if you would follow our guidance here, we would like you to observe certain of these concentrated areas of light."

Following the direction and guidance, Peter sees different essences that seem to be larger spheres of light, some more brilliant than others, and yet others that seem to either be just forming or just fading.

"Good observation. Excellent evaluation of what you have perceived, Peter. Next, we would like you to join us closely, and we will follow this immediate area of light here, which has some juxtaposition to our own group."

Curious, Peter follows the group and is surprised to find that the spokesperson is turning away from the Earth to an area that Peter perceives as being above them. Startled, he perceives clearly what he believes to be another group remarkably similar to their own, yet positioned somewhat above them. Off to the side, he notices a bright ribbon of light undulating and moving. He follows it in his own consciousness to its point of reference and finds himself at the outer parameter (so to say) of the Earth once again. The slender, almost delicate, filament of light is entering the Earth at a point far below him.

He turns back up to the new group and, under the guidance of the spokesperson, opens himself. Suddenly, he realizes there is familiarity here. With a rush of joy, he recognizes his friend Bobby, from whom he receives a warm greeting, and then begins to sense that he has met this entire group before.

(At this point, you might realize that it is our group that Peter perceives, called the Lama Sing group and that the delicate ribbon of light is the Channel by which we are communicating to the Earth in the present.)

The spokesperson studies Peter for a bit. "These are brethren, Peter. They will be of considerable assistance to us and the works that lie ahead. You can think of them as being in service to others in the Earth. In some respects, many of those you perceived on your journey here (in what you humorously discovered was called the astral body) were and are people with whom this group works, serves, and guides."

"You mean, this group there and ours will work together? That they, in turn, will represent real people in the Earth?"

"Yes."

"You mean like Abe and the others?"

"Possibly so."

"That is incredible! Will they know of our presence?"

"They are being told of it at this very moment."

"All of them? I mean, how are they being told? What's

the mechanism? Do they speak to one another? Do they have some sort of connective link? I only see one ribbon of light here. Are there many of them? Do they all know me?"

Zachary's spontaneous laughter fills the circumference of the group, followed by Paul's and Elizabeth's and all the others who are forming the outer periphery.

"Oh, forgive me, I guess I lost control there a bit, and my habits crept in again."

(Laughter continues, not only from this group, but we must admit from our own—this, as called, the Lama Sing group—and undoubtedly will be shared by you in the group who are following this, the "Peter Project".)

The group comes to a state of more ordered discussion, and the spokesperson turns to Peter. "We would like to show you something at this point, Peter, again to broaden your comprehension."

"Very well." Peter is now in a jovial mood and very light and expectant.

Zachary comments off to the side a bit, "This is the real Peter you see before you now. As you've reviewed in our previous works and will no doubt have the opportunity to experience, he's just a delight to work with."

Aware of this communication, Peter asks, "What previous works?"

"We'll get into that later, Pete, but let's see what lies ahead here."

Peter senses that they are moving towards some specific destination. "We are getting very close to the Earth now. I can tell from the intensity."

"Yes," responds the spokesperson. "Good perception. We are moving close to the surface of the Earth now, closer to the source of mass-mind thought, closer to the people."

They are moving swiftly over the surface of the Earth.

Peter perceives it to be probably a mile or two above.

"Somewhere in that range," responds the spokesperson, again hearing Peter's thoughts.

"Forgive me, sir, for all these little inward reflections. It's just my nature."

"That's a part of your endearing qualities, Peter. There is no need to apologize for that which is a trait of admirable nature. Observe now, as we pass over this particular area."

Peter feels in his essence a heaviness, a thickness. He perceives it as dark, murky, yet it's in motion, not stagnant, a full array of swirling colors, heavy, thick, syrupy. They seem to buffet one another, abrading as they do, creating a roaring cacophony of sound that is caustic and grating. Peter withdraws his perception to the degree that makes this tolerable while yet being able to observe it.

"We are in an area of rather concentrated and intense thought," explains the spokesperson. "It is generally in conflict with itself. Many facets of intent and purpose are at odds with one another and, as you will note from occasional flareups here and there, many people terminate their existence here as a result."

Peter turns to see what the spokesperson is referring to. He detects occasional flashes of light followed by the familiar upward ascension of what Peter now knows to be a departing entity. Here and there, he can see delicate wisps of light flutter down into the mire, the mass quagmire of raucous thought and color. "Don't tell me those are new, uh, babies? Those aren't entities coming to be born into that mess?"

Studying Peter carefully, the spokesperson simply nods.

"Why on Earth would they ever want to move into that?"

"There are many reasons, Peter. And we shall encounter a great number of those in our experiences ahead. But for now, continue to observe, and we'll move just a bit further."

Gradually, Peter begins to detect the outer periphery of a circular pattern of light. Its edges are irregular. There are rivulets of darkness that seem to course into the circumference of light. The outer periphery appears to be in motion, undulating, shifting, pausing, hesitating, as though the greater density of the mass-mind thought and this light were in some sort of struggle against one another.

"Aptly put," comments the spokesperson. "It is, indeed, a continual struggle. It is not like two warriors battling one another, but then again, it is not unlike that either."

Fairly overflowing with questions, Peter contains these as the motion continues. The light becomes brighter until they reach what Peter calculates must be the center of the source of light. Here he sees great beauty. He can see the purity of the colors working more in harmony than anywhere he has seen to the present point upon the Earth. There is a simplistic beauty, a harmony with the essence that surrounds the Earth beyond the mass-mind thought. Peter finds it refreshing. He feels the urge to move into this light and more or less bathe in it or cleanse himself.

"What is this?" he asks the spokesperson.

"It is called by many titles. But it is, in the simplest of terms, a place of light, Peter."

"How did it come to be, sir?"

"This particular place of light has, for the most part, always been, Peter. Some in the Earth think of this as a power point or as a light center. Others call it by other names and titles. Some have no particular title or descriptive name for it, but just know it to be a place where they are joyful or feel good or well."

"What sustains this light?"

"It is, in a sense, self-sustaining, Peter, by those who are attracted to it and, thereafter, by their intent and purpose and their work. So, as they contribute to the light, it expands and grows and sustains itself. As they take from the light, as you saw on the periphery, and give not back to it, you see the continual shifting and struggle that appears at the periphery of the light circumference. Do you understand this?"

"I believe so. It seems straight forward enough. Are there many such light centers upon the Earth?" Peter detects what he believes to be a most subtle hint of sadness from the spokesperson as he responds.

"Would that there were more or even that the entire Earth were of such a light, Peter. To a degree, you could say that this is our group's ideal: that we might bring such light into openness. For even as you look beyond here," the spokesperson gestures back to the darkness, "within the darkest of the dark, there is a light similar to the most brilliant below us. It is within the entity who dwells in darkness. As we know this and go forward with this quest in our heart, as a part of our intent and deed, we might then remove the mantle of darkness from the true light within."

Pausing to gaze around at the immensity of the darkness, and then, at the seemingly small area of light below them, Peter looks up with all due respect to the spokesperson. "This looks like quite an undertaking. It appears to me that it will require far more, if you will forgive me, than our company here and even the group above us."

"Peter, it is that kind of thinking that limits, not to be judgmental, for you are responding from habit. It is habit that is one of the forces that we shall deal with."

Peter is a little embarrassed that he would think in limited terms.

"Not to worry. That's part of the reason you're so good at what lies ahead. You can feel and respond and remember. You can react and equate things in terms that are most valuable to the work ahead."

Pausing for a much longer period of time while reviewing, observing, Peter finally turns back to his group, specifically to Paul, Elizabeth, Zachary and the spokesperson. "Where do we start? How do we begin?"

"We begin wherever we are with what is asked of us,"

responds the spokesperson.

"Asked of us?"

"Yes. There are continual requests for our participation, for our service as a part of the intent and work of those who are seeking to bring light first to themselves and then, through their actions, words, and deeds, to others. That is where we can begin, and that is where we will."

"How do you know these places to work?"

"Observe." Peter turns to look in the direction of the spokesperson's gesture and, in a moment or two, he hears a sound. It is somewhat musical. It is, in a way, enchanting to him. "Move towards it with us."

Suddenly, Peter finds himself only a few meters above the Earth, looking down to see the source of this strange essence of sound.

"Listen carefully, Peter. Open yourself as completely as you can. You have become accustomed, for several Earth years now, to communicating in ways that are not the norm in the Earth. What you are experiencing is the thought, the word, of a person in the Earth in joyous prayer for another."

"Really!" Peter opens himself even more. Sounds give way to tones, and these give way to rhythmic patterns, and suddenly he is amazed to hear the spoken words. He had forgotten how defined and crisp and succinct they were in comparison to the breadth and depth of the exchange of thought-forms between him and his colleagues.

"God has permitted us, Peter, to answer this prayer. And that will be where we shall begin."

Peter, in wonder and awe, simply observes.

And so, dear friends, here we shall conclude for this gathering. In our next, the true work shall begin.

May the grace and blessings of our Father's wisdom ever be that lamp to guide your footsteps.

CHAPTER 12

Channel of Blessings

JUNE 2, 1994

Just as prayer creates what could be called an orb or a circumference around you that is like a field of energy, so too does a joyful way of living, a joyful attitude, do much the same. Joy allows the opening of the creative flow, and that creative flow is ever one with God wherein all that you do bears the mark of His Spirit and the essence of the Christ as a light in your activities in the Earth. No matter how you are challenged or what seems to burden or limit you, claim your right to be joyful inwardly and express it outwardly.

Also, it is not well to struggle with those things that seem to limit, for the only way they can truly claim any of your power, individually speaking, is if you relinquish it to them. It is a matter of functioning in the arena of their choice or in the arena of your choice. They will not seek to follow you into the joyful state. But if you engage them at their level, there is the possibility of their gaining power from your efforts.

We believe that what shall be given next will illuminate this even more clearly. We will now return to Peter, his group, and the larger one with whom they have recently joined. For your reference, essentially no time has passed, perhaps several Earth minutes or so.

Peter has studied, observed, and even moved into and out of the flow of prayer as he was being taught. Again, we must emphasize that this is translated not from the spoken word but from thought-forms exchanged as a means of communication among these entities. Let us join them, then.

eter is addressing the spokesperson of the group that has joined them, which is still positioned in a circular pattern around him, Paul, Zachary, and Elizabeth. "This is an incredible experience. It is what I would call in the Earth a paradox. I can hear and understand only too well the words and the emotions that are pouring forth from this person in prayer. At the same time, I can hear what I guess to be the manner in which it moves or is expressed beyond the Earth with its more defined and limited expressions of that prayer. Is this how all prayer might be observed or experienced?"

The spokesperson responds. "It is what could be considered a basic format of a sort. Remember that all souls are unique, so there are to be expected certain variations. One variable is the purpose or intent of the prayer. There can be other variables, as well, that we shall no doubt encounter as our experiences proceed."

Nodding, Peter turns to observe the beauty, the melodious harmony of sound, color, light, and many other forms of expression. "You said that God has permitted us to answer this prayer. Might I ask how He notified you or gave us permission?"

"It is not by verbal communiqué nor is it in any form of what you would call in the Earth a message. It is more an attunement of our group and our group intent to what is often referred to as Universal Consciousness or God Consciousness. When we know that we are in harmony—similar to harmonizing in the musical sense, as in a balanced chord—we also know, based upon our past experiences, that we are able to meet the need. That is how we are, in effect, given permission to respond to this prayer."

Still puzzled, Peter displays his curiosity.

"Ask further if you wish, Peter."

Happy to be afforded the opportunity to ask questions, Peter begins, with Zachary chuckling softly in the background. Turning to smile at Zachary, knowing full well his thought, Peter carries on. "Can anyone answer prayer? I mean, can anyone use that procedure to determine whether or not they are in harmony or capable or ... have the *right stuff* (I guess I could call it) to answer a certain prayer?"

"Basically, yes. Of course, this is simplified, to be sure."

Again Peter nods and then asks several more questions. "Is the procedure for answering prayer like checking one's inventory of solutions or healing energies or abundance or whatever those things might be, and then drawing on those essences or reserves to fill the need? Or is it something beyond this, as I suspect it is, where you would draw resources from elsewhere to fill the need or request of this wonderful person in prayer here?" As he speaks, he is looking at the source of the continuing flow of wondrous prayerful light.

"That is very well put, Peter. Perhaps one of the others here might wish to offer some comments on that." The other two entities who had come to the forefront to speak to Peter are now illumined by the spokesperson.

The entity to the spokesperson's right smiles and nods warmly at Peter, a smile that seems to reach out and literally embrace him. "Peter, it is very interesting to observe how you have expressed your question. Certainly, one can draw a parallel to your past association with the Earth. For a moment or two, consider that we are not dealing with inventories or even reserves that are idling or in neutral, as you call it in the Earth," at which Peter receives another warm smile. "Rather, it is more a continual flow of energy, like an indescribably immense flow of light that is continually passing through all of existence. It is like a gentle wind, a breeze, winds of light that are ever offered to those who would seek to be sufficiently at one with them in order to know them and to apply them. So, returning to your terminology, this would be the inventory you referred to that we would turn to in that regard."

Digesting this explanation Peter is quick to follow with another query. "How then, does one know where this wind of light might be, and how does one partake of it? Must you be balanced or in harmony at a certain level, like a gradient as perhaps one to some number, with one being the lowest and let's say ten being the highest? ... Is my question clear?

Again the entity to the right of the spokesperson responds. "We comprehend completely your intent, Peter, and we would answer in this way: It is not so much that one ascends and gains credence, or that there is a hierarchy in the sense of an ascension. It is more the inner openness of the entity who is seeking that enables that one to be sufficiently selfless and joyful in their intent to allow this to manifest in their work, in their prayer, and in their intent."

The entity turns to look back at the spokesperson, and nods. The spokesperson resumes the commentary. "We are at that point now wherein it would be better for you to experience than for us to simply offer you more thought-forms and explanations that are only a part of it all. Certainly, we can offer you profoundly detailed and revealing information in the form of a massive thought-form, or we can give you an experience in the sense of a concentrated form of energy.

"In other words, we can fashion a massive amount of awareness in the form of what you would perceive as a great sphere of light for you. Once you accept that sphere of light into your being, the knowledge therein is yours. But since we are in the Earth and, as you may recall, we are also involved with others both in our group here and in the group adjacent to us ... " *(He is referring to our group and, of course, to you who are following this work in the Earth.)* "It seems only proper that we engage in experiences serially that can be better understood by those in the Earth and, as well, be beneficial to you as a sequence of events. Is this acceptable?"

Peter glances at Paul, Zachary, and Elizabeth, and receives a gentle smile and nod from them. He turns back to the spokesperson and the others. "I would be honored to participate in any works with you, but you must know I would consider my worthiness to answer anyone's prayer questionable."

"Listen carefully," responds the spokesperson. "Anyone can answer any prayer. Prayer is a giving of self. How one chooses to manifest that giving is, of course, the individual's choice. It is not a question of being qualified to answer the prayer. Our previous comments to you, in which we pointed to the mechanism we used to determine if we were permitted to answer the prayer, deal with the non-finite, non-physical aspect. From the individual standpoint, all entities are as one in God's sight, and therefore, undoubtedly you are worthy."

Peter nods, even though he is still hesitant about his ability to accept this completely.

Zachary places a hand upon what would be Peter's shoulder. "Not to worry, Pete. Let's just flow along with this and see what happens."

Peter smiles his readiness.

Without another word, the spokesperson and those to his right and left move directly into the flow of the prayer, and Peter is amazed to see that, where there was the beautiful flow of prayer expressed in the form of what he would describe as pure energy, he now sees it amplified many-fold. It is as though each of the three entities, now a part of that flow, has added unique qualities to it.

Peter is startled as he observes the spokesperson motioning to him to join them. He feels himself (in essence) freeze up. His companions move to his side, and he can hear their encouragement. Bolstered by this support, Peter moves, albeit slowly, to join the trio in the midst of this now much larger expression of light.

As he approaches the flow of wondrous prayer, he starts to feel as though, at the outer essence of his own consciousness, a gentle electrical current of some sort begins to energize his spiritual cloak (the outer energy level of his being). At first, it has a tingling sensation, gradually moving in tiny rivulets of energy inward towards the center of his being.

Again, he tenses just a bit. Elizabeth helps him balance. He feels her rosy energy of loving, healing warmth, which immediately calms him and he feels more balanced. Opening himself again, utterly placing his faith in his companions, he feels the memory of something like static electricity. It is not disruptive. This is more like a charge of energy trickling here and there but very rapidly all through his being.

"What is happening, Zachary, may I ask?"

"Of course, Pete. You can't disrupt a thing here, so don't give it a second thought. I might add as well that you are in no danger, of course. So, allay your concerns and just relax, observe, and enjoy. This should make wonderful fodder for your future questions." At this, all express their amusement.

Realizing the truth in Zachary's encouragement, Peter relaxes. The more he releases himself, the greater he experiences the energizing effect of this prayer. He pauses and looks towards the source of the prayer, marveling at the person. "Do you mean to say, Zachary, or any of you, that this one in prayer is producing all of this wonderful energy?"

Peter receives nods and gentle smiles from his companions. Continuing to move more towards what would be defined as the center of the flow of energy, Peter again marvels. "I feel utterly ecstatic. It is like being in the flow of a majestic chorus or symphonic production, where I could take all of the wonderful things I could remember from the Earth and form them into some master symphonic work."

"Aptly put," responds Zachary, "for the person is praying in the Master's name."

"Does that make a difference? Supposing they hadn't prayed in the Master's name, would there be a difference?"

"Yes, there would indeed be a difference. It would be detected differently. It would have a different resonance, and all of the effects that you have experienced would be varied somewhat. Later, we'll show you how different people with different belief structures have a uniqueness in the flow of energy or the essence of their prayer."

"But I thought that all prayer was answered by God and that for anyone who prayed, generally speaking, believing in God, the prayer would be essentially the same."

"That is also true. But essentially the same is not exactly the same, is it, Pete?"

Peter reflects for just a moment. "No, I suppose not. So basically there is a foundational essence to prayer, and then there are a number of variations that can be placed upon it? Including the individual in prayer and, as was indicated to me a moment or so ago, the intent and purpose, and all that sort?"

"Yes," responds Zachary. "And if you will, note your other questions so we can continue here."

Glancing about, Peter quickly realizes he may have held things up, so to say. He nods, slightly embarrassed.

"Remember what you were told, you cannot block or impede things here. The measurement of time is very different here. We can move, as you would call it in the Earth, perpendicular to linear time, so we have considerable latitude within the expression of one moment or second in the Earth. We can have the equivalent of minutes or hours or much more here, yet the entity in the Earth will have experienced in their consciousness but a moment or two."

"I do recall some experiences dealing with that, Zachary, but as you said, habits and being in this close proximity to the Earth seems to have re-awakened them in me, and they seem a bit difficult to shake off."

Zachary moves close to Peter. Reaching out with deliberateness, he brushes his cloak. "Here, I'll get a few of those off here and there. Nothing more than a bit of lint, don't you know, on the spiritual cloak."

All gathered express their amusement, especially Peter as he realizes Zachary's playful demonstration carries an implicit meaning. "So, these things are superficial. That's what you are saying, right Zachary?"

"They are unless you take them within and make them a part of you. There's not a thing wrong with a habit as long as you've chosen it to be a part of your life, and that you realize that it's there and is functioning for you as an extension of your intent, your will or purpose. But when habits are imposed, as they often are by one's environment, then they are all too quickly accepted subconsciously as being what you call 'just the way things are'. We'll deal with this over and over again as we function here in proximity to the Earth."

There is a pause in which Peter is allowed to reflect on all of this. Then the spokesperson gestures to him to move to a position immediately next to him. As Peter does, he feels the sensation of movement. Studying Peter carefully, the spokesperson invites his questions.

"I can feel a sensation of movement. It feels, in Earthly terms, like an upward movement of some sort."

"Yes, please continue."

"Well, shall I allow myself to simply flow with this? It seems to be moving me as though I might be some sort of magnetically charged particle in an electrical current or something like that."

"That's a good analogy, Peter. Do let us move now and let God's Spirit guide us."

"Truly? Are you saying that we will be moving in or by or within God's Spirit?"

"Yes."

There is a bit of fluttering of light, color, and sound around Peter and, once again, Zachary comes forward, aided by Elizabeth on the other side and Paul to the rear. "Settle down, Peter. This business of worthiness needs to be put in proper stead. We've dealt with it many times and it is a bit of lint on your spiritual cloak, if you know what I mean."

"I do, Zachary. Please forgive me, all of you. I am learning but obviously this habit is reluctant to leave." With a bit of humor and a swift return to their activities, Peter relaxes.

He can hear the spokesperson as though he were now in a suspended state. It is as though their communication is *dream-like* (is the best term Peter can think of). This is a blending of consciousness between the group and God's Spirit or Universal Consciousness. Because of this blending, there is a temporary sensation of the dulling of the individual consciousness as the group consciousness now moves into a balanced state among all the participants.

"I feel as though I am a bit numb. Almost as though I'm, uh, well, I recall in the Earth being put under an anesthetic, and that slowed my thinking and caused me to drift or float. And I find myself having difficulty in expressing thought-forms to the rest of you. Am I doing something wrong?"

"No," the spokesperson responds. "No, you are not actually doing anything, Peter, and that is why you are experiencing what you are. What is happening is that we are all joining together to become as one. In essence, the uniqueness of our combined individualities will, ultimately here, form into one group individuality or group consciousness. By so doing, we can become without finiteness as it is associated with individuality and, therefore, we can move in what you would understand to be a more infinite form of expression. Thus movement and motion and other such references will have totally different meanings. We might suggest that you simply allow yourself to experience. If you wish to express yourself as this unfolds, you are certainly encouraged to do so, and we shall respond as best we can to your question."

Peter, feeling a bit more as though, indeed, he were anesthetized, continues to simply float. He reflects inwardly that this is not unpleasant, just foreign. He finds himself a bit giddy, lighthearted. An essence of childlike spontaneity rises to the summit of his consciousness and then down somewhere into his being to a position within him that is balanced and harmonious. Again and again, wave after wave of these unique essences pour through him.

Finally, he comes to a point where he feels remarkably at ease. As he now attempts to bring a form of communication to his colleagues, it is as though he can hear himself speaking off from a distance and as though he can perceive himself from many different perspectives all at once, like a reverberation chamber that echoes over and over again but all simultaneously. It is a delightful experience, as though he has now become stereophonic, as if there are many Peters and yet, still only one.

"I feel like I have exploded and yet I am intact. I feel like I am in many places all at once and yet here I am. I feel like I can see and hear and know myself as I have never ever seen and known myself in the past. Is the person's prayer having this effect upon me? Or is this God's Spirit? Or what?"

(At this point Peter will perceive in a very unique way that we find is virtually indescribable in words. So we shall condense what is happening, offering explanations where we can to help you understand. This is, indeed, a wonderful opportunity for all. We pray that we are capable of conveying it to you.)

Peter hears and he knows that the response is from the spokesperson. Yet it seems to come from all of existence, as though he might be hearing, seeing, perceiving from the center of a massive hall in which perhaps dozens or even hundreds of speakers are positioned all at different angles and directed specifically at him. Each of these seems to be the source yet, together, all of them are the source.

The spokesperson responds. "By engaging in service as a group and moving into the flow of this prayer, we have become as one, Peter. So, the multifaceted expression of Consciousness that you are experiencing is because you can, at this moment, experience through any of us and all of us simultaneously, including yourself as you are known as Peter."

"This is stunning. I feel as though I am many Peters and yet that you are all one with me. I feel as though I know each of you in a way I have never known anyone, including myself. It is not a knowing that has the specifics of reference that are so common in the Earth. It is a knowing of the result, the outcome, the end effect of one's sum total of experience. It is a kaleidoscope of colors and patterns, a mosaic of brilliant light, a symphonic resonance of many wonderful symphonies all gathered together simultaneously and conducted by one common conductor. I presume that that central focus that I have just attempted to identify must surely be the Master, or God's Spirit, or something of that sort. Is this true?"

Peter is given a single word response. "Yes."

"And now I feel we are moving. Are we moving along in the flow of that person's prayer, so to say?"

"Yes."

"Where are we moving to?"

"To the object of his prayer."

Peter marvels, reveling in the uniqueness of this expansion of his being. He reaches up delicately to experience from many different individual points as he is able to identify them. Each is individually exquisite, delicious, wondrous. It is as if a healing balm were thrust into his total consciousness. Each new point of awareness affords Peter a new understanding, somewhat like placing himself at the center of a massive stage, where he can instantaneously move to any position and view himself. Simultaneously, he understands and perceives his uniqueness from the point of perception he chooses, which he surmises must certainly be one of the other entities.

Suddenly, as he moves to yet a new point of focus, he feels a rush of familiar energy. He hears a sort of echoing communication coming to him as though it were spoken into a long cylinder or pipe, and yet is extraordinarily clear and understandable. Peter knows immediately that he has positioned himself in oneness with Zachary. He feels the humor, the incredible wisdom, the uniqueness of Zachary's spirit. As quickly as he recognizes this, he can tell that he has moved instantly, beyond an instant, and the flood of rosy essence energy from Elizabeth becomes a dynamic part of his awareness. Her gentleness, the many wonderful works that he now realizes she has performed for others in service to God, her bond, her uniqueness, her past experiences, her memories. Then, swoosh! Suddenly he feels the calm, wondrous surety of the entity he knows and loves as Paul. He hears a communication from Paul and remembers his experiences with him at the very onset of his journey into other realms. There is a collage of color, an essence of the wisdom of antiquity. Peter realizes that he can pause at any moment to study and be one with any one of these. He becomes aware of a great hall filled with what he would call wondrous records and entities of light. He feels that he could move there at this very instant because he is one with Paul.

In the next instant, he is back to his former position of awareness in the multifaceted sense, as though all of these entities here and he himself are all a part of Peter's consciousness simultaneously. "I could not imagine that such an experience could be. There would be no way for me to express this. It has to be experienced. It is like I am moving in all directions, or so it would seem. And that I am capable of understanding from all perspectives, though I suspect that I, in the individual sense, am not understanding and experiencing, but we are experiencing and I, therefore, as a part of the we, am sharing in this."

"Good," Peter hears from the spokesperson. "That is the essence of becoming one in a group work or in service to God. It is the sensation of unlimited movement, of being unfettered, free to simply be. And all that is, is a part of that being. And all that shall be is within that being as a potential. Now, I call your consciousness to focus just a bit upon this destination."

Swiftly Peter complies, eager, exuberantly so, for this to continue. He perceives the object or target of the entity in prayer, the intent as a part of that prayer. It is a person who seems to be somehow burdened or diseased. While Peter can sense a physical form, he cannot perceive it in the finite. He simply intuits that this must be a physical form. At the same time, Peter can perceive it from what seems to be an infinite number of perspectives.

"Open yourself now to the conditions here, Peter."

"How do I do that?"

"You do not need a procedure. You have the consciousness of the group. Simply allow it to be."

Realizing that because of the group consciousness he can use the faculties, the conscious awareness, of any and all of the entities therein, he opens himself. Almost instantly, he sees and knows an incredible array of information. It is as though all of the records, all of the karma, the needs and wants of this person, the purposes, the opportunities, everything, are before him. He is swept with a flood of compassion and love for the person. He understands the struggle. He realizes that this is an opportunity for this person, as an eternal creation of God, to progress, to throw off some limitations.

Peter asks, "What is the specific difficulty?"

Before he can perceive an answer, the answer is before him. Turning inward to the body, he is amazed to see its internal functioning. He perceives a tube-like passage, perhaps as a part of the digestive tract that seems to be swollen and distended. Immediately he realizes that it is disintegrating, actually being consumed. Again he feels a wondrous flow of love and compassion for this one and the immense desire to see this perfect again.

"What you are experiencing at this very moment," explains the spokesperson, "is the intent of the person who is in prayer for this one who is in need."

"How utterly beautiful. There is no ... How can I call it?

at would be the word I would use? Reservation? It is a completely selfless wish for this person to be well and perfect, in a state of joy. The word that comes to me is *ease*."

"Now simply let yourself be, Peter. You'll be capable of observing all that is transpiring in the next several moments here. For this period, simply let yourself be and observe. We can discuss it afterward. Is this acceptable to you?"

"Certainly."

Peter shifts himself into this new but now familiar position of oneness with the group. He is ecstatic. He feels as though whatever capacity to feel exuberance or joy that he had as Peter, the individual, has now been multiplied by the number of this group and more. His thoughts, his awareness, drift back to a time in the Earth when he was listening to a sermon about releasing one's ego and becoming a part of God, letting go of the individuality and the desires of self to be one with God's will and God's purpose. He remembers as clearly as though it were happening now instead of many Earth years ago, that when he heard those comments in the sermon, he was fearful, reluctant to release his consciousness. He could not comprehend simply *not-being!* He had always considered it like being more or less lost, a ridiculously tiny molecule in the immensity of an eternal sea that is God ... insignificant, meaningless, forgotten, and probably eternally lost thereafter.

But this, Peter marvels, *is utterly the opposite. I am the sum and substance of the totality of this group. I am not lost. I am amplified by the wonderful beauty of each entity with whom I am participating. What wonders must lie beyond? What if this group were twice its number? Would I experience twice this majesty, twice this joy? How could that be?*

These and many similar thoughts pass through him. Then he is drawn back to focus upon the person in need, as he senses something familiar, an energy at first, a bit of light, a resonance similar to sound. A flow of consciousness passes all through his being, and it grows and glows beautifully—silver, blue, glorious golden colors. They are embraced literally by what Peter thinks must surely be an enormous circumference of light. Instantly, he knows this to be the Master. He feels and knows this wonder, the immensity of the love of the Master Himself. Every particle of Peter's being vibrates in resonance with the presence of the Master, as though he is wrapped in glory, yet he is unlimited. It is as though he is a tiny diamond-like clarity of light and brilliance, yet he is in all places at all times throughout the universe. He cannot find any reference to define this to himself. So he does not even try, but humbly and joyfully he simply flows rhythmically.

He feels himself moving, now wondrously expressed as an incredibly pure rose or red light. Next, it is as though green were the substance of all existence and vibrations that seem to be uniquely associated with it. Now, a bit of this color and that sound, and Peter feels as finite as the smallest particle of existence and then as immense as all of the solar system he has known, within which is expressed the Earth. This paradoxical shift from the finite to the infinite seems to undulate in a rhythmic pattern. Associated with it are glorious expressions that, to the senses in the Earth, would embrace all the capacity of the physical body to comprehend; that once these reached their limit or limits, they would expand, again and again, ad infinitum.

Peter sees before him molecules, tissue, fluids, cells. He hears their resonance. Where there was a discord over here, an undulating shaft of light embraces it and it is instantly in simpatico with all about it. And on and on, until he realizes that the tiny spheres, forms, and shapes together comprise tissue. In that instant, he recognizes that he can perceive at the tiniest level this person's physical body. In the next instant, it is as though he is looking upon this body from billions of miles distant in time and space, yet with every bit as clear and crisp a perspective as being immediately before it.

What seems to be a long, lengthy series of experiences, to Peter's utter joy and fascination, is actually but a moment or two of Earth time. Suddenly, Peter is a distance away from the person, again looking upon this one with compassion and love pouring from him. Amazed, he sees before him now a person who seems to be rejuvenated. A light is about them, unquestionably the Master's own essence. Then he hears this thought-form expressed to him:

Peter, I thank you for joining us in service to our Father and to the need of this, our brother. It is my joy and my prayer that you shall remain to work with us here, in and about the Earth and, as well, in the future in other realms of expression in yet other commissions. My love and spirit are ever with you, Peter. Farewell for the present.

Peter is in a state of numbness as he realizes that he has done exactly what he was reluctant to do in the Control Center with Zeb. That invitation had been accepted and has been fulfilled as of this moment. Before him and the group is this person, healed, perfect in every respect.

Peter is aglow. In this moment, he realizes that each of them is expressed in the individual sense once again. He can feel a touch of flavoring within him as a memory of the group consciousness, and he instantly realizes that he can call upon this connectivity of group consciousness as needed. He turns to gaze at each of the other entities in true wonder and joy.

The movement is now swiftly back to the person who initiated this prayer, and we hear the spokesperson communicating as follows. *Give this entity that which you have received, Peter, that they shall know their work is done.*

Turning to ask how and what he should do, Peter suddenly is flooded with the group consciousness again. Almost as though it were automatic, he reaches within himself and directs something—a thought, a love, something—to this dedicated person.

To Peter's wonder, he can perceive a shaft of golden

light. He is stunned as he realizes that it is the Master's light coming from *him*! The person who had been in prayer becomes alert, straightens up. Peter can see the follicles on the arm of the person bristle with hair standing erect. *Goosebumps*, Peter thinks to himself with a bit of humor.

He can hear the person state softly, "Thank you, Father, and dear Jesus for having heard and for answering my prayer. Amen."

Peter's joy is overwhelming.

At this point, we shall conclude for now.

But we wish you to know that you have been a part of this work and that Peter's joy should rightfully be shared by each of you.

CHAPTER 13

Group Consciousness

JULY 12, 1994

We return now, dear friends, immediately to Peter, wherein no measurable time has passed since our last meeting with him, and we find him having just moments ago been the channel of blessings to the person who was in prayer, in a way notifying the person that his work was and is complete.

Peter, as is his nature, is bursting with questions and utter jubilation over his experience. We turn now to his comments and questions, translating these from thought-forms into terms and words intended to be the best we can find here for your comprehension.

G enerally directing his queries towards the entire group about him, Peter asks, "What can exceed this? How can one even begin to comprehend, much less measure in any form, the vastness of what we have just experienced and shared together?

"My immediate thought," continues Peter without pause for response from the group, "is that I intensely wish to go back to the state of group consciousness. This was like nothing I have ever experienced before. At least, not to my current recall. How is it that any entity who has experienced such a consciousness could find the … perhaps I should call it, courage or willingness to return to finite expression ever again?"

Here Peter finally pauses, looking deeply into the countenance of each of those surrounding him, his own group as well as the greater group of entities Peter is now moving with while yet in the Earth realm. They are once again expressed in an individual form. Peter probes them, queries with his mind, his perception, remembering as he so does the uniqueness of each of them, and then startled just a bit by what he detects as a subtle reflection of his own being, now apparently a part of all present. He moves deep within himself to consider this. It is for him like peering into a looking glass, a mirror, and seeing a portion of himself along with the immense beauty and wondrous mystery of potential that must lie beyond this one single group consciousness experience.

By your measure, a considerable period of time passes, and none of the entities present—neither Zachary nor Paul nor Elizabeth, the spokesperson, nor any in the group—make any effort to respond to Peter, for they are aware that the process of Peter's deep exploration of them is more important than responding to a specific.

As Peter's gaze continues to gently flow over each of these companions, it seems to bring a renewal of that just-past experience into his consciousness. He feels a heightening within himself very similar to what he felt when he was a part of the group work in the healing process of the prayer.

He pauses at Paul, Elizabeth, and Zachary, who are immediately beside him, and waits, not because he is expecting an answer necessarily, but because the majesty of this glorious experience, even in the recall of it, is simply too deliciously wonderful to disrupt.

Finally, Zachary speaks. "Sort of like tasting your first birthday cake, eh wot, Pete?"

Startled by this finite and obviously deliberate effort by Zachary to center Peter, so to say, an outpouring of laughter gushes from Peter, so vigorous and spontaneous that it surprises Peter himself. It echoes and rolls and causes a rapture of gloriously cascading colors all throughout the group. Just as quickly, everyone erupts in joyous expression, and the laughter reverberates in the time and space they are positioned in adjacent to the Earth.

After the laughter settles down, Zachary comments

again. "Well, that certainly should have caused some reaction in the Earth, maybe even short-circuited several fuse boxes in our general vicinity."

At this analogy, Peter again laughs heartily. "Zack, is there ever a time when you do not have a humorous thought to interject or some sort of left-handed comment to the most staid or even glorious?

"Well, let's see, Pete. I'm not sure. Let me reflect on that. I suppose there have been some instances where humor seemed inappropriate and escaped me. Paul, perhaps you can recall as an observer better than I as the creator of humor."

Paul is smiling very broadly, shaking his head slowly from side to side, obviously delighted at his involvement here. "There is not a single time that I recall, Zack, where humor has failed you or escaped any event."

"Truly, Paul?" feigns Zachary. "Not one time?"

"Not that I recall," continues Paul, still smiling broadly.

Turning exaggeratedly swiftly to Elizabeth, Zachary asks the same question. She, radiating humor in the form of her beautiful rosy-colored essence, repeats the same thing essentially, that Zachary never seems to be without humor.

Again feigning a serious countenance, Zachary turns back to Peter and states matter-of-factly, "Well, there you have it, Pete. Obviously, this is my nature. Probably one of those habits you have in the Earth. So deeply ingrained, who knows if I'll ever shake it off."

Rivulets of laughter come from this rather impish-like commentary from Zachary.

Peter, aware that when Zachary displays his impish side, he is up to something, smiles. "Zachary, I know you well enough to know that all this has an objective. True?"

Looking down, discovered, Zachary fidgets about. "Well, I suppose it would be good if we used the energy we've just created and, you know, sort of direct ourselves to something productive." Looking up at Peter, "What say you, Pete?"

Peter mimics Zachary's typical nod and wink, and finishes with his own broad smile.

The spokesperson of the group speaks next. "We have some works to attend to, and you are about to have your own unique experience that will not require our attendance, so we shall depart for a bit. One of our group," gesturing to an entity on the right, "shall remain with you, if it is to your pleasure. You can call upon us through this entity at any point, and we shall return."

Without waiting for comment from Zachary or any in the little group, the spokesperson and the group with him begin to drift off, as though many beautiful lights were beginning to move in motion, then swiftly gathering together and amassing themselves as one beautiful, brilliant light.

Peter gasps in awe as he sees their movement—the beauty, the essences of perceptible qualities of sound, light, color, music, all that would stimulate the physical senses of the Earth and far beyond. In a very brief time, measured by the Earth, they are beyond his perception, and Peter believes that he can detect that, here and there as the group moves away from them, one or two seem to move off to the side or down or up, in this direction or that, until he can no longer perceive the group's light in the collective sense.

Impacted by what he perceives as the loss of his newfound group consciousness, he turns to find that the remaining entity, the new spokesperson, is gazing intently and lovingly at him. A soft communication comes to him.

"You cannot break a bond such as we have fashioned together, Peter. Now throughout all of existence and beyond we shall be capable, one and all, of coming together when there is the need, the purpose, or the desire to so do. Do not allow your memories of finiteness to cause you to react in a sense that you have lost something, for you have not. You will learn, as we continue in our mutual works, how untrue that is. And the breadth and depth, if not the majesty, of our group consciousness, is simply repositioned. That repositioning never diminishes nor weakens, in any sense, the original power."

Peter is moved by the sure, gentle, loving compassion coming from this one. Quickly in his consciousness he sorts back through his just-previous experience with the group and remembers this entity only too well. "If you will forgive me, were you ... I mean, uh, was your ... the physical body that you might have had at one time or another, was it feminine?"

A compassionate smile of understanding comes from the entity. "Yes, but of course, as you know and have often exemplified in past, these things are moreso essences than relationships to physical form that have to do with, as you call it in the Earth, gender. Now, you might sense this in the true qualities of what is intended between the masculine and the feminine that have no specific relationship to the physical body, its anatomical structure, or any such."

"I do understand what you are stating," responds Peter, "and I thank you for indulging me in my curiosity. As my friends would tell you, it is one of my predominant characteristics."

A little humor comes from the group, and Zachary states, "Well, Pete, how about a little exploration involving humor? After this little outing, you will understand why I feel so reverent (if you will) towards humor and good cheer."

"That should be quite an enjoyable discovery, and as ever, I'm ready for another outing."

"Good. Then off we go."

The group begins to move slowly, with Zachary somewhat to the forefront and with the spokesperson (or perhaps we could more appropriately call this the spokeswoman, with a note of loving humor) having positioned herself immediately to Zachary's right just a bit distant from him.

Moving along, Zachary begins pointing out this and that to Peter as they pass over the surface of the Earth some distance above it, perhaps you'd call this about 1.7 kilometers perpendicular to its surface.

Peter looks about the velvety richness of the evening sky, rich with celestial bodies. Shifting his attention back to the Earth, he can detect where there are populated areas by the illumination there. As he is observing this, he feels the group slowing, and his consciousness returns to Zachary's communication.

"For our first experience, Pete, I have chosen this location because of, you might say, its lack of or need for humor."

Puzzled at what he is leading up to, Peter simply nods at Zachary, who is now turned and directly before him. "You see, Pete, often I have found, as have our colleagues, that the most intense and dire situation in any realm, not the least of which the Earth, can be transformed in a moment or two with a bit of humor, and that the greater is the absence of humor, the more intense is the potential effectiveness of negatives."

"Negatives, did you say, Zack? Could you be specific?"

"Nothing's more specific than an example or two. Follow me."

Peter is caught a bit off guard with the abruptness of Zachary's movement but swiftly follows with utter faith in his colleague. Darkness is all about. Peter feels a whirling, tenacious resilience to the group as they pass through, even though he has complete transcendence, in terms of his power, to penetrate virtually any any energy. "What is this stuff we're going through here, Zachary?"

"Thought," is the single-word response from Zachary.

Shocked, Peter turns and looks. As he does, Zachary, completely alert to Peter, abruptly slows the group to a very deliberate downward angle.

"Take a good look at it, Pete. What do you see? What do you perceive? What do you feel?"

As Peter attempts to follow Zachary's suggestions and answer his questions, he reaches out from his inner consciousness to extend his awareness into the thickness surrounding them. As though he had touched a hot cook-top with a finger, he recoils in shock. "That's nasty! That's as nasty as I've seen or experienced for a very long time. In fact, I might state that I can't recall anything quite that nasty since I've left the Earth. The closest thing that comes to it, as I recall, was Jack's approach, initially. Remember that?"

All nod, including the spokesperson. Peter makes a mental note to inquire about this later. Somewhat surprising Peter, she is the one who addresses Peter's question and reaction. "This essence, Peter, is what we would call a form of mass-mind-thought. It tends to have certain identifiable properties that could almost be defined as physical properties. Certainly, within the realm of the laws of physics in the Earth realm, it would be definable and would, therefore, be considered as a viable substance, in the sense that all forms of energy and/or matter are categorically defined there."

Surprising to Peter, he actually understands this, and questions back, "When you say 'thought', I remember the comments about mass-mind thought and that the agreement between entities can ultimately form a realm or create a consciousness of existence. And I remember how, in the Crystal Workers' Realm, by sort of eliminating their sense of limitation or finiteness, they began to almost magically progress into higher consciousness and thereby greatly enabled their works to be more meaningful. Not to imply they weren't previously, but well, I suspect you understand what I mean. So this is, somehow or other, the collective thought of the people in the Earth at present?"

"It is certainly not the collective thought of all people, but some. Some who are in the Earth at present, some who are adjacent to the Earth at present in realms of more limited expression, more confined potential, like a cloud or essence that is the cumulative result of what has gone before."

"Excuse me," questions Peter, "but when you say 'gone

before', are you talking about entities who were in the Earth previously, or some essence that went before? You know, like a storm or conflict?"

Nodding gently, a beautiful essence moves to Peter from the spokeswoman. "We could answer that question, Peter, with a simple affirmative, that all of the statements you have just made are, in essence, accurate and correct. But to give you a better comprehension of it, I offer you this: Time and space do have relativity and purpose to the progression of a soul in their quest upon their journey, might I call it, of 'intended return to oneness with God'. And as the effects of all of the souls who have sojourned in the Earth and in adjacent realms to it could be considered as a living essence, somehow connected to each who have perpetuated and supported that, then it moves in time and space along with or parallel to the perpetuators and supporters."

She turns to gesture downward in the direction of their now very gradual movement. "As Zachary intends to show you, as entities in the Earth continue to support—or perhaps I should say provide sustenance to—this mass of energy or this thought-form, it has continuity. It has what it needs in order to continue to be an expression. Is that understandable?" She pauses and studies Peter carefully.

Peter senses this as tiny little rivulets of light passing through him, seeking out portions of his being, his consciousness, to determine if, in fact, he has comprehended this. Before he can speak, he feels the withdrawal of those rivulets.

"Good. You have comprehended it well." Without waiting for a comment from Peter, she turns to Zachary and simply nods.

At this, Zachary begins to take command of their entire group and accelerate it forward again.

Suddenly, Peter feels as though they are bumping, jolting, passing through what he remembers to be like different strata of thoughts, as though one has this reaction upon their group, another has that. The group remains exactly as it was before, but Peter senses this as *passing through layers of different types of resistance*, is the best he can think of it.

"Pretty bleak, wouldn't you say, Pete?"

"Bleak isn't the word for it, Zack. It's like what I imagine it must be like at the bottom of a coal mine."

Humor does not follow this comment, but rather a sensation passing through the group, and Peter suddenly realizes that he has given the group a unique perspective of understanding that perhaps only he could have given to this group.

"Very good," comments Zachary.

"Indeed," responds Paul.

Peter recognizes that he has contributed understanding to the group. His memory, his experiences, have just been shared with all of the members of the group.

As though they are abruptly, almost bouncing, to a stop, Zachary can be heard chuckling a bit, and he comments in his inimitable style. "Sorry for that bumpy landing. Things are a bit turbulent here," and he continues on as though he were an airline pilot, bringing forth a bit of lightness in the group.

"Now look over here, if you will, Pete," not pausing for but a moment.

Peter moves to Zachary's side, and the spokeswoman moves with him so that Peter is between the two.

Casting his consciousness forward in the direction of Zachary's motion, Peter sees nothing but a swirling collage of muddy, thick, syrupy essences. "Yes, I see them."

"See what?"

"I see the energies, the muddy, swirling, junk out there. That nasty-looking stuff."

A tinkling of laughter spews forth from Zachary. "That's not what I meant. Very descriptive, Pete, but what I'm asking you to do is look through it, beyond it."

"Oh, I see. Pardon me, Zack," and he attempts to penetrate what is before him. As he does, he feels strange, as though he is straining. It is as though the more he attempts to thrust his consciousness forward, the greater becomes a force, perhaps on the other side of this *stuff* (as he's called it) that seems to be opposing his forward movement with an energy or force that keeps matching his.

"How are you doing there, Pete?"

"Well, it's as though I am actually laboring here. I had forgotten what that felt like. It's like I'm expending energy in a finite sort of way. The more I try, the more I make an effort here, something, some power, seems to match that, and I get very little forward progress."

"Why do you suppose that is?"

Peter pauses, still holding his energies before him. "Hmm, let me see if I can discover this." He moves within himself, looking for the light within, and he feels the presence of the golden light, which he now knows is always present when he seeks it and even when he does not. He knows that in the activity of affirming the presence of the light, this seems to bring to the situation the power and majesty of its presence.

"Very good," Paul comments softly.

"Yes, well done," responds Elizabeth.

Peter, seemingly oblivious to these comments, continues to bring this golden light to the forefront. With remarkable ease, what had resisted Peter now separates, as though it is retreating in the face of this power, this light, as though it seeks to withdraw rather than to be exposed! With as much ease as he comparatively felt diametrically opposed resistance, Peter moves without a bit of effort, easily, through these energies.

Suddenly, here is the Earth, immediately before them. They are just above street level in what appears to be a very large, probably east coast, city. Peter opens his senses and perceives the essences ... the asphalt, the exhaust fumes, the various odors from the many buildings and shops along the way here. His faculties are incredibly sharp, he notes, as he can even perceive a bit of the sea in the air, and on and on. With each of these, he instantly receives a vision of the originating source. On this goes until his consciousness focuses on a small group of people loosely gathered over in a darker recess of several buildings in the dim illumination of a streetlight. Here, Peter's perception stops and lingers.

"Very good," comments Zachary. "Now to exemplify my earlier comments, tell me what you perceive in this group and, conversely, what you do not."

"What?"

"What I'm saying, Pete, is tell me the qualities you find present and those which you discern as being absent."

"Well, you've proven your point here. I can't find a bit of humor here, much less joy or happiness. There's the distinct feeling of competition, aggression, dominance, and other qualities I can't quite grasp. They seem foreign to my consciousness, and yet, somewhere I seem to understand them, but I can't find that somewhere, if you know what I mean."

Nodding an understanding, Zachary turns to Paul.

"Peter, if you will, for a moment recall our experiences together as we passed through the colors for the first time."

Peter swiftly draws from within him the array of those memories, as though he were vividly reliving them.

"Remember the lower level of colors that we passed through. They were among the first. Compare those to what you're detecting from these people."

As Peter follows Paul's suggestion, there is an instant correlation within him that defines the memory. "These are similar to what I would think of as very basal energies. You know, like survival instincts that might go all the way back to what we think of as the caveman … you know, food, shelter, clothing, survival at its most basic level."

Peter detects Zachary slowly drawing the group closer. "Do two things next, if you would, Pete. Listen and perceive.

simultaneously."

Pausing for a moment to grasp Zachary's intent, Peter turns his attention to the group. He can hear their conversation, though he doesn't quickly understand all of what the intent might be. They are using terms, perhaps slang, that are not totally familiar to him.

"Just a vernacular, Pete. You know, a localized set of terms that have meaning to these and other such groups."

"Reminds me of what we used to call 'jive talk'."

"I suppose you could call it that, Pete. But now, try to perceive as well as hear. That will act as a sort of translator, and you'll understand."

Peter finds this amazingly easy to do. As he locks on to each of the people, Peter discerns that this seems to have a visible impact upon each one, even if but for just a split-second. One, in particular, Peter notes, actually turns to look about, as though someone had tapped them on the shoulder.

"What was that?" he hears from the kid, who appears to be perhaps 15 to 17 years old.

"What are you talking about?" asks one of the others.

"Something just came by me. You know, that spooky feeling when someone's watching you. Maybe it's the fuzz."

Looking around, the group becomes alert, until after a time they calm themselves and go back to their conversation.

"Zachary, that young lady knew when I made contact with her. How's that possible?"

Zachary simply shrugs, as though he either has no answer or doesn't have one that immediately suits him to offer.

The spokeswoman moves up beside Peter. "While you are here in the Earth with us, Peter, you will find more and more that some people can perceive more than others. This young female, in spite of some of the habits and activities that might be thought of as limiting, has always had the capacity for perception beyond the normal, perhaps uniquely attuned to be aware of our more subtle energies. So, when you reached out to perceive her thought-forms, her degree of attunement enabled her to know of that, while the others of her group, as you could detect, felt nothing at all."

"Are you saying that some people can know of those of us who are no longer in physical body?"

She simply nods and smiles.

Peter's thoughts race over his past incarnation, and he comes up with an answer. "You mean like mediums and psychics, fortune-tellers, the tea-leaf readers and all that sort of thing?"

Again, the spokeswoman nods. "And more."

"What do you mean, 'and more'?"

"You have witnessed an example of your own doing," she responds gently.

Somewhat taken aback, Peter then recalls that he was the channel through which the entity who was in prayer realized that their work was done.

"I understand what you're saying. It's a pretty incredible discovery. The whole concept of people being cognizant of our presence and, perhaps, of our intent or our works ... this will require a further expansion of my understanding as relates to my memory of the Earth."

Elizabeth comes forward in her usual warm style. "Peter, it is no different in the Earth than in the many other realms we have experienced together. If you will recall, some entities are very much aware beyond their realm of expression. If you think about that for a moment, it would be logical to conclude that this certainly must also apply in the Earth."

"Yes, I suppose you are correct. I remember hearing of and reading about, and actually observing on several occasions, people who seemed to possess extraordinary powers. I remember one woman who was particularly adept at concentrating some form of energy and causing people who were ill, often very ill, to be healed. Olga was her name, I think. Marvelous person. Extremely dedicated, from what I read. And very impressive. Is that what you're referring to?"

Elizabeth radiates her understanding to Peter. "Precisely so, Peter. And there are many, many others. And I might add, many who are in varying stages of development of the reclamation of their unlimited side."

"Do you mean they are doing this while they are in the Earth? You know, walking around alive and all, they're reclaiming this?"

Elizabeth nods. Peter can hear Zachary muffling his laughter off to the side. Undeterred by Zachary's obvious humor, Peter is now intense. "Why do I get the feeling that this somehow involves us?"

"Consider how wonderful it might be if we could form a bond of consciousness, if we could create a connective link between those people seeking, striving, and wishing to do God's will and purpose in the Earth; that we might come to their aid as companions, as co-creators with God and with them in bringing a healing energy or light into that darkness that you just experienced. For example, look at those people right over there," gesturing to the small group.

The instant she does so, the young female once again turns abruptly, startled, obviously reacting to the essence of Elizabeth's contact with her. "Man, there is something spooky here tonight, I tell you. I've got this strange feeling we're being watched."

Again, the group becomes alert. One of them states, "Let's go over by Porky's." The group moves swiftly around several bends and down a dark alley.

Peter sees the piles of trash, a few people propped up in doorways holding something wrapped in a brown paper bag, another over here barely clinging to life. He can see their energy almost out of the body. Suddenly, he can also make out the luminous forms of several entities hovering just above him. On and on, there is a collage of experiences. Finally, he makes out the dim neon tubing of which several letters are not completely illuminated, but perceives that it's called "Porky's".

After a time, the group settles down again, perching themselves on various boxes and containers and just, as Peter thinks of it, lounging about.

One he hears ask, "What you wanna do?" A conversation ensues, and there seems to be disagreement. All the while, the female keeps looking about.

"She can detect our presence, can't she, Zack?"

"Yes, Pete, but she doesn't know what she's detecting. It's just not normal, so it has heightened her attentiveness."

"Well, is there some way we could help her, help this group?" looking from one to the other.

Paul responds. "Yes, I understand that there will come to be a time when we can help them. But it isn't now. If you'll look at them carefully again, and don't dwell too long on that sensitive one there, you should notice a familiar essence ... somewhat like Jack, if you'll recall. It's unyielding. It's forceful, almost impenetrable. Unless you were to call upon the light within, you would have considerable difficulty reaching to a point of inner consciousness or contact with them. Try it and you'll see what I mean."

Immediately Peter understands, as he reaches out to probe, so to say, each of them. As he comes to the female, he carefully avoids any direct contact and notes that she is still, forehead wrinkled, eyes squinting, in a strange state of consciousness, knowing that something is taking place.

He swiftly moves back away from the group.

"As I said, Pete, no humor here. Don't you think they'd benefit from a few good laughs, a bit of humor, perhaps an outing in the Realm of Laughter?"

"No doubt about it. I do understand what you mean."

"Good. Let's go, then."

"What?"

"Let's go. We can't do anything here. They're not ready,

and until they are, the others over there will keep watch over them."

Glancing around, Peter observes the group of entities not unlike themselves.

The spokeswoman explains, "Those are, as you might call them, workers. I know them and have made contact with them. When something changes, and we can assist, they will call us, and we can return."

Peter is surprised to hear himself say, "Oh, good. I'd like to help them, particularly that young lady."

Without comment, Zachary gathers up the group, and off they go.

Peter feels the passage through the *stuff* again, the thick, gooey collage of energies, and suddenly they are free of this and in a much more pleasant environ, again maybe 1.7 kilometers above the Earth.

"Whew, that is awfully unpleasant stuff."

"Why do you say that Pete?"

"What do you mean why do I say that, Zachary? Isn't it obvious?"

"In what way?"

"Well, it's not pleasant, it's not joyful."

"You mean there's no humor?"

Laughter comes from the group. "You're right, Zachary. I couldn't find a bit of humor in any of that stuff."

"So am I on a reprieve for wanting humor so often?"

Peter chuckles. "You have an eternal reprieve, as far as I'm concerned, Zack. I have never found reason to complain about your humor, anyway. It just surprises me at times."

"That's another key ingredient, Pete."

"What is?"

"Surprise. The unexpected. Habit breaks easily when confronted with something new. When habit is confronted with the unknown and the new, something like fear can block the light, can block the presence of an opportunity for change.

You know, the Earth is in a marvelous time of transition and change."

Without pausing, Zachary continues. "It is a time of enlightenment, of joy. It is a time to look for the seat of laughter within one's being and to bring that laughter and the seeds of it into one's life. It is a time to venture forth, to explore, to question, and to ask of self greater than what has become the accepted."

Peter studies Zachary. "Of course, you realize those were some pretty profound statements you've just made. And of course, you must also, therefore, realize, that I have a score or two of questions about what you've just said."

"Good. We'll answer every one of them, Pete. Just follow us, and we'll provide the answers for you graphically."

Without a moment to object or question this, Peter feels himself drawn, again, by Zachary and the spokeswoman ... moving, moving. He perceives below himself a change in the terrain. The thick, syrupy substance that he was told is collective thought, or mass thought, seems to be changing, broken up here, a bit lighter, purer energy there, not necessarily light in terms of light and darkness, but not thick and heavy, lighter energies, not dense and burdensome. Finally, they come to an area that Peter feels is very pleasant.

"You like this, eh wot, Pete?"

"Well, it's certainly better than where we were."

"Just hang in there a moment or two and observe."

Peter reaches out with his consciousness. Without truly thinking about it, he is wondering where they are, geographically, what part of the Earth and which continent. He begins to perceive rolling hills and ever-increasing elevation, beautiful streams, a few lakes, and far less density.

"In a rural area, I gather. Right, Zack?"

"Right, Pete."

"In the foothills or such of some mountain range."

"Right again, Pete."

Slowly, they begin to decrease their forward movement, and Peter, as he looks down, begins to see the movement of light slowly coming upward, a little here, a little there, over here, some a bit brighter. And over in the distance a bit, he sees several luminous essences that seem particularly bright.

"Like to visit those, would you, Pete?" asks Zachary.

"Yes, I think so, Zack."

They move to be positioned close to the light without disturbing it, just several dozen meters (as you'd call it) distance from them.

Peter counts. There seem to be about five or maybe six focal points of light here. "What is that, Zachary?"

"It is the example I wanted you to see. What do you think of it?"

"Well, it's quite lovely. It is most refreshing compared to where we just were."

"Good," responds Zachary, and he turns to Paul, inviting him to take over the commentary.

"Peter, if you will, we should like you to experience the essence of what you perceive before you. If you would reach out again in your consciousness, we can then discuss what you experience."

Peter swiftly and easily moves to be among these lights. He thinks, *There are six. They are very distinct. They are unique. They are individual, and yet they seem to have some common purpose.*

Obviously hearing all of Peter's reactions and thoughts, Paul continues. "What do you feel from these people, as you certainly know that this is the life-force of people here."

"Well, I feel that I am in the area in the Earth called North Carolina. I feel that this group has come together for a common purpose. I feel the presence of joy and laughter, but I also feel some sense of purpose, as though they are working on something. They do not seem to be laboring in any way, but rather totally at rest. In fact, the best way I could describe it to you is that they are almost all asleep."

Laughter spews forth from Zachary. After he settles down, he comments softly. "I'm certain that some of our colleagues in the Earth will find that to be a unique and perhaps appropriate definition for the process they call meditation."

"What?" asks Peter.

"Meditation. They're meditating, Pete."

"Oh, I see. Well, it's hard to tell from sleep, isn't it?"

Laughter spews forth again, this time from all the group.

"You may be more right there, Pete, than most people are willing to admit. But suffice to state that meditation is, as you well know, by definition at least, a process of becoming quiet within, calm, tranquil. Not unlike when you reach within and find the Master's Light. They are doing the same, as best they know to do. They are exploring, learning. They are finding the Way. And they are working together in support of one another, just as we support one another in our works here."

"How wonderful! That's just marvelous. I wish I could have been a part of one of those in my last go-round in the Earth."

A little laughter comes from the group, and he remembers the comments previously about his actual activity of meditating in his study. "What's the commonality I sense here? What is it that they are doing together?"

"Well, Peter," responds Paul, "they are coming together in joyous prayer on behalf of people who are requesting prayer for varying needs."

Peter is obviously touched and amazed by this answer. "Which people have asked them to do this?"

"Well, it's difficult to define to you briefly, but let me answer that in this way. They have made it known in a limited sense that they will pray for others and their needs. And so, periodically, they come together as a group and do so. When they are not together, they remain bonded by this common intent as they individually and severally pray for the needs of others. They have a request list that circulates among them and other groups and individuals like them, and they do their best to be what we would call a source of God's Light, as you did when we joined to answer the prayer in God's name of the person in need just a short while back."

"I see. Does that mean that they will experience what I did while they are yet in the Earth?"

"It is possible," responds Paul sincerely. "And it is possible that they might do this and more."

"More? They in the Earth might do that and more?"

"Yes, why not, Peter?"

"Well, uh, I don't know. I mean, I had just never thought of anyone in the Earth as being able to, you know, experience what we did. I mean, the thought of that while yet in the Earth seems almost impossible."

"Excellent. Define why it seems impossible."

"Well, it's just unheard of, Paul. No one would ever believe any such thing. How could that be? The Earth is very physical, in case you've forgotten, and such things are not given a second thought, as far as I know."

"By some, it's given much more than a second thought," continues Paul. "In fact, it has become a way of living, a way of directing their potential. And as they do, they become unlimited. The greater they work with what they are given, the more they are given. Just like you. Understand, Peter?"

Obviously toiling a bit to place all this into his consciousness, Peter responds, "I comprehend it, Paul, but I can't, if you'll forgive me, believe it's possible in the Earth."

"That's it," exclaims Zachary. "If you can't believe it's possible, how is it ever going to be? Believing is the key. And when an entity is joyful, perhaps inspired by, if you'll forgive me, a bit of laughter now and then, they tend to release the previous shackles of limitation, and their joy goes before them as a great light. You'll find what you are looking at now among this group, if you will explore it, is the peace and joy of each of these people gathered together that is rising up from them, so to say, and eventually will connect with the Master's own Light."

"Wait a minute! The Master's own Light?"

"Yes, Pete, why not?"

There is an obvious and awkward silence as Peter is very apparently striving to digest all of this in the sense of a conception. "Do you folks really understand the Earth? I mean, I know you are all wise, far wiser than I. And I know you've all had many experiences and done many good works in and about the Earth and other realms.

"But what I'm asking you is, do you really understand what it's like to be in the Earth, and to walk about each day needing to tend your body, feeding it, cleansing it, clothing it, interacting with other bodies, other needs, other wants? The challenges of mundane things like, for instance, paying your electric bill, sending payments off for this and that, and struggling in traffic and crowds, dealing with cross and irritable people? Do you comprehend those things? And forgive me for being so direct, but it seems impossible to me that you could understand these things and suggest, if you did, what you are suggesting to me."

"Well, Pete," responds Zachary, "perhaps that's a good work that you could contribute here. Perhaps you could be a bridge of understanding between the consciousness of the Earth and our less current consciousness of the Earth."

Peter again is covered with different lights, and sparks begin to flow from him as he is obviously trying, as best he can, to balance and comprehend all this.

"Don't struggle, Pete." Zachary comes forward as he speaks and brushes Peter's cloak. "There is no better way for you to comprehend things, as you well know by now, than to be a part of an experience. And so, let me suggest here that we come in God's name and call upon the group. If you look, they are returning to join us now."

Peter perceives off in the distance the beautiful light of the group with whom they had answered the prayer previously, returning.

"Let's work with them. And let's follow their prayer, and let's see if we can be a part of that. Acceptable, Pete?"

Peter slowly nods, incredulous but feeling a sense of joyous anticipation.

———————————

And so, dear friends, it is our hope and prayer that you, too, will share this anticipation as we strive to come into interaction with you as perhaps never before.

Fare thee well then for the present.

CHAPTER 14

Learning the Power of Prayer

AUGUST 20, 1993

We believe you shall find what occurs in this meeting to be of some particular significance to you. Some portions may well be quite revealing in unique ways, and others you may find to be quite reinforcing, supportive, and encouraging.

As we return to rejoin Peter and his group, by the measure of your time, only several dozen minutes have elapsed since our last meeting with Peter and his entourage. There has been considerable discussion regarding the events having just unfolded and Peter's inquiring mind having probed the specifics of the situation to some considerable degree, as you might well expect of him by now. We shall now convert what is in thought-form moreso than the spoken word.

Peter turns to Zachary. "I find what is happening to be incredulous, even with the many explanations you've offered. Perhaps, as you say so often, experience might be the better approach to helping me understand this more fully."

With a gentle smile, a nod, and another of his exaggerated winks, Zachary sweeps Peter up, so to say, and brings him to a position close to him. Across from them is the spokeswoman of the greater group, which has now returned in its entirety and is surrounding Peter's more personal group, comprised of Zachary, Paul, Elizabeth, and Peter himself.

Zachary, without comment, moves to the periphery of the now well-formed shaft of *prayer energy* (we shall call it) that is flowing up from the group in the Earth just below, the small study group in North Carolina.

Peter moves to where his *nose* (so to say) is up against the outer periphery of the light. "What a wondrous essence."

"Indeed, Pete."

"And these people are collectively generating this? Is that correct, Zack?"

"Generating could be an acceptable expression, but perhaps more accurately would be that they are allowing themselves to be in a collective state of joyful passiveness, focusing only on their desire to be one with God's will and purpose in service to any soul who might be in need."

Peter is only marginally nodding, mentally digesting Zachary's explanation while remaining somewhat intensely focused on the majesty of the light before him.

As abruptly as before, Zachary now sweeps Peter directly into the flow of light.

Peter ooh's and ah's as he sort of rolls about, allowing himself to be utterly fluid in the beauty of this upwardly flowing column of light. It effervesces all throughout his consciousness.

After a time, he notes that the others of the group have also moved into the light, and it appears to him that the light itself has expanded enormously to accommodate the entire group.

"How marvelous!" exclaims Peter. "And the feeling of group consciousness seems to be returning, but with a new *dimension* (for lack of a better word). Is this dimension added to by the people in the Earth?"

"Yes, and by their oneness with the Master."

Peter stares at Zachary, trying to understand the thought-forms. "This is most curious, Zack, for you have mentioned several times the inclusion of the Master or the Master's light in this group. Yet, while I can relate to the Master's light and perceive it to be a part of this, I cannot perceive the Master in the individual sense."

Zachary nods and smiles with gentleness. "The Master is

a part of all entities. What you are perceiving of the Master is that essence that is within each of those individuals below us," gesturing back to the Earth.

His curiosity now piqued, Peter asks, "Are you saying that the quality or the essence or the spirit of the Master, perhaps in some respect a particle or grain of His essence, that is within each of those individuals, by doing what they are doing, they have released that to combine together? And that it has formed, not a handful of small particles of the Master's essence, but one greater-sum particle?"

"Well put."

Paul adds, "Indeed, Peter, that is very well put. If I might add an addendum to that, it is not simply the addition of, for example, two small particles of Consciousness to three to sum a total of five. In this, as the *particles* (so to say) come together, they are much greater than the sum of the five. They are magnified many times over. The immensity of this is the light that you perceive."

"I am beginning to … "

Abruptly, there is a contact of some sort, and Zachary gestures for Peter to pause for a moment.

Zachary attains immediate communication with the spokeswoman and then swiftly turns back to Peter. "We have a call, Peter, and it would do us well to answer it. We have this vast prayer energy offered by this group here, plus the sum of our own potential, to offer to a need that is about to occur. But before we can respond, I must have your approval, your willingness to engage in this service."

"Sure, Zachary! If you believe this call would be good for us to answer, then of course."

Peter can feel the group unite their consciousness and then a swift movement.

Zachary communicates to him inwardly. *Peter, there will be no pauses in this journey for sightseeing or explanation. We are moving immediately to the need.*

Peter detects then that they come to an abrupt stop. They are still surrounded by the prayer power, the light, of the North Carolina group. It is, from a visual perspective as you would interpret it in the Earth, as a huge ray from the point of its focus in the small group in North Carolina to this point on the eastern coastal area of North America.

Peter is stunned to recognize that this is the very same place they were just a bit ago, where the somewhat sensitive young woman could continuously discern their presence. Gazing outside of the beautiful light surrounding them, he sees the same people, still fairly much in their previous positions but now somewhat agitated. He detects energies bouncing off of them in a strange way and also notes a profound dullness, for lack of a better description, off to one side. To the other side of this scene, he notes other entities like the group now moving with his own, who he thinks of as workers of Light in the Earth, guides.

He ponders the intensity here and feels Zachary nudge his consciousness. *Pete, let's you and me, Paul, and Elizabeth, move out of this prayer power for a moment or two so that you can understand from multiple perspectives what is about to occur.*

Somewhat overwhelmed by all these events happening in rapid succession, he nods.

They all, then, easily sort of slide off to the right, perpendicular to the golden prayer power.

A brief shudder of energy passes through Peter as he again perceives the, as he calls it, nastiness of this energy. As he allows his perception to move about the group, it falls upon the young woman, who, again, jolts to alertness and looks about. Swiftly, he withdraws his energy that has had an effect upon her, and she begins to settle down again. He whispers, "What is going on here?"

Zachary chuckles softly. "There's no need to whisper. She can't hear you, Pete. It's that she senses or perceives our presence. When you focus on her that makes a connective link of sorts, albeit somewhat muted. So you can communicate with me normally. To answer your question, though, there's about to be a conflict here, and several other events are possible. We had knowledge of this aforehand because the group over here," gesturing to the guides, "are, you might call this, close to a number of the people in this group and, therefore, would know of the opportunity that is about to be presented to several of the entities here."

"Presented? Opportunity?" stumbles Peter in his questioning. "Just what do you ... ?"

Zachary's hand comes up, signaling Peter to pause, and he gestures off into the darkness for Peter to focus his perception there.

Peter is stunned by the emergence of a similar band of young people racing across the short distance from the darkness to where the other band of individuals is gathered.

Peter hears all sorts of yelling and cursing as the groups begin throwing things at one another. Then he hears several shots fired. He struggles to focus amidst the intense energies crashing all about in this conflict between these two rival gangs. Violence begins to happen at a rate that horrifies him, for he had forgotten such events. They attack one another with a vengeance that Peter cannot fully comprehend. Several young people are wounded. "What is motivating all this?" he asks Zachary in incredulity.

"Who can say, Peter?" Zachary responds, with a hint of sadness in his communication.

Suddenly, Peter's attention is drawn to the sensitive girl again. One of the attacking gang members has lunged at a young boy and, without a moment's thought, the sensitive girl throws herself in the path of the attacker, receiving a violent razor slash across the neck.

Screams and shouts are spewing forth, at which point several employees from Porky's burst out with bats in their hands. One has a revolver and fires it into the air. The gang members scramble off in all directions.

And there is silence.

The young boy who had just been protected by the girl is kneeling, sobbing, over her body, blood gushing from the gash across her neck.

In that same moment, Peter notes that the ominous darkness off to the sides seems to take on various forms, and they move closer and closer. Simultaneously, the group of guides begins to move forward.

"What is this, Zachary? Who are those dark forms?"

"They are Earth-bounds, Peter, and they want this girl to be a part of their group for reasons that are complex in one respect though incredibly simple and basal in another."

Peter turns to look at the now seemingly lifeless form covered with blood and hears the weeping of the young boy beside her. "Oh, God. Please save her." Other such prayers are coming from him, most unexpected from one such as he.

In the midst of the prayers from this young boy, Peter begins to see the life-form of the girl taking shape above her body, appearing as a collection of rising translucent energies. Peter watches, spellbound, as he sees her take complete form so that there are now two expressions of the girl before him, the one motionless on the ground and this translucent one now developed before him.

The dark, foreboding group of entities moves closer and closer.

Suddenly, Peter hears the spokeswoman of his own group state with remarkable authority, *That is sufficient!*

From one of the ominous group, incredulously, Peter hears a response. *She has chosen to live much of her life in darkness. Therefore, we are here to escort her to our level, which is one with her choices. It has been a part of her consciousness. So this is our right. That is the Law.*

Still spellbound, Peter hears the spokeswoman counter,

You have heard the prayer given by the young lad in her name. You know full well that the Law of Grace is now enacted. Therefore, you have no oneness with this one, for she is in God's Grace at the request of a person in the Earth. Should you wish to proceed further, you are of course welcome. But, as you are aware, you shall thereafter immediately dwell in God's Grace, and the darkness in your minds and the desires in your hearts shall be in-filled with the Light of God's Grace and Christ Love.

Peter can hear cursing and accusations, threats and all sorts of outpourings from the ominous group. At the same time, the entire band of guides moves closer and closer to them, and the light around the entire scene becomes brilliant.

It's the prayer power, Peter exclaims to himself. *It's that group in North Carolina. Their prayer is engulfing this whole scene, this whole situation!* He watches as the band of guides adeptly direct this power of God's Love and Light, intended and generated by the group in North Carolina to do all manner of work here.

The group from the darkness moves off a considerable distance, but they are yet out there on the periphery, cursing, hoping, waiting.

Suddenly, Peter hears a voice he knows to be the girl's whose body now lies on the ground, appearing lifeless. *I knew this. I knew it would come to this,* he hears her speaking, *I knew it would be like this.*

Peter whispers to Zachary, "What is she talking about? Can you explain this to me, Zachary?"

"WELL YOU SEE, PETE ... " responds Zachary in what Peter discerns to be a booming voice for the purposes of indicating to him that she cannot hear them, "the light of this prayer that we are using," now in a normal volume, at which Peter chuckles, getting the point, "that we are using, in effect, as an energy for this work is all that she perceives at present. She can perceive neither you nor I nor, individually or severally, any of our group, be they those of our group of light or those out there," gesturing to the periphery. "And this is, as they call it in your novels in the Earth, the moment of truth."

Peter perceives one of the guides move forward, approaching the girl. He can see the girl peering at this entity, trying to focus. *Grandfather, is that you?*

Simultaneously, Peter perceives another movement. Something within him, very familiar and well loved, begins to stir, and he knows the movement is the presence of the Master, just above and behind this guide, the entity the girl has identified as her grandfather. The grandfather is standing before the girl, now being over-lit by the Master's presence.

She begins to sob, reaching out to embrace her grandfather as he gently strokes her head and caresses her, soothing her. *Oh, Grandfather, I feel free somehow. The pain ... it was so brief, and now I am with you. I always loved you so, and I know you loved me. Where do we go now, Grandfather? What comes next?*

Peter hears an incredibly loving voice speak to the girl, communicating this approximate translation: *It is your choice, my dear. You can return and continue on and perhaps, knowing what you know now, do something of goodness for yourself and for others in the Earth. Or should you choose otherwise, we can leave here and go to a place of consciousness I am certain you will find most beautiful and joyful.*

She looks up adoringly. *Oh, Grandfather, why would I want to go back? It is so cold, and I have done such wrong. I have nothing I can contribute to anyone, much less myself.*

Her grandfather indicates his disagreement. *You have a moment of glory, of love, that shall stand throughout eternity. If you have nothing else, and there are many others I can identify to you, this and this alone should be a light in your heart forever. For you gave your life, willingly, for that young lad there who is now embracing your body.*

She turns under the guidance of her grandfather to see

her body being embraced by the boy, who has literally thrust his fingers into her physical anatomy to stop the pulsing blood from gushing any further. Desperately, tears streaming and falling upon her body, he offers up his repetitive prayer to God, which she can hear.

Slowly, she becomes aware of a bond between herself and this young lad who she had, curiously, looked after in the previous years but never quite knew why. Now she can see that in a past time it was by his action that her life was saved, and by his kindness and generosity that she and her family were freed from what would otherwise have been life-long bondage. It was he in another past time, in his position of some stature and wealth, who saw to her education, that she would know the basic art of healing, how to do various works that could be therapeutic to those in need, acquiring the basic medicinal needs for her to continue her work and obtaining the proper documents that allowed her to do so.

Flooded with the memory of this, she sees now the love pouring from him, not just gratitude for giving her life to save his, but she feels at the very fiber of her soul a love that spans eternity. Mere moments passed as she reached out and felt all of this, her grandfather nodding and confirming here and there her discoveries. Among these she has just discovered is that the one now holding her body is her own soul mate.

This event unfolding before Peter enthralls him. He is deeply touched and moved, even though somewhat over-whelmed by the grisly, brutality of some of it. He sees the grandfather, still over-lit by the Master, gently nurturing this girl, now nearly fully departed from her physical body, en-couraging her to search out and discover. At one point, he sees her reach out to embrace the lad in a gesture of such en-dearing warmth that Peter cannot remember ever having known before. It is not the love of one person for another, though yes, this is a part of it. It is not the care, the concern, the well-wishing of one person for another, though yes, this, too, is involved. Nor is it the desire to heal the sadness and remorse of one in need, although, again, this is a part of what Peter perceives. Above all these more finite aspects, he is drawn by the observation of this event back to the Beginning of their time, their very consciousness, as though he can perceive a beautiful light, resplendent in its aura, its coloration, its vibration and sound, seem to divide itself, yet he knows that it was two in unison as one. He now perceives this unified light as being these two entities, soul mates, who have found one another again, or at least one has found the other.

The girl rises from her embrace of the boy, who cannot perceive her embrace fully but seems somehow comforted by it, for his sobbing has stopped. His fingers probe her neck to continue to contain the life-giving blood within the body. He is rocking, caressing her hair, her face, picking small fragments of debris from her as he does, looking up at the others standing there, shouting, "Tell them to hurry. Tell them to hurry."

The girl turns to her grandfather. *I understand, Grandfather. I must go back. I must walk on the Earth for a time and do what I can. I will do this willingly for my brother,* turning to gesture at the boy. *And for any others who might ask of me, I will try to serve them, too.* Looking up at her grandfather, her guide, *Grandfather, as I do this, will you walk at my side? And at the end of this walk, will you be waiting for me?*

Peter is overwhelmed. The sense of love and the depth and breadth of compassion evident in this young woman are utterly stunning to him.

He hears the grandfather answer, *I shall always walk with you, as shall those healing angels of God's own service also walk and serve with us.*

At that moment, Peter perceives two brilliant, beautiful lights, whom he immediately knows to be from the angelic host, gently descend to stand on either side of the girl. Nodding, aglow from the light of these two orbs, she embraces her grandfather a last time and communicates something to him. Then, without a moment's hesitation, she turns and moves easily back into her body, as the two orbs of light position themselves on either side of her still lifeless form.

Barely perceptible by Peter at this time, two men in uniform with a stretcher rush to take over the boy's position of holding what appears to be a major vessel in the neck, then quickly inserting tubing, which Peter presumes contains blood, and performing other works. But they cannot pry the boy from his grasp of her.

One of the attendants stops and looks with care into his eyes and touches him upon the head. Simultaneously, the girl becomes over-lit. *Is this an angelic light that has been overlaid, in a manner of speaking, upon this body? Or is it the body itself that is now somehow glowing from within? What exactly is this light?* Peter cannot tell.

The attendant places an arm about the young lad as he reaches with the other for the stretcher. "Come with us," he states. "She'll need you when she wakes up."

In wonder, the boy's eyes open awide. "When she wakes up? You mean … "

"Yes. There's a pulse. It's weak, but I can tell you, had you not stopped the bleeding, she wouldn't be here now."

Until now, Peter had not noticed, but in this moment he can see this girl's entire body pulsing with the golden light of the prayer. With what Peter now thinks must be at least one of the angels at her side, the ambulance doors slam shut and off into the night, bellowing its wailing cry, the ambulance disappears.

In the moments that follow, there is stillness. A few people are gathered here and there, questioning, gesturing, pointing, as people in the Earth will do when such trauma occurs, and a few of the other members of the girl's group are being tended to by a second emergency unit.

In the scene that Peter reaches out further to perceive, he

realizes something that touches him ever so deeply: This group in North Carolina has been, at least in some direct sense, involved in not only returning the life to the body of this teen-aged girl in a dark corner of a city on the east coast of North America, but they have contributed, by so doing, a brilliant light of hope for the future. Peter knows this, for he knows that this girl will surely do much to change the lives of others in times ahead.

Suddenly and for a moment, Peter feels strangely empty, with a sense of sadness and longing.

Paul addresses this reaction. "The essence of your spirit is now a part of that girl, Peter. You and we and each of the members of the group in prayer so far-distant, and seemingly so remote from this place, are all one in a beautiful work that carries a potential for the future. A light of hope has now been illuminated in this corner of darkness on the Earth. Perhaps those in the Carolina group may never fully, consciously, know what wondrous works they have taken part in, and that they, in harmony with the Master Himself, have perhaps changed the destiny of, not only this young woman and her friend, but also that the grace of their blessings and this work will be seeds that these two shall sow throughout the remainder of this lifetime and an indeterminate period thereafter."

Peter nods that he understands. "Will we, you know, uh, see them again," almost in a whisper, "or maybe even work with them?"

"As it is your wish, these things and more we shall surely do, Peter. I can tell you that the next time we are in her presence, she will not only subtly know of our presence and your contact with her, but perhaps much more than this will now be possible. For she has, you see, created a channel of blessings between herself and our realm. And the one she defined as her grandfather, which is, in fact, correct and true, is also, you see, a part of this group, our friends here now around us."

Peter looks up to gaze at the entirety of the group gathered around, radiating their love and understanding and joy. Slightly embarrassed that he had forgotten that they were even present—and even more importantly, in his thinking, the wondrous work that they had contributed—Peter emanates thankfulness and greetings to each and receives them in return.

Zachary breaks Peter's flow of communication with the group. "Well, Pete, there's a final stage of work here, if you'll recall, and I should think it appropriate that we now complete that."

Peter looks at Zachary and suddenly remembers from the last work they shared that there is importance in identifying to the workers in the Earth that the work is now complete.

Just as swiftly as they had arrived in this city, do they now return to a position above the North Carolina group, who are still, as Peter perceives them, in varying stages of rest. Some, Peter notes with humor, appear to be utterly asleep.

Zachary chuckles over Peter's discovery. "The more at peace and rest they are, perhaps the more open and pure channel they become ... at least, Pete, that offers them an excellent excuse."

Peter laughs at this, which he finds is well-needed. The seriousness, as he defines it, and intensity of the just-previous situation has left him feeling strangely depleted.

"You put a lot into that, Pete, as have these people here in this gathering. So, let us summon up some joy, a bit of joyous laughter at the good works and beauty of that which has just been accomplished." Swiftly, Zachary creates the light of his joy, and it abounds among the group, accepted and accelerated by each, individually, until Peter feels refreshed and re-balanced.

In that moment, Zachary contacts Peter and guides him gently down to the core of the group of people. Though Peter cannot perceive them in the physical, detailed sense, he can perceive their essence, their energy, and the uniqueness in the individuality of their personage and their bond in the direction of their intent and work.

"Tell them, Pete, that the work is complete."

Without a moment's hesitation, Peter reaches within himself and centers there. As he does, he perceives himself generating a warm essence that he knows to be tangible in the Earthly sense. He sees first one person stir, and the area round and about the heart to the solar plexus glows. Then, another over here. Then the larger one over there in the corner (his favorite spot) shifts his position and groans or something, and the energy cascades over him before dancing on to each of the others. Peter can sense, not see, each of them looking at one another. And he hears only this word: "Wow!"

With that, Zachary nudges Peter, and they soar instantly up to rejoin the larger group. A time of joy and re-balancing takes place. Peter delights in the time now spent in joyful ease as they exchange commentary and gladness. And he comes to know some of the group whom he now identifies as Earth-workers or guides, and he knows them in a very individual sense. Each of these guides relates to Peter their own experiences and those who are yet in the Earth unto whom they, individually and severally, often strive to serve with.

Peter, sincerely and genuinely interested, asks all sorts of questions, of course. And he makes inquiries about you, dear friends, for these of the larger group are your guides.

And what of you, who are not a part of this group so uniquely identified in North Carolina? What has been your role, your participation, in this work? Let us presume that you have asked this question, that we might be afforded the opportunity now, here in this moment with Peter, to answer it. We'll answer it in this way, as Peter inquires of one of the guides who serve with a person from a place called Texas.

"You mean to say," questions Peter, "that her prayer, in other words, her intentions, were also a part of the work we have just performed?"

Smiling and nodding, the guide affirms this to Peter.

"So it was not only the group I perceived from North Carolina but this one in Texas, as well? Her prayer, her power or light, also contributed to this work?"

"Just as surely," responds the guide, "as that of the prayer work of the North Carolina group. For you see, they are part of a common group who are unified in their intent to serve others in need and do so in God's name regardless of where they are geographically whether or not they all hear the call at the same hour or time. Her prayer and the sincerity of her intent to serve freely and willingly, according to the needs of others, was every bit as important in that work as any of the others'."

"Amazing," responds Peter.

"And if I might add," continues the guide, "the same is true for all the others of my group, and others beyond them that you did not perceive as being present but whose energies were directed towards this work, as well."

Peter, pausing to attempt to orient all of this in his consciousness, tries to envision this. "As I saw the small group in North Carolina direct their prayer and it becoming more or less a golden shaft of light, if I might paraphrase it as such, then might I assume that the one you are serving with in Texas was also a golden shaft of light or something of that sort, which at some point came together with the light of the North Carolina group? Would that be a correct assumption?"

The guide nods. "That is a very accurate analogy, and from the finite perspective, it is understandable and excellent in that regard."

"I see. Well, then, I might draw this a bit further afield to include the prayer energy or power of all of the other people involved in the Earth, so that I might envision many lines of light coming together to form one massive light-force that was, in effect, the light that I perceived surrounding the entire event that prevented those dwelling in their own self-imposed darkness from entering. Is that correct?"

The guide responds. "Yes and no, Peter. Yes, in terms of the analogy and comparisons you have drawn in the graphic sense; but no, in the sense that the light does not invade or pervade, as such, or create a barrier. To the contrary, it is warm, subtle and yielding. It is inviting. And it is those qualities that are ... well, that the entities in that darkness abhor. It would suit them to better combat the light were the light to oppose them. See? For then they would be able to deal with that action with mechanisms of their own familiarity, use, and control. Their intent is to modify, re-shape, or re-direct the intent of God's Law, that it is no longer pure Truth. And that is what causes the appearance of darkness and the emanation of limitation. They are, in fact, every bit as much in the light and unlimited as are we. But it is their own acceptance or intent that causes the appearance and the reaction you observed."

"That is most fascinating," responds Peter, after a period of reflection.

At which time, Peter hears Zachary. "Well, I see Peter has found a willing source of information here," and he chuckles. "Hey, Pete, do you have enough to satiate your curiosity for a moment or two?"

Peter flushes a bit with self-consciousness. "Yes, I do." Then he turns to the guide with whom he's been speaking, "Excuse me. I may have kept you from something. Perhaps you need to return to your, might I call it, ward in Texas?"

"I am with my ward in Texas," replies the guide, smiling softly.

"Oh, uh ... uh, I see."

At which, Zachary, of course, laughs. "Think about it, Pete. Remember what you've learned. There is no problem whatsoever for this fine guide here to be in Texas and also be represented here."

"Yes, yes," responds Peter authoritatively, though awkwardly. "I do remember that. I just don't quite have the hang of it yet, you see. But I remember the basics."

"Anytime, dear Peter, that you would like to explore that further, I should be honored to assist you in that regard," comments the guide, smiling broadly.

"You may regret that offer," chuckles Zachary. "I can tell you, sooner or later he will take you up on that."

Everyone breaks forth in laughter and good cheer, and Peter feels lovingly warmed, becoming buoyant, uplifted, and losing a bit of his focus.

Reveling in the laughter and joy, Peter knows that Zachary, Paul, and Elizabeth are right near him and joyful also, and he utterly relaxes, and he feels as though he is floating gently upwards.

Time passes, by your measure, and Peter hears a voice gently calling: "Peter. Hey, Pete, are you going to wake up or stay there for the rest of, let's say, this year?"

Stirring, Peter turns to look into the broad smile and radiance of his friend, Zeb, looks around and finds he is back at the Control Center. And laughter and good cheer abound.

We are pleased, if not joyful, that these shared experiences between Peter and his group have brought you some insight and joy unto the potential and unlimited power that is yours to call upon in prayer. For as oft as we and others before us may have given that there is no greater work, no more omnipotent power than prayer in God's Name, until such is delicately experienced, until the wonder of this power in action is observed and partaken of, it is difficult to comprehend the richness, the fullness, and the omnipotence of it.

CHAPTER 15

Duality of Expression

SEPTEMBER 5, 1993

As we prepare to return to join with Peter and his group, we should like to express to all of you our profound and humble thanks for our opportunity to be one with you in this way. So as you here or there have a moment of question or doubt, be assured that we stand with you, openly offering, so as is your need and so as you are willing to accept same in that or any other moment.

In that which shall follow, you will discover some other perspectives that we believe will add another dimension to the understanding of your uniqueness and beauty and of the oneness of your group, regardless of those things that appear to limit, not the least of which can be your own thoughts or feelings in this way or that.

But this is sufficient precursive commentary, for there is more to be gained, we believe, by moving forward and re-joining Peter in his experiences, reminding you that Peter discovered upon focusing his consciousness that he had returned to the Control Center.

Zeb is listening intently as Peter discusses with him the recent events. "I tell you, Zeb, it was like nothing I can express. The transformation of this young woman was virtually unbelievable. Had I been told beforehand that she, in her former rebellious and introverted personality (no offense intended, of course) would shortly thereafter return to the Earth after being offered this, I might call it, window of opportunity to leave that place—meaning the drabness of the life she was dwelling in—chose consciously, to return, I wouldn't have known what to make of that. And not only that, Zeb," continues Peter, "she did so with a light no less than some of the greatest I have observed to the present. I tell you, it was wonderful."

Zeb nods, looking at Peter in a way that Peter recognizes, and he realizes that Zeb had prior knowledge.

"Of course, Zeb. I forgot. You're aware of all this, true?"

"Yes, I was, you could say, appraised of them."

Peter, quiet now, reflects, studying Zeb. "I am intuiting or something of that sort that there is more here to your being … how did you state that? Appraised?"

Zeb nods again, smiling.

"Would you care to confirm or deny my feeling, Zeb?"

"Yes, I will confirm that for you and more, if you'd care to accompany me. I'd like to show you something that I think will help fill out your understanding of this experience."

Peter becomes excited, visible in his cloak.

Zeb turns swiftly and proceeds in a direction that you would perceive to be off to the left. Peter looks at the surroundings and again notices the beautiful mass of undulating, living light, like beautiful clouds that are somehow back-lit or lit from within. They seem to be continually swirling, subtle hues of colors interplaying with one another almost as though they are playing some sort of children's game like hide-and-seek or tag. Peter delights in that thought as he continues to follow Zeb.

He hears Zeb. "It is, indeed, beautiful, isn't it, Pete?"

"It truly is."

"Would you say that it is an essence, or an energy, or how would you define the substance?" motioning at the white cloud-like formation.

Peter hesitates for a moment, so Zed answers his own question. "It is an essence perceivable from various levels of consciousness, spiritual awareness." Still moving along with Peter and the rest of Peter's companions behind him, he continues, "It is a confluence, a coming together of thought-forms or vibrational essences that are associated with entities of a certain level of awareness. You see, properties associated with entities tend to come together. When those properties have a common point of reference or intersect, then the result is a somewhat particle-ized collusion of light, color, sound, and vibrational energy.

"To attempt to carry the technical explanation beyond that, one finds great difficulty, for the terminology and understanding in the Earth are not yet present. So, let me turn back to the spiritual quality, which is merely a different form of expression of an entity's consciousness, do you see? And that consciousness, for example of you and I when in conjunction with one another, forms that bit of cloud-like looking substance right here." Zeb stops so abruptly that Peter nearly cascades into the back of him. "See it?" He turns to look mirthfully at Peter.

Peter, startled by his own abrupt termination of movement, turns to look. He perceives a small section of the greater energies or cloud, that is seeming to respond to Zeb.

"I do see it, Zeb. Is there significance or meaning in my being able to do so, or in the fact that you pointed it out?"

Pausing a moment to study Peter, Zeb places a hand on his shoulder or the visual translation of this in the physical reference of the Earth. "Watch this." Zeb quickly withdraws his hand from Peter and the smaller sphere of energy that Zeb had pointed out to Peter a moment or two ago changes as quickly as Zeb's motion changed his position. A sort of pastel shading comes and then gradually seems to be absorbed into itself, the smaller sphere of cloud-like substance merging back into the greater sphere.

Peter's interest is now clearly piqued.

"Questions, Peter?"

"You know there are. What just happened? Somehow or other, the combination of you and I or our energies is represented out there," pointing to the massive beautiful white, shimmering essence before them. "And when you did whatever it was, a corresponding response occurred there. True?"

Zeb simply nods.

"Then that would imply that we, individually and collectively, have some control over this very beautiful and immense essence."

Zeb simply nods again.

Pausing for what seems to be a lengthy period of time, Peter turns to study Zeb. "I understand what you're expressing to me, but I fail to see your purpose for having shown this to me."

Zeb seems to now be somewhat removed from the situation, withdrawn. He has paused, and the pause grows longer and longer, until Peter asks, "Is there something amiss here? Something wrong? Did I ask an inappropriate question?"

Zeb, still silent, gazes at Peter.

Suddenly, Peter gets a sort of inner sensation of activity, slowly at first, but growing until he is acutely aware of the inner light he has come to associate with the Master.

Still silent, looking with a loving expression at Peter, Zeb slowly extends his arm to point back to the vast white substance before them.

As Peter, now quite energized by the goldenness within him, turns to follow Zeb's gesture, he is surprised to see a growing sphere of golden light on this majestic white cloud before them. Realizing that Zeb is showing him rather than explaining to him, Peter asks no further questions. He just observes the golden sphere, now quite pronounced on the whiteness.

Suddenly, the goldenness is gone, and to Peter's wonder, what he sees is a hospital room. There is a bed and on the bed is the teenaged girl whose experiences so moved and inspired him. At her side, holding one of her hands is the boy who virtually saved her life, according to how it would seem in the

Earth, but Peter knows it was the Master's light that saved her and made this event possible.

"There. Now I've answered several questions for you, one you had previously when you asked me how did I do that … Remember? When I created the opening in the clouds?"

Transfixed on the scene before him, Peter simply nods, so vigorously he can hear Zachary chuckling in the background. "You look like one of those pet birds in the Earth when they're exercising their neck. If you don't stop that soon, Pete, we'll have to get you some sort of attention."

The entire group laughs at this, and Peter, his perception still focused upon the grouping, acknowledges Zachary's comment with a chuckle of his own. "They're here! And how wonderful she looks. She's well, then?"

"She is as you see her, Pete," responds Zeb.

Studying the scene, Peter moves a bit forward and begins to lean, as though to look out a window.

Muffled laughter comes from Zachary. "Zeb, you'd better make an adjustment there before we have to go after Peter because he's fallen out of the Control Center."

Startled back into a fuller consciousness, Peter looks at Zachary with a bit of self-conscious awareness. "Oops. This is just such a beautiful scene, and it brings back the memories of the entire experience."

While Peter is speaking, Zeb has, at Zachary's request, adjusted the picture, so to say, so that Peter, as he turns, states, "Oh, I can see them very clearly now. What is happening? And, Zeb, why are you showing me this here?"

"Well, Peter," explains Zeb, "you had asked if you could be aware of or part of their works again in the future, so I was just contributing my small part to that request, along with answering some of your earlier questions. The power, as you would call it, to do any work is always within you, Peter. And that is why I helped you to call upon the consciousness within you that is at one with the Master, so as to make this possible.

All of this was within you always, that is to say, prior to any involvement on my part. All I did was make it known to you by joining with you to amplify it as you now perceive it."

Peter turns to study Zeb. "So you're saying that before, when you sort of swirled your hand around, that was just a demonstration, that you would have had to do nothing."

"That is true, although sometimes we find a little joy in embellishing these things a bit. Not to be accused of any impropriety, but there is much to be said about a worker finding joy in what they do. Sort of the personal touch, wouldn't you say, Zachary?"

"Oh, I would, indeed. You know me … I'm always in favor of having a bit of joy, a bit of humor, in all we do. So, yes, I support that, Zeb."

Peter turns to look at Zachary, who is bobbing his head up and down vigorously in imitation to Peter's own recent antics. "This is a good exercise, I'll say that for it, Pete, but somewhat of a meaningless application of energy." He stops and gives Peter a exaggerated wink.

"Okay. I understand, now that you've both lightened the experience, for which I'm grateful, as always. But why is this event unfolding? I know you both only too well to not realize that this is not an idle event."

"No, indeed," responds Zeb. "You have us, as you say in the Earth, cold on that one, Peter. What's happening is that we are being permitted to be present during the next stage of her evolvement."

Peter turns to observe the girl and the boy at her side. "She is in the Earth. True?"

"Oh, yes," Zeb responds quickly.

"And we are here, wherever this is, in the Control Center. Also true?"

"Yes, yes, good assessment."

"So we are observing them through mechanisms similar to what you have shown me in the past?"

Both Zeb and Zachary express confirmation.

"Are we, in some respect, to participate in that?"

"Yes," replies Zeb, "as you are willing, of course."

Zachary steps in. "Wait a minute. I know what this is. It's that game you play in Earth, *Twenty Questions*, right?"

Peter, totally caught off-guard by Zachary's off-the-cuff humor, bursts out in laughter and the others join in. They all move in close together until Elizabeth, Paul, Zachary, and Zeb are now standing very close together with Peter, Zeb on his right and Zachary the left.

For what seems to be some length of time they simply observe the situation before them. They can observe the thought-forms being expressed between the boy and the girl, who is upon the bed, attired as is typical for a hospital stay, and with tubes and such.

"She looks good." Peter attempts to break, what he feels is a bit of awkwardness with the passage of time.

"Indeed," responds Zachary.

"He looks good, too, don't you think, Zack?" adds Zeb.

"Yes, yes. He does look good. Though, you know, in some ways I think she looks better than he does."

Zeb tilts his head. "I'm not sure I can agree with that, Zack. He looks a bit more energetic, more ... "

"Wait a minute, you guys." Peter interrupts. "What is all this? What's with all this, as they say in Earth, small talk?"

"Uh-oh. Some of that influence from you is rubbing off on me and Zeb, Pete. I knew it. I just knew it would happen," at which, Zachary steps away and begins to rotate and spin.

Peter watches, dumbfounded. As Zachary spins, little lights and bursts of energy cascade off him, like the fireworks displays that Peter remembers, and little whirligig-type things give off illumination as they spin furiously about.

Then, as abruptly as he started, Zachary stops and brushes himself off here and there. "There. I've gotten rid of some of those habits, a bit of the flotsam and jetsam, cleaned my cloak. Oh, I feel so much better. How do I look?" turning about for Peter and the rest of the group.

Zeb, calls out over the back of Peter's shoulder, "You look marvelous, Zack. The best I've seen you in a long time."

"Truly? As good as *they* look?"

Peter glances down at the girl and the boy.

Zeb answers. "Every bit as good."

"Excellent. Then there'll be no problem if I join them."

Zeb nods. "Without question, you'd be no intrusion whatsoever."

"Good. Let's go, then, Pete."

Peter realizes now that he has been set up, but before he can speak, he feels the swift motion, as Zachary seems to pull him, and they dive into the opening in the cloud-like mist. Nearly instantly, they have stopped and are in the corner of the chamber in which the girl, the young woman, and the boy are positioned.

"Good. I'm glad that I was able to do that without being any offense," Zachary states off to the side, a hint of impish humor in his voice.

Peter can hear Zeb's voice, as though coming from some distant point deep within him. "You look good, Zachary. They look good, too, but you look just as good."

A bit of humor rolls off of Zachary, and Peter can feel it. It quiets and calms him, and he realizes that his dear friends have greatly simplified an event that he, in his questioning, might well have complicated to the point where this movement might not have been possible. He turns to Zachary with obvious affection in his eyes. "Thank you, Zachary. I understand now what that was all about. I can see that our consciousness can be one of our greatest limitations, and that trying to think out each point, to compartmentalize each little aspect of something, can become so significant, if not intensified, that it becomes an obstacle."

More serious now, Zachary responds, "That's a good observation, Pete, and I'm proud of you for having made it. You will forgive the little antics between Zeb and me, but we had made the decision that that would be the best way for you to get that. But now let's turn to what's before us here."

Peter simply nods, as he feels Elizabeth moving to a position immediately at his side, and at her side, Paul.

As they observe the young woman and boy, many thoughts come to Peter as his consciousness moves about the room, awakening within himself memories of the past of a hospital room such as this ... the birth of his children, the various illnesses of his parents, having visited friends.

"Brings back memories, does it, Pete?"

"Oh, yes. Excuse me, dear friends. It does, indeed. It awakens many things I find difficult to express, but feel free to share from my consciousness as you wish."

"Thank you, Peter," responds Zachary, as does Paul and then Elizabeth. For a brief moment or two, Peter can feel their consciousness move to be one with his own.

Zachary smiles. "Ah, yes. That does give one a perspective of the finite compared to the infinite, doesn't it?"

Gently, remarkably calm and tranquil, Peter just nods.

"Raises other experiences within you, too, doesn't it, Pete?"

"Yes. A lot of things sort of flash by, memories, you know, emotion ... sometimes joy, sometimes anxiety, sometimes a little fear. Emotions like that when one is expressed in the Earth."

"How do they feel to you, Pete? I mean, do you feel lighter, heavier? Perhaps a bit reticent? Try to express it to me if you would."

"It's not like that, Zachary. My reaction, as best I can share it with you, is one of being ... well, you said it, sort of like expressed in a simultaneity of form."

"Interesting."

"Indeed," responds Paul.

Again, Peter invites them to share his experience, and so they do.

A few moments later, Peter becomes conscious of someone entering the hospital room through the door off to their right, as they are a bit over in a corner of the chamber. Peter sees that it is a radiant young female carrying a tray. She moves over to the opposite side from the boy and places the tray upon a table, talking all the while.

Peter notes with interest and joy that the comments from her are as much visible as they are verbal expressions. "Look! You can see the thought-forms from that nurse almost as clearly as her speech."

"Yes, you are correct. We see them, as well."

Paul confirms this as, of course, does Elizabeth.

Elizabeth, who has been silent for some time, moves closer to Peter. "Watch her carefully, Peter, if you will."

His interest piqued again, Peter focuses his perception upon the nurse. "She's quite lovely, almost radiant. If I didn't know better, I'd say there's some familiarity here."

"Just keep observing," Elizabeth encourages softly.

Next, Peter hears the nurse say to the young woman, "Well, Cara, how are you feeling today?"

To his joy, Peter can now reference the young woman by the name Cara. He perceives her respond to the nurse, "I feel very good."

"Well, let me check you out here." She reaches for the bandaged wound on Cara's neck.

The boy becomes uneasy and begins rise to his feet.

"No need to leave, Tim. This won't take but a moment and, you won't be able to see it, so don't worry about being queasy."

Sheepishly, the boy now identified as Tim blushes and awkwardly sits back down, almost sliding down in his chair. Obviously, all this makes him very ill at ease, the hospital, the wound, and all of it.

Busy about her work, the nurse continues a running commentary, which Peter finds amusing. "Well, Tim, I suppose you've been told many times that, had it not been for your intervention, this young lady might not be with us here."

Tim, now embarrassed, looks down. "I didn't really think about it. I don't even remember doing it. It was automatic."

The nurse, still talking, looks quickly at Cara, smiling, and sees that Cara is smiling warmly.

Cara can remember some portions now, and she begins to speak. "You know, when I lost consciousness, I had this marvelous dream. I dreamt I met my grandfather, who died many years ago, but who I always loved and remember as being very special to me. It was so beautiful. And there were angels, and they promised to help me."

Without a moment's hesitation, the nurse answers, "And I'm sure they will. If they said they will, you can count on it. I've seen these things before. All that's needed is faith, faith from you, young lady," at which she reaches up and ruffles Cara's hair a little.

Cara is obviously touched by this gesture of warmth. The nurse smiles and, to Peter's surprise, gives Cara an exaggerated wink as she sweeps up her tray and leaves the room.

Peter turns quickly to Zachary. "You know, Zack, if I didn't know better and you weren't standing right here, I might have thought that nurse to have been you in some other form. Or at the least, maybe a twin sister."

Humor rolls from the group.

"Who knows, Pete? Anything's possible, but there's more interesting stuff to happen here. Let's watch."

Cara raises herself up on an elbow and asks Tim to adjust the bed. After they've settled themselves, she says, "I have to tell you something, Tim, and I want you just to listen. Don't let it affect you. Maybe it was all a dream or something, but I have to share it with someone."

Tim, somewhat shy by nature, just nods.

Cara then relates her experience, as much as she can recall, and then tells Tim how amazed she was at herself for choosing to return.

After a while, Tim, without much visible doubt, asks, "Why do you think that was, Cara? Why do you think you came back?"

"Your prayer. It was your prayer, Tim. They told me it was your prayer that made that all possible."

Tim shakes his head. "I remember it and yet I don't. It was like I was dreaming, too. Maybe that's because everything happened so quickly. But it was like I wasn't alone. Everything I did, it was like others were doing it with me. Does that make any sense to you, Cara?"

She smiles lovingly at him.

"You'd better rest now, Cara. Remember, they told me only a few minutes. You lost a lot of blood, and they're concerned about other things. Complications, you know. But I know you'll be okay, don't you?"

Again, Cara simply smiles and nods.

Tim gently holds her hand and places another hand on her forehead. "I'll go now so you can rest, but I'll be back this afternoon. Okay?"

She nods.

As Tim leaves, Peter can see Cara begin to relax. As she does, he perceives the energy around her expand brightly. In that same moment, Peter becomes conscious of the fact that there are several other entities, lights, in the opposite corner from where they are.

"Look there!"

Zachary nods. "They've been there all the while, Pete."

"They have?"

"Yep."

"Why didn't I see them?"

"You weren't perceiving at that level. You were focused on Cara and Tim."

"Yes, you're right."

Studying the forms, he recognizes two to be the angels who promised to stay with Cara, and a third form, reaching out with his consciousness, Peter now realizes to be her grandfather.

Cara's eyes are closed, and suddenly she speaks. "Grandfather, you're here. I can tell."

Peter sees a single glistening tear of joy trickle from the corner of her eye, and he sees the grandfather move slowly to position himself at her side.

"Grandfather, you have always been so special to me. In my heart, I always felt your presence. It was the gentleness of your love, like an island of hope, an island of love, in the midst of the despair of this city with all its anger and hatred, its violence. I so wish you could have stayed here with me. But I know we don't always understand these things, and I'm just grateful to know that you're here with me now."

Peter sees the grandfather expressing his light to reach out and touch her. And he can see Cara react gently to the infilling of warmth. He sees now, as well, these two luminous forms, beyond beautiful. "Angels. I can recognize them after my experience with them. They are so beautiful."

"Indeed so," nods Paul.

Then from Elizabeth he hears, "Observe them, Pete. Carefully, now."

Turning to look at Elizabeth, whose own warmth radiates an equally beautiful essence as the angelic realm, a loving compassion that embraces every molecule of his being, he then turns to observe the two forms. Remembering Zachary's earlier teaching, he reaches within himself to attune to the center of light within. Then he more or less reflects outward, to perceive from the fullness of his being.

At once, he is taken aback, for, at the left, he thinks he sees Hope! Unable to restrain himself, he shouts, "Hope, is that you?" Instantly, Peter perceives her clearly. Without thinking about anything else, he hurls himself across the room to embrace her, and an exchange takes place much in the nature as you might upon discovering an old friend in an unlikely place. "How are you? What are you doing here? How did you get here?"

Engrossed in his discussion with Hope, he then hears, "Peter, what about me?" Turning, he sees Rebecca, radiant, glowing, emanating love and fellowship to him. And he does the same with her, literally crashing himself into her position, and joy radiates from their exchange.

Then Peter hears Cara. "The angels are here, Grandfather! They're here! I can feel their joy. They are so beautiful and so loving. Love is bouncing around this room like rockets on the Fourth of July."

Embarrassed, Peter now realizes that Cara has detected his unfettered, full force demonstration. He stammers to Hope and Rebecca, "Please forgive me. I do pray I have not upset anything."

He is quickly assured that this is not so, and he asks, "Please, how is it that you are here? And how is it that I could not perceive you?"

They explain to Peter that they came in answer to a commission and that the *prerequisite*, if you will, was that they would move inward and, in essence, create a cloak of Christ Consciousness that would be virtually impenetrable. They go on to share more, each one offering this or that— their journeys, their travels and works in other realms and for other entities. Then they received a call from Zeb explaining that there was a good work to be done in the Earth that required the position of consciousness of one from the Angelic Host, and asking if they, Hope and Rebecca, would accept this commission? Joyfully and without hesitation, they did so, for it was precisely what they were seeking. And now here they are in the Earth to work with this entity called Cara for the remainder of this lifetime.

Peter is awestruck. "Are you saying that, for as long as she is in the Earth, you will remain at her side?"

"Yes," they respond.

"What a beautiful, dedicated work. I'm sure it will be a mutually fulfilling and blessed relationship. I've seen some of the potential of this one, Cara, and I can think of none other who would be as worthy as both of you to serve with her."

A rosy glow so familiar to Peter comes from the tranquil, loving smile of Hope and gently flows over to him, and similarly from Rebecca, as though they were expressing their gratitude for his kind confidence.

"You are Peter, then," he hears behind him. He turns to see the grandfather directly before him.

"Yes, sir. Forgive me. I hope I haven't disrupted anything here."

"Not in the least. Delighted to have you. I want to thank you for your part in the works for Cara, my granddaughter of my just-previous incarnation. And do thank all of your companions for the beautiful light that they offered in her name."

At that point, Zachary, Paul, and Elizabeth move to be beside by Peter, and greetings are exchanged. Not surprising to Peter is the fact that Zachary and the grandfather seem to know each other well, as does Paul.

Peter's curiosity cannot be contained, and he asks the grandfather about this.

"Oh, yes, I know them quite well. We worked together in preparation for those events and for the work that lies ahead."

Peter turns in wonder, first, to look at Paul and then at Zachary, who sort of shrugs his shoulders and smiles at Peter as though, *What can I say?*

Peter smiles. "You'll be explaining that to me, won't you, Zachary?"

"Oh, yes, of course, Pete. Intended to do it some time ago but, well, we were busy and all."

Peter smiles and shakes his head at Zachary's jesting.

The grandfather continues. "It is so nice that you could all come for this stage of Cara's progression. If you will just take a position over here (gesturing to the space beyond the foot of the bed), we'll proceed."

"What's he talking about, Zack?"

"Watch and observe, Pete. Better than that, reach out and perceive it, and you can be a part of it if you like. All you could do would be to contribute. No possible way you could detract from this."

Peter glances over and sees Hope and Rebecca smiling broadly at their old friend Peter.

The grandfather turns now, and Peter sees him move gently over to Cara, and then seems to lean forward so far it's as though his face is nearly pressed against hers.

Cara's eyes pop open. "Grandfather, did you speak to me?"

The grandfather is still bent over, as though he is speaking into her ear.

"Grandfather, I hear you!"

This continues for a time until Peter can hear what the grandfather is speaking. *Interesting comments,* Peter thinks. They're like encouragement, support, like instructions, almost as though the grandfather is instructing some portion of Cara for reasons that escape Peter's perception just now.

Shortly, Cara's eyes slowly close, and she states softly, "I hear you, Grandfather. I hear you."

Then, Peter observes her consciousness begin to fade, and he realizes she has fallen asleep.

She moves deeper into slumber, and Peter gasps as he sees, again, a second form slowly rise up above her physical body, becoming defined. The grandfather reaches for it, gently turning and positioning this luminous body, the mirror image of the physical. Finally, the grandfather has it positioned such that it is immediately before him. The eyes on this luminous body are still closed.

Then, Peter hears the grandfather call very loudly, "Cara! Cara! Cara!"

The eyes flutter on the luminous form. A smile floods her the face, and she hurls herself upon her grandfather. As the forms come together, Peter can see beautiful lights cascade off of them, and they begin, to Peter's amazement, to dance around the room, singing, laughing, arm in arm dancing.

"What is this?"

"Just watch, Pete."

After a time of effervescent expressions of joy and love from Cara, the grandfather and Cara seem to rise up several feet above the floor. Around them, Peter can see a beautiful meadow form, flowers and trees in the background. It is beautiful and he is deeply touched.

"Here," the grandfather suggests. "Let's sit here. This is a lovely place."

Peter glances from where they are to where Cara's body is and estimates the distance to be no more than five or six feet measurement. Yet, when he focuses on Cara and the grandfather, they might as well be a thousand light years away, for the purity and beauty is no less than Peter's own Garden Realm.

The grandfather appears to be explaining things to Cara. Then they arise, and he appears to lead them back down to floor level and over to her body. He reaches up and gently touches her face, at which point her body begins to float. The grandfather repositions it immediately above the physical body in the bed, and it slowly descends until the luminous body and the physical body are as one.

Peter sees the aura change around Cara, and he perceives her deep rhythmic breathing. She has fallen into a deep sleep.

The grandfather then turns, bows to Peter and the others, expresses his gratitude and honor that they should have been present, and slowly begins to dissipate before Peter's eyes.

"Is he ... leaving, Zachary?" questions Peter.

"Not in the literal sense, but he no longer needs to express himself in the just previous manner, so he's moving to a position to be one with Cara."

Peter does not fully understand. Glancing back, he is joyful to perceive Rebecca and Hope fully radiant. He moves over to them. "Could you explain to me what took place here? And why the grandfather was honored to have us present?"

"Well," replies Rebecca, "it's that the grandfather is in the process of helping Cara to open herself to be a channel of blessings. Hope and I will serve with her in healing works, and the grandfather will, of course, always be present and oversee these. A bridge of consciousness has developed more clearly now between the two of them, a preliminary foundation of sorts that will enable good works to be accomplished."

"I see," Peter responds. "Well, this certainly has been an incredible experience. May I ask, must you always stay here? You know, can you come and spend time with the rest of us? Maybe in the Control Center where we wouldn't bother anyone? I would love to hear of your experiences, and I would just like to be with you again for a while."

"Most assuredly, Peter," smiles Hope. "There is no difficulty in our being in the Control Center and here, as well."

Pausing for a moment, Peter realizes that this duality of expression seems to be very commonplace. "You know, I need to find out more about that. Perhaps I could contribute something at some point or another in a future work."

"We'd be glad to share what we can with you, Peter," answers Rebecca, "and Elizabeth can help you considerably, as well."

Peter turns to look at Elizabeth and remembers their earlier experiences in the formless realms, and her joy and fondness for the freedom of being one with existence. "I understand now, I think, Elizabeth, what you were saying way back in those experiences. Is what I am considering correct?"

Smiling very broadly, Elizabeth nods.

He turns to look at Zachary and Paul, who are also smiling and nodding an affirmation.

"Well, then, is this a good time for me to practice?"

Of course, all gathered agree, and we find them moving to be at one with Zeb in the Control Center.

Zeb greets the group with great cheer, and all in the Control Center celebrate the work with Cara.

Peter is introduced to many new entities and is told that they will assist here and there with varying works. He notices that the gathering includes the wonderful group of entities, the Earth guides, with whom he has just sojourned. Greeting them, he asks, "Will you be involved?"

"As we are permitted," answers the spokeswoman from his previous works.

"This is wonderful. Just wonderful," and they turn to join the larger group.

And so for the present here, dear friends, we shall conclude, asking as we do that the joy, love, and glory of God's oneness with all be awakened within you, just so as it has been within Cara.

CHAPTER 16

Forms of Healing

OCTOBER 13, 1993

In the works that are to follow there are many things that Peter will encounter and participate in. The extent to which you might also participate depends only on this: First, it is your willingness. Then, it is your affirmation that it is you who makes the way passable, you who opens the door. So, it is your willingness and affirmation that makes it possible for you to participate in spirit, mind, and perhaps even in body in some instances, with Peter and his colleagues. This as a part of the forthcoming works shall be our intent and our offering while Peter has many adventures.

Among these, we find that Peter will likely have one or more visits to what is called, in the Earth, the Akasha, or the soul record of those who have sojourned in the Earth and elsewhere. We believe he will participate in and be present for numerous forms of healings, and it is possible that Peter and his company may come to the aid of one or more in your own group in those days ahead.

Peter and his colleagues are in the Control Center. Zeb has been busy sharing information about Peter and his companions' works with virtually all who would listen, and after the most recent experience with Cara and Tim, Peter is elated to meet and discuss with anyone gathered the events and even the possibilities he sees as lying ahead for Cara and her works. He is in the midst of a group comprised of Zachary, Paul, Elizabeth, Rebecca, Hope, the Earth guides, and a dozen or so others. "I'm wondering about just what Cara and Tim might do in the days ahead.

Zachary tells Peter that the questions in Peter's mind are certainly valid and that the specifics could be explored in the literal sense if Peter so desired.

"What do you mean by the term 'explored in the literal sense', Zachary?" queries Peter.

"Well, there are several ways I can answer that for you, Pete. The first, probably my favorite, of course, is to go and experience the potential. The second would probably be my second-most favorite, and that is to go and observe the needs and wants of those souls who might be served. I could continue, ranking them in order of my preference." He stops and smiles at Peter.

"Well, since you listed the first as your first preference, that is likely what we should do."

Zachary is humored at Peter's response. "Perhaps it is what *I* would like to do best of all because I know that *you* will find the greatest potential joy in doing it. And as I see that you would be joyful, then my joy is doubled."

Peter smiles broadly. "Well, when could we take such an excursion?"

"At this very moment, if you'd like, Pete."

"I would like. What about the rest of you?"

The spokesperson for the Earth guides answers, "Some of us would be very joyful to accompany you and assist where possible."

Hope and Rebecca come and embrace Peter and the others, stating that they feel they should return for the moment to be completely focused with Cara, and the others in the Control Center express their own individual works and purposes, leaving Peter and Zachary, Paul, Elizabeth and several of the Earth guides.

Zachary looks about at the little group. "Well, we have a good entourage here. "Ready to go, then, Pete?"

Peter, ready but, never knowing what lies ahead in one of these *outings* (as Zachary calls them), nods, mustering his most radiant smile possible.

This causes Zachary to laugh aloud, and then Paul and Elizabeth, which causes Peter to realize his effort is utterly obvious.

Two of the Earth guides move close to Peter, the spokeswoman being one of them. "If we might, we do have a work in the Earth, and we would find your company a wonderful addition as we respond to this call in God's name."

"Excellent," responds Zachary. "That way, Peter won't think that I have coordinated this somehow and just directed him to where I wanted, as he usually suspects," with which, he gives Peter one of his exaggerated winks.

They gather together with the Earth guides, two of them at the forefront and two others a bit to the rear. The movement, while it is swift, is not so much so that Peter cannot sense the passage through the varying layers (as he thinks of them) of consciousness.

"You might notice here," Paul points out, "that some of these realms are more active than when we last passed through them."

Peter nods his realization of this, and Paul continues.

"This is due to an impending time of change or, more accurately, an opportunity for progression that affects the Earth and realms adjacent to it. Since many of these outlying realms are in their current position because of memories, habits, and such as are relevant to the Earth, any change or impact to Earth and Earth consciousness would therefore also impact these other realms."

Peter contemplates this and then nods again to Paul.

"So, Peter, as we continue our progression, you might take a moment or two to reach out to perceive the impact that this might be having upon some of the inhabitants. Since you already have a consciousness of them and their essence, you should be able to perceive if any significant difference has transpired here."

"Good idea," echoes Zachary, "and of course I'll assist you as you wish, Pete."

"Thanks, Zachary," Peter responds. "Some of this seems a bit … well, unpleasant. Just a hint though, mind you," laughing at his own choice of words.

"Not at all, Pete. It's good for one to evaluate, to have some criterion on which to base their choices, their direction in life or any experience. Goodness, we can't have everyone just floating about, being buffeted by whichever forces might be dominant in that area of expression, can we? Sooner or later, if that were to be the case, some of these realms would be severely overcrowded, if you follow what I'm implying."

Peter reflects. "Yes, I believe I have the full cognizance of that, Zack."

"So, it seems it would be helpful to have a literal expression here and determine if, in fact, some such effect has taken place," Zachary motions for Peter to follow him. "Just reach out with your consciousness now. Don't think of yourself moving necessarily, just let your consciousness expand and let it just get a feel or a reading of the situation, and allow your senses (as it were) to perceive. Thereafter, you can compare this to your earlier perception."

"I can?"

"Certainly." Zachary laughs. "It's there within you, as all things are. You have only to go within and find it to actualize it again. Collect the data first and analyze it second."

Remembering that this is even good advice from the Earth, Peter reaches out with his consciousness, commenting here and there about subtleties that he feels, suddenly feeling an impact here and there as he encounters what he presumes must be clusters of intensified emotion or thought-forms.

"Good perception, Pete, for individual entities can concentrate and generate very dynamic fields of energy. Some are more accomplished at this than others, yet all have this as a potential, whether innate or active. The value of you experiencing this and recognizing it will be a reference and a tool, sort of diametrically opposed to their use of this ability in future healing works."

"How so?"

"Well, consider that here you have, for example, this entity right here." Peter feels a jolt, as though Zachary has grabbed onto something and slowed the entire procession. "Oops, sorry about that, Pete. But this is a good place to pause a moment to perhaps make use of this opportunity."

Receiving an affirmation from the Earth guides, who now move closer to Peter and Zachary, Zachary continues. "You see this fellow here?"

Peter, taken aback, turns to look in the direction that Zachary is gesturing. To his amazement, it appears as though Zachary has grasped ahold of a massive collage of colors, lights, and patterns, not necessarily unpleasant but very disorganized and raucous in their vibrations, not at all like the harmony and beautiful symphonic resonance that Peter is accustomed to while working with his colleagues.

Zachary is aware that Peter has caught this. "Good, Pete. One of the first things you can use as an evaluator is no harmony. See that?"

"Yes, I do. Gosh, these colors are bright and ... Say, wait a minute! Do you have ahold of that fellow, Zachary?"

Zachary laughs. "Well, yes and no. You could say that he has ahold of me."

"What?"

"Look. He's attached himself to me. Though it looks to you that I have grasped him, to the contrary, the entity has taken hold of me. I have, of course, allowed this to happen. Knowing his intent and his personality, I was sure he would grab onto anyone or anything moving into or out of the Earth because of some habits he has associated with the Earth."

"Habits? You're not talking about habits like Jack's, are you? I hope not because that was very disarming at first.

dust on a mirror

Can't say it was too bad at the latter stages, but goodness, for a time there … "

"No, not like Jack. Quite different, yet, much the same."

"How can it be quite different and much the same? Wouldn't it be one or the other? Are you saying there are similarities, but they are expressed differently?"

"Good reasoning, Pete, but take a closer look. Try a bit of this red here." Zachary reaches into the blob of color and seems to just casually extract a large blob so that his hand and forearm are immersed in this ball of red color.

"Good grief, Zachary! What are you doing? Won't that hurt him? Or you, for that matter?"

Zachary is smiling, and Paul and Elizabeth are giggling. Even the Earth guides are amused at this.

Quickly noting this, Peter responds. "Well, the impact of seeing you do that was a shock. But now that I think about it, of course I know you wouldn't do anything that would hurt him or injure yourself in any way. You must admit, though, that's quite something for me to have seen."

"Why is that, Pete?" questions Zachary.

"Well, you reached in and took a part of that fellow!"

"Not really. I didn't actually take anything. These are just essences that are surrounding the entity. You know, like lint attracted to a surface in the Earth. If I took some lint off a table, would you say that I had taken something away from the table? Or that I had done the table a service?"

"Well, I suppose I would say that the table would be relieved to have some of the dirt off its surface. But we're not talking about a table. We're talking about an entity, and that looks like a vibrant, living essence I see at the end of your arm there. Oh, wow! It seems to be consuming your hand and forearm!"

"Not at all, Pete. Watch." Zachary raises his arm, swirls it around and snaps it forward, and the red blob goes hurtling off into time and space as though someone had fired a rocket.

Dumbfounded, Peter watches the blob grows smaller with each millisecond. He turns to look at Zachary. "You threw that away, Zack, but that belonged to this fellow."

"Not to worry, Pete. Just a moment or two here and you'll learn something about the laws of ethereal physics."

The group is now consumed with laughter, everyone except Peter. Curious and mystified, he looks about. Zachary is simply rocking back and forth on his heels, as you would call it, and the rest are utterly at ease, enjoying this little event.

Suddenly, Peter thinks he hears something … distant, soft at first, then growing and growing. Puzzled, he turns to look to Zachary and is about to speak when Zachary raises a finger to his mouth indicating to Peter to be quiet. Then he points straight out into space.

Peter, still perplexed, turns to look in the direction that Zachary is pointing. Suddenly, he can perceive a tiny, tiny red speck growing larger and larger as the sound and other essences with it also seem to be growing. Peter realizes, of course, that it is the red blob of energy or light or whatever it is, and that it is hurtling back at them at an incredible speed. "We'd best get out of the way, don't you think, Zack?"

"Not to worry. It'll pass right through us if need be."

"Well, I don't want that thing passing through me!"

"You wouldn't feel a thing, Pete. But if it concerns you that much, step just a bit back a step or two. Briskly, now!"

Peter awkwardly moves backward, and there is a very powerful swooshing sound along with other sound-oriented energies and a flash of color. He turns, though not nearly fast enough, to see that the color has struck the large sphere that is the entity Zachary has ahold of, or it has ahold of Zachary, and it's right back in the same place where it was before Zachary removed it.

"What in the world is that, Zachary? What's this all about?"

"Ethereal physics, Pete."

The whole group now breaks out in boisterous laughter.

"Okay, I know you're all having a good time here. I realize it's not at my expense, but how about an explanation."

Zachary nods a bit more vigorously than necessary. "Like attracts, Pete. Just like some things in the Earth. No matter how hard or how far I would try to throw that thought-form energy, if I might call it such, that red blob, because of its affinity, its attraction, to this entity and the entity's claim —in other words, he *owns* that red blob—there's no way I could throw it hard enough or far enough that it wouldn't come back in short order.

"You could question me as to whether it's the same red blob of energy as the one I threw, and I couldn't rightly answer that specifically for you, except to say that it has precisely the same properties as did the original blob of energy. It is the collection of those properties that the entity needs or wants or desires that causes that expression of energy to be attracted to him. And the place it's positioned on him, so to say, if you would think of this as this entity's cloak, represents about where that entity has ranked this emotion or this energy in the hierarchy of their thinking or desire.

"Now, look here ... " Zachary spins the large sphere so casually, which Peter knows is the entity, that Peter's mouth falls open (so to say), and Paul and Elizabeth laugh loudly again, "and let's stop it, hmm, right here." The sphere's rotation is instantly stopped. "Now, look up here." Zachary plucks a smaller blob of reddish-colored energy, though not the same, and seems to cause it to be suspended in mid-air before them. "And I'll take a little bit of this, orangish but still definitely red, that's hovering just above the sphere, close to me, and let's see, hmm, one more from ... column C, I believe would do it," with which, he plucks another reddish-colored energy and (to Peter's perception) just simply tosses it into the air.

[Now, mind you, here is this great sphere, perhaps 15 to 25 feet in diameter, which Zachary's one arm is imbedded in, and in front of Zachary are these three much smaller spheres, perhaps about the size of small melons, and they are rotating in front of the group, just suspended in mid-air. Peter is in wonder, awe, and great curiosity.]

"This is incredible, Zachary. I don't understand what it's all about, but I can tell you, if you could do this in the Earth, you could make a fortune."

Of course, laughter ricochets off of everyone here, as they find delicious humor in Peter's thought-form. Zachary, rising to the occasion, executes a few antics as though he were a performer, and then appears to juggle the three smaller spheres with the right hand that is free and unencumbered.

"Well, that's good, Zack, but that's old stuff. Now the first things you did, that's new! That's marketable!"

"Well, enough of all this humor for a moment, if you will, Pete, and let's get down to business here."

Peter, smiling broadly, simply nods.

"Okay, let's see … " With one arm still inside the sphere, Zachary puts his other hand on his hip as the three spheres continue to appear as though he were juggling them and, then, and as swift as can be, he reaches out and plucks one of the three juggling spheres from their midst, while the other two continue on. "Take a look at this one here, Pete. Nice color red, wouldn't you say?"

Peter studies the sphere as Zachary holds it in an out-stretched hand before him.

"Here, hold it a minute," and Zachary tosses it to Peter.

Startled, Peter reaches out and gingerly positions the red sphere of rotating energy in the midst of his two hands.

"Cup your hands over it or whatever you need to do to sort of ascertain an essence from it."

Peter follows Zachary's directions.

"What do you feel, in Earth terms now, Pete?"

"Well, I feel something flowing from this. I would say it's like is an emotion."

"Oh, nicely done. But a bit more detail, if you will. All this stuff is emotion, after all."

"Oh, yes, of course. Forgive me."

"Not at all, Pete. Just having a bit of fun."

"Hmm. It feels like an emotional energy that is, uh, well, it's a, it's sort of like a ... no, no, it's not like that. It's a ... "

"Come to the point, Pete. After all, we're holding the entire group up."

"Well, Zack, I can't tell you what this is like in specific terms."

"Why do you suppose that is?"

"I don't know."

"Take a look inside yourself for your greater consciousness and bring that forth. Learn to do that as much as you can as an automatic reaction to that which you don't know, to an encounter that is out of the ordinary, or to answer a need."

Peter nods. "I guess I got caught up in the specifics here and forgot that good training you've given me in past."

"That's a good lesson, Pete, and good for all people in the Earth, as well. For it's often the focus, the intensity of the moment or the situation, or the relationship, or what have you, that causes one to move out of the desired pattern and into a reactive mode. So it's a good point, and I'm glad you haven't taken offense but are, rather, following it. You are following it, aren't you, Pete?"

"Yes, of course," responds Peter, with everyone smiling. He closes down his outer perception and moves inward until he finds a sensation of wondrous peace, a glow, an essence that seems to have a sort of vibrational undulation, a rhythmic eternal pulse. Finding this and feeling the wisdom therein, he draws himself back to the surface of his consciousness, opens his perception (you could consider this opening his eyes) and now he sees this through greater wisdom and perception.

"Now can you tell me what this is, Pete? How do you assess this?"

Peter now can determine the source and the nature of the energy, and his response is sure and swift. "This is an emotion that has to do with love. It is a feeling of having failed or lost something. It relates to an opportunity that was presented to this entity, or someone that the entity did not respond to. In fact, I would say the entity rejected this somehow or other. It is, summarily, unfulfilled love."

"Excellent, just excellent. Toss that back, if you will."

Peter does, and Zachary grasps the next sphere and tosses it to Peter, who simply nods, knowing he should follow the same procedure. Only a moment's pause and he has it. "This has a similar flavor to the first, but somehow or other this was an action or a violation of a trust or love. This has something to do with transgression. There's an essence of action here, whereas the first was more the withdrawal or denial. I would say that the entity did something against someone, or transgressed against someone's free will. Probably someone who loved him."

"Very good!" Zachary then gestures for that one back and tosses Peter the third, with which Peter follows the same pattern, describing the emotion, the energy, and the probable circumstances.

Zachary continues. "If you will consider that this entity has quite a collection of all of these energies all about him, you could conclude here that he has many things that he considers to be failures or errors. If you continue that line of reasoning, you would ultimately have a good assessment of where this entity is in terms of what his limitations are, enabling you to far better assess how you might help the entity when there is the readiness for progression.

"Now, if you take this as a whole and look at it from a distance," at which Zachary removes his arm from the large sphere, the smaller spheres having been returned to the surface of it, "at a certain point you'd see all this sort of blend together and form what could be called the primary essence of the entity giving you the outer appearance of what you call in the Earth the personality, the id, the ego, the consciousness. Are you following all that, Peter?"

"Yes, so far. But what's the purpose for knowing this, other than to, as you say, be informed and aware, in order to respond to an opportunity?"

"This entity is about ready to release some of this, we could call, it 'stuff'. What we've been showing you has to do with the mechanics, if you will, as relates to healing. Who is the guide here, please?" Zachary looks off into space.

Peter is surprised and curious at Zachary's call, and even more surprised as he begins to see first one sphere of light form off in the emptiness on one side of the larger sphere, the side with all the red, and then a second off on the right side, both growing in brilliance. Peter is familiar with the essence of these spheres. Very swiftly they take form.

"Greetings," Peter hears from the entity on the right. "How are you all? And you, Zachary?"

Peter quickly looks at Zachary, wondering many things, of course at the forefront of which is the question, *Does everyone know Zachary?* This makes Peter smile warmly, and his fondness for Zachary is self-evident.

"Hello there, Frederick. How is this fellow doing? About ready to make a little progress?"

"Yes, I'm certain of it," responds Frederick. "He's been showing signs of being willing to release some of these limitations. Quite a collection he's got, wouldn't you say, Zack?"

Zachary laughs aloud. "Yes, we were just exploring some of them. I'm sure you saw all that?"

"Oh, yes, saw the whole thing. How did you find the experience, Peter?"

"Oh, uh, very valuable, sir. I learned considerable from

it, though I must say I'm not sure how to apply it yet."

"Well, you came to the right place," Frederick laughs. "Zachary and I and my friend over there will show you."

Without waiting for a response from Peter, Frederick begins to glow brilliantly, greater and greater, as does his colleague on the other side of the patch-quilt-looking cloak over the entity, who has, as Peter realizes to this point, not as yet been identified or even contacted. The two spheres emanating from the guides on either side of the subject intensify until Peter realizes that the entire group—the guides, the subject entity, and even Peter's own group—are all contained within a larger sphere of light.

"Now, then, let's move into a different level of consciousness, if you will, Zachary, Peter, and all of you. Slow your essences down until you can perceive the entity in finite focus."

Peter looks from Frederick to Zachary, then to Paul and Elizabeth, to get at least a hint of how to do this. Zachary just looks quickly over at Peter and winks, indicating, as Peter perceives it, to follow his lead.

Zachary seems to shut down, as best Peter can define it, and Peter attempts to emulate this. Remarkably and very swiftly, he finds that he is, indeed, able to control his expression and, therefore, to control his perception. Continually referencing Zachary as a gauge and then glancing to look at Elizabeth, who smiles at him, and Paul, who also smiles, he can see that they are all slowing their essences. It looks as though they are drawing the light within themselves, concentrating it within so that outwardly they are not as luminous.

Then, Peter hears Zachary say, "Good enough, Pete. That should do it."

"Yes, nicely done," Frederick remarks to Peter, which gives Peter a sense of accomplishment and a bit of joy.

Instantly, then, Peter realizes that the entity in the patchwork-like cloak is now expressed fully in a form before them.

jubilant, expectant

"Hello, Frederick," says the entity.

"Hello, yourself," responds Frederick. "How are you doing with the things we discussed last time?"

"I think I understand them, and they make sense. The more I reflect on them, the more I realize that this is just a repetitive habit. Apparently, somehow or other I have absorbed a lot of guilt. It's deserved in many cases I think, but the things you gave me to study, Frederick … I saw that that guilt wouldn't help anyone. Not only am I slowing myself down, but I'm also hanging onto several others in the process."

"Very good," responds Frederick. "Let me introduce some of my friends here." He introduces Peter and the others and then turns back to the entity. "Well, are you ready to leave this consciousness to experience what lies beyond? Or if you prefer, we can do it another time."

"No, no! I've had enough! I truly have had enough. With your help, Frederick, I think I can release these things."

"Well, good. Let's get at it."

Peter can feel the almost jubilant anticipation emanating from the entity.

Focus on that quickly, Peter, urges Zachary. *That's a key here, and you'll find it to be an ever-present essence that makes the way possible and passable for such movement. That entity is unquestionably ready to move on. And this essence right here …* Zachary motions to the jubilant, expectant energy manifested in front of Peter, beautiful, wondrous, *will tell you every time if they're ready.*

Got it, Zack. Thanks for pointing it out. Peter watches with delight and amazement as Frederick and the companion guide seem to merge with their ward, as though their light is now over-lighting the subject. Peter can see what he interprets as flare-ups of energy become manifested and then diffuse off this way or that.

Those are his thoughts, his energies, his limitations,

Chapter 16 – Forms of Healing

Pete. Now keep watching. See if you can tune in to the blobs of color that we were working with a bit ago. You should be able to because you handled them.

I understand, responds Peter. With remarkable ease, he can perceive the entity in the midst of the over-lighting from the two guides, and he can also see the cloak. He watches carefully as the larger red sphere of energy slowly begins to dislodge itself from the cloak. It hovers and wobbles and floats about in a sort of orbit around the cloak, as though it were looking for a way into it. Slowly, the large sphere moves out, and it begins to drift away further and further. Then the second sphere of energy with the bit of orange in it, and then the third, all drift away. Peter can feel the lightness that results as the after-effect.

Over on the other side, Peter perceives a few more similar spheres of different color, which also drift off. He turns his focus back to the entity's cloak and marvels at how much better it looks. There are yet some distortions here or there, and the harmony isn't what Peter knows it can be, but it is so much brighter. The raucous, discordant nature that Peter felt at the first has been greatly diminished and in its place the beginnings, Peter thinks, of a beautiful symphonic harmony.

Good assessment, Pete, comments Zachary. *Very good. Now, if you will, let's move back a bit and just watch.*

Peter does so, along with the rest of the group. He begins to see the over-lighted entity rising, slowly rising, and marvels at how luminous the joy of the entity is.

"It's such a joy," Zachary remarks sweetly, as the entity and his guides drift upwards, "to see one progress, to see subtleties of understanding and comprehension begin to return to them. It's like you've given them back a part of their being that they have long forgotten, a virtuous nature hidden within themselves that they've newly discovered. Ah, yes, it is a beautiful privilege to partake of."

After some while, Peter can perceive them no more.

"How long will they move? How long will they continue to *rise* (if I might call it that), Zachary?"

Paul responds this time. "If you will, Peter, recall again our own journey through the colors. They will do the same until they find that point at which they can proceed no further and still sustain harmony. Or, if they are capable of passing through them completely, they will break free of this level of expression, which involves the Earth and many other realms and sub-realms, and move on to the next, just as you and I did. Remember?"

Peter nods, smiling. "Yes, I do. And I realize a little more with each experience here how much you gave me, Paul. I shall always be grateful for that and give you my love and dedication in return."

"Those things you have given me in past, Peter, and I thank you for that. But there is no need, for we are as one. What you and I have are possessions of one entity, not two."

Peter, reflecting and studying Paul, has no words to express his admiration, his fondness, his love, for this one. He can feel the timeless nature of their relationship together and the unshakable solidity of Paul's faith and oneness with God.

Turning to glance at Zachary, who is obviously pleased and joyful right along with these two, Peter cannot help but compare these beloved friends. Amazingly, as he does, he finds they yield their essence to Peter utterly, that he can search out and understand what it is that holds his interest at this point.

In the sweetness that follows, Peter comments, "Thank you for that and for all that you have given me, all of you," turning to include Elizabeth in this. "I think, from what I understood from this just-previous experience, that you are intending for me to see a similarity to what can be associated to healing works that might relate to the Earth, or to any other realm, and that these things might be tools to use in healing works … or, more broadly, spiritual works."

"Good assessment," responds Zachary. "And of course, as you know from your experience just now in becoming one with Paul and, to a degree, with myself and Elizabeth, this is an important part of Paul's continued dedication and work, and mine and, of course, Elizabeth's. Both Paul and Elizabeth have been steadfastly dedicated in service to such works for, well, by Earth time measure, thousands of years."

"Really? That is a lot of dedication."

"All of it is joyful, I assure you." Elizabeth smiles. "And the greater is our service, the greater becomes our joy. That goes without saying. Right, Peter?"

"Yes, I do understand that now, Elizabeth."

"Very good," Zachary chimes in. "Now, let us let our Earth guides continue on with our journey."

The spokeswoman smiles and, without another comment, the movement continues. Peter has more observations along the way, but for the most part, his focus is upon what we would call the destination, which he can see is the midst of a city, many tenement buildings lining the streets. Their movement is swift, and they are now positioned just a short distance from a middle-aged male who is leaning against a wall of a building, hands in pockets, looking down.

"Take a look at this cloak, Peter. We'll begin there."

Shifting his focus, Peter now sees a large sphere covered with a haphazard pattern of colors and energies. "Goodness, this is dense, and not at all in harmony. Is this fellow alive?"

Zachary chuckles. "In the physical sense, he's alive, but not by many more standards, as you have well seen."

"How do I equate this to healing? I mean, I know I can assess each one of these, as we just did with the last fellow and the little spheres of color. I don't think I'd care to do that here though, Zack, because that stuff does look nasty."

Laughter comes from the group again. "Nasty it is, in most every interpretation of that term. What I'd suggest to you now is to carry your perception one stage further."

"Okay … uh … how do I do that?"

Zachary chuckles again. "Follow me"

Peter sees Zachary begin to change. At first, Peter thinks he must slow down or reduce his energy, as he did in the Sea of Faces in order to perceive the entity. And he hears from Zachary, *You've got the right idea but the wrong direction, Pete. Move the other way. Increase your essence. In your terms, increase your vibrations.*

Oh. Okay. Peter focuses on the thought Zachary has given him, and his luminosity increases.

Keep it up, Pete.

Peter concentrates and closes out all other essences and focuses on this increasing energy. He is calling upon his own spirituality. He is drawing it unto himself as an expression of light, of energy. As he is so doing, which is a concentrated activity on his part, he notices that all the others are doing the same, as is Zachary, who is setting the pace.

A little more, Pete.

Peter concentrates on drawing this essence from within and manifesting it outwardly.

Right about there, instructs Zachary. *Hold at that point, if you will, Peter.*

Not knowing exactly how to do it, Peter simply does it.

Good. Now, if you will, just take that expression, Peter.

Swiftly looking over to Zachary so as to emulate him, it appears as though Zachary reaches out and somehow grasps the light that has gathered around him and draws himself unto it or it unto him, so that Zachary becomes this light. Once he does, he takes a form of a physical expression, which Peter realizes is merely for interactive purposes.

(What Peter does not fully realize is that Zachary is doing this for ease of our reference to comment back to you, dear friends in the Earth.)

Peter emulates this and looks about himself quickly. He is amazed, utterly dumbfounded for a moment or two, to find that he is in the Great Hall. "We are in the Garden Realm! This is the Great Hall!"

"It is *a* Great Hall or a *part* of the Great Hall. It is also what is called the Hall of Records."

"The Hall of Records? We are there?"

"Yes, otherwise known as the Akashic Records, or two or three other names popular in the Earth at the present, though I suspect there will be some new ones shortly," chuckles Zachary.

Glancing around in amazement, Peter looks to find resplendent entities moving about and other entities that some seem to be working with. He finds all manner and form and shape of recordings—books, scrolls, leather-bound, virtually every creative type of record-keeping craftsmanship seems present.

"The next intent here, Pete, is to find that Keeper of the Records for this entity," pointing to a rather dull spherical shape that has no errant energies anymore, just the muted form of the entity from the Earth.

"That's not the entity, is it, Zachary?"

"No, no, it's the spiritual expression of him."

"Greetings."

Peter hears a voice melodiously, yet almost thunderously, behind him. Startled, he jerks about, to find himself looking into the eyes of a wonderful, gentle, warm entity whose essence seems ageless, timeless. Peter marvels at the eyes of the entity, how they reach out and embrace him and seem to know all about him.

So, when we return, we will explore the Akasha. Who knows? Perhaps yours will be the records of choice.

CHAPTER 17

The Akasha

OCTOBER 13, 1993

As we are preparing to rejoin Peter and his colleagues, we might briefly comment that in the information that is about to be given, you will find a number of references to varying terms, concepts, thought-forms, that may have been referenced in past by varying title or description or name. In most instances, we believe you will be able to draw some parallels from those previous reference points. But you will also find in that about to be given other explanations that may, indeed, go beyond the known and enter into areas that are little known in the Earth except but by a few.

The experiences that are about to be shared here can most assuredly be accomplished by all of you, to the extent that your ideal, purpose, and goal are aright, according to Universal Law.

We turn then to Peter, who we find just as he was when we last met with you. He is observing the entity, fascinated with the essence that seems to be radiating from what you would call his eyes, his perceptive consciousness. Peter ponders all this. Here is an entity obviously of timeless wisdom. The countenance, exuding immenseness in some curious way, is not the literal expression of the entity in terms of size or manner, but that is the impression Peter gets, coming from something that is not explicitly expressed at the moment, and perhaps from something that Peter is intuiting rather than perceiving from without. Another quality that Peter observes in the entity is the sense of utter patience and love, a compassionate ease that is radiating and seems to be, in this very moment, permeating all of Peter's being.

It is Peter who breaks the momentary silence, as is somewhat traditional for him. "Greetings, sir. I am joyful and excited to be here and in your presence."

The entity of radiance and gentleness responds to Peter quickly and directly. "You are most welcome, Peter, now and always, as are, of course, all your friends here." The entity makes a slow sweeping gesture to the rest of Peter's friends who are gathered just to the side of Peter. "I gather that you have come to explore the status of this entity?"

Paul nods. "Yes, we wish to inquire about the status of this person who, as you know, we have just recently observed in the Earth. This is a part of the developmental process for our friend Peter here and, of course, a part of the expanding consciousness of all of us as we determine any possibilities of contributive work that we might offer the person."

After but a brief pause, the entity glances at the group and in that swift moment Peter feels as though the entity utterly knows him and each of the others. The entity nods. "Very well," and moves with such swiftness directly past Peter that it feels to Peter that he is almost pulled along behind.

Just a short distance ahead, Peter and the group come to a stop at what Peter perceives with a mixture of amazement and curiosity a massive array of what could loosely be called great books.

The entity reaches up and extracts a single volume.

Peter focuses intently upon the book, perceiving that the *book* (as such) has a sort of emanation, a sort of aura or sphere of energy expressed around it. He also determines that the energy seems somewhat dormant, inactive, lacking vibrancy or life.

With his back still to Peter, the entity comments. "That is quite an accurate assessment, Peter." He turns, holding the book. "For you could consider that the person is and has been for some measurable Earth time in a state of dormancy."

Slightly flustered, remembering that such entities can easily perceive his thoughts unless he takes deliberate action to block them, Peter attempts to move as easily as he can into an exchange with the entity, as though he was not caught off guard in the least.

Zachary smiles at this, off a bit to Peter's right, arms folded, and just rocking to and fro, as is often his habit under such circumstances.

The entity, now fully facing Peter, directly in front of him, turns the book to position it and open it to Peter, completely surprising Peter.

"Here." The entity looks down at the pages and with a luminous hand indicates his point of reference. "This is the position of the person at present as compared with some of the earlier experiences." The entity begins to shift the earlier pages in the book, back, back, back, until Peter has had a glimpse of numerous experiences that have gone before. (You would understand these as past lifetimes.) He pauses with his hand flat against a page and looks up to meet Peter's eyes in a full, warm, understanding gaze. "Do you have questions about this procedure, Peter?"

"Well, uh, yes sir, as a matter of fact, I do."

A bit of tinkling laughter can be heard from Zachary, still rocking on his heels, so to say, along with the soft remark, "He always has questions."

This arouses a bit of humor in the great radiant entity, and Peter is quick to join in and share that with him.

In the few moments of humor that seems to engulf the entire group, Peter moves to a new level of ease and relaxed expression with this entity. He knows from past experiences, the energies of humor and joy, when shared, can do much to bond entities, and this is just what he feels now to this great, beautiful entity before him. "I would feel very honored, sir, if I might submit some questions here. I'm certain they would help me gain a better foundation for future works or events."

"That is very wise, Peter, and I could not agree with you more. Please do proceed with your questions."

"May I first, sir, ask if there is a name that I might use to speak with you, rather than this more formal reference, which is a habit of mine, of calling you 'sir'?"

Again, a bit of tinkling laughter comes from Zachary and smiles from the remainder of his company.

"You can call me Beu-Wheil, if you wish, or just plain Beu."

"Bowheel, did you say?"

The entity, smiling softly, nods.

"If I might," adds Zachary, "you would actually, Pete, consider that two words or two names, and it would in the Earth actually be spelled B-E-U and the latter part as being W-H-E-I-L, which is probably not going to make a lot of sense to you. But it is the most descriptive definition of the vibrations of Beu here. Most of us simply call him Beu."

Peter nods and smiles. "Well, Beu, could you tell me where this name comes from? It is unusual."

"Its primary usage, Peter, was in the times that are mid-point in the references of the Atlantean time. So, just shortly after the second great upheaval, a noteworthy point of reference in the chronological flow of the Atlantean times."

"How curious such a name would be to the current times in the Earth."

"Why is that, Peter?" asks Beu.

"Well, it's hard for me to equate it."

"Only because of your reference. If you would look at some of these other countries and their means of communication, you would find it to be far less than extraordinary." The entity, while speaking, turns to gesture to what Peter sees as an assembly of almost colossal books of strange emanation, a collection that seems to be apart from the other records and yet here in the same general confines of the Hall.

"What are those huge books Beu?" asks Peter.

"They are the collective thought-form—past, present, and future, so to say—of the essence of those groups that are associated, in the Earth, to countries, philosophies, theologies, and all that sort of thing. You might think of them as a cross-referencing work that combines soul group work and things like that into a manageable reference. So they are depicted as you perceive them in rather substantial volumes."

"Most fascinating," responds Peter.

"Would you like to observe some of those, Peter?"

"Oh, yes, I would, indeed."

Zachary interjects, "If I might, perhaps it would be well to conclude this work before we begin another."

This brings humor to the group again, and Peter back to the point at hand.

"Wisely suggested," responds Beu. "So, Peter, if you will look here again at this person's records, you will find that there has been a continual pattern of seeking to break free from a tendency towards, you might call this, isolation. But in fact, the person longs, perhaps in the Earth called a burning desire, to be one with others, to have lots of friends, to receive and to give love. But his pathway, as you see here ... "

The entity seems to be turning pages of the book, which is held now quite close to Peter, and Peter can perceive the inscriptions on each page as the entity is turning them. "Right here, for example, at this time in what's called here Persia. Currently, political lines are dividing the area in the southwestern portion of Iran and several other countries, but the point here is that the person in this lifetime led a very nomadic life, which was not unusual. But if you will look at these several entries here, on occasion, when his heart was filled with longing and sadness, the universal forces brought to him an answer to his prayers, yet he shunned it. And here, you will see why."

Peter, very intrigued and very caught up in this activity,

strives to focus on where the entity's finger is now pointing. He sees a dialogue written, and he can feel it as he attempts to look at it. "What strange writing."

Beu responds without comment by passing his hand over the page.

Peter notices as his hand moves across the page left to right that which now appears as words—crisp, clear, and typed in English. "That was incredible!"

"Not at all. Just merely adapting the essence of these records for your specific interaction here. You wouldn't actually need this book, Peter, but since we are dealing here in forms that are expressed somewhat finitely for purposes that are several-fold, it follows, I should think, that you should be able to literally read the book."

"Wow!" Peter turns to focus intensely upon the words. He finds himself consuming them at a remarkable rate, even for him, in the sense that in the Earth he was a voracious reader with rapid absorption. But this far outpaces any previous ability. "How interesting. The moment I focus on reading this, it's as though it sort of responds to my intent and is almost instantly in my consciousness. It's not like my eyes move across the page to read each word and form them together into sentences, but that the experience leaps out from the page and imprints itself somehow in my consciousness. Do all these records do the same?" Peter turns to look about the immense array of great volumes around him.

"It depends upon the reader," responds Beu. "For you see, not all are willing to perceive as you are. For example, if you will glance over there ... " Beu lifts his hand from the page to point somewhat over Peter's right shoulder, as Elizabeth and Paul step aside a bit.

Peter perceives a group of entities, perhaps five or six of them, gathered about some works. Several of them are very luminous. Others have luminosity that, as he looks back at his own group for comparison, seem very much the same as he and Elizabeth, Paul, and Zachary. But one entity seems to be different than these. While there is some degree of luminosity, it is different. It is like this one has no firmament within the luminosity, only partially expressed.

"That one," responds Beu to Peter's unspoken thoughts, "is a reader from the Earth."

"A what?" exclaims Peter.

"A reader, one who has come to observe the records for purposes of certain Earth works. Here, we call them, loosely and lovingly, 'readers'."

Puzzled, Peter turns to Zachary and the others.

Zachary responds with a twinkle. "If I might, Beu, let me interject here a corollary to something in the Earth that Peter will understand. "Hey, Pete, remember the time when you were in, what's that called, Chicago, with your friend Damon, from the trading company, and he took you to that little place out of the way, that cafe? You had the wonderful dinner, the music, strolling violins? And the one in gypsy attire came and read your tea leaves?"

Peter is taken aback at this detailed reference to a point that he indeed remembers very well, surprising himself. "Well, yes, I do. I might ask you how you would know that to such detail."

Zachary shrugs impishly. "Part of the trade, Pete. Sometimes on holidays, I do a little tea-leaf reading here and there."

"What? You're not telling me that was you?"

"Well, you know, a person keeps their hand in this and that. And what the heck, it was a lot of fun, wasn't it?"

Peter is in a state of bewilderment before breaking out in laughter, and all share in this humor.

When it subsides, Zachary continues on. "Well, whether or not that was me as the tea leaf reader, that's what Beu is referring to here. People like that in the Earth, you know, who can close down the conscious portion of their mind and emotion so as to perceive things about people for whom they are attempting to do a certain work. Also in that category would be intuitives or psychics, and all that sort of thing that people do to invoke their own guidance or perception. Not the least of which, in the category of readers, should also be pointed out to you that people in their sleep state very often will come here and do a bit of reading, aided by their guides. That group over there are gathered around the ward they are guiding, so the ward in the dream state can gain guidance for their current life by building on understanding and references to the past. How's that? Does that make it clearer for you, Pete?"

Peter, absorbing and digesting what Zachary has shared, continues to observe the group in the distance.

"Would you like to join them?" asks Beu. "Perhaps that would afford you some clearer insight and understanding."

Swiftly turning to look at Zachary, as though to say, *Could we do this? Is this current work for this entity at a point where we could move over there?*

Zachary shrugs and nods. "We can always come back to this one from the Earth. He's been at this for several hundred Earth years, at least three or four concurrent lifetimes. A few Earth minutes more or less wouldn't make a great impact on him, don't you agree?"

The others of the group all nod, but before another word can be spoken, Beu seems to place the book somewhere, turns almost flowingly, sweeps by Peter, fetching him by an arm as he moves by, and more or less drags him along behind him. (Although we must indicate clearly that you can't drag one. It's merely the expression of a form for descriptive purpose here that we are dealing with.)

The small band of Peter's company, and Peter himself being carried along by Beu, swiftly arrive beside the group with the reader. Peter tries to focus on the group and their communications as quietly and unobtrusively as he can. Several of the guides are commenting between themselves, attempting to show various symbols.

Moving into complete silence now, Peter and his group focus on the others. One of the guides, who appears to be in charge in some way, communicates. "It is important to give him the understanding of the encounter he had here, for it's an opportunity to break free of a habit pattern."

"I agree," responds the other guide. "Let's build some thought-forms here and present them to be played back later."

"Good," agrees the other guide, and the two turn to two others who are expressed more luminously near them. Without communicative exchange that can be perceived, these entities summon up a brilliant orb of light that flows forward and envelops the reader entirely, yet Peter can perceive the reader through this light.

The two guides move quickly to become a part of the light, and just as swiftly, and before Peter can hesitate, Beu tugs at him, and they enter into the light also, followed by Zachary, Paul, and Elizabeth.

Peter marvels that the light, which seemed physically very small, could embrace them all. He has visions of, in the Earth, a dozen or so college students trying to climb into a Volkswagen of some antiquity. The thought-form raises a bit of humor from Peter's group and also from Beu, and also from Peter himself.

Beu responds. "It is simply a question of a need, Peter. If there is the need to embrace five or fifty or five thousand in this light, it is instantly done. It is not like the automobile you pictured in your thought-form that is finite, that is defined in rigid terms in the thought-form of the Earth. Here, thought-forms are not rigid, not restrictive, but ingratiate the needs and wants of those who are here as workers, readers, and helpers of any sort. Now, if you will, observe, please."

Peter turns to perceive what looks, for all practical purposes to him, to be a gigantic screen of some sort. The reader seems to fade in and out, sometimes more clearly defined, other times as though the reader is drifting back and forth. He can also perceive that the guides are attempting to direct the reader ever so gently, as those who tend a flock of domestic animals in the Earth do to gently guide one back to the flock.

Swiftly now, Peter begins to perceive activity on the "screen", which is actually a luminous white backdrop, so to say. As he does, he is amazed to see what appears to be real life experiences portrayed on the vastness before him. The experiences seem to come alive, taking form according to the experience the guides are striving to impart to the reader—a brilliant flash, symbols, spinning and whirling colors, a muffled explosion, darkness pierced by a light, strange sounds, all sorts of things. "May I ask what this is, Beu?"

"It's a past-life experience that is being shown to the reader, Peter."

"If you'll forgive me," probes Peter further, "in what form of realm was that life expressed? I've never seen anything like this that I can recall."

"It was an Earth incarnation some several hundred years previous to the current time in the Earth, Peter."

"In what form? In what country? I cannot recall anything of this nature."

Beu turns to Peter and simply looks upon him gently, softly. Peter feels something emanating from Beu that has a delicate luminescence, bathing Peter in this essence which Peter perceives as coming from Beu's eyes. In just a moment or two, Beu turns back to focus upon the great screen that Peter was observing previously, stating, "If you will look again, Peter, perhaps that will help."

Peter turns and is startled to see before him the scene of a great battle. The warriors appear to be in some sort of foreign clothing, using weaponry that is antiquated. Peter remembers having seen them in museums and history books. "What is this scene, and how is it that I now see it as a scene where previously it was nothing but symbols?"

"What you saw first is the summarized essence, so to say, of the impact of this experience on the reader. Some in the Earth might think of that as having reduced the experiences into expressions of finite coded color, sound, and energy. And these essences of color, sound, energy, and quite a significant array of other vibrational forms of expression are the effects of this experience upon the reader.

"Look at the reader as carefully as you can in this past life experience, remembering that we are only looking at their shadow form, not their 'real physical body'. You can see some of this circling around right over here," with which Beu points to about the middle to the lower back. "Notice right here the concentration of energies that are similar to what you perceived previously."

Peter does see the flashes and colors and the sort of heavier energy expressions. "That is fascinating. Might I ask, uh, the reader … they are unaware, right, of you and me and the others and what we are doing?"

"Yes, correct. The reader's guides have seen to that. But if I might call your attention here to these energies concentrated right here, notice beneath them." Beu makes a motion with his hand and Peter can see a line of spherical light forms. "These are the energy centers of the physical body depicted in this shadow form, the sort of paralleled composite energy that is being impacted by this other dense, chaotic energy overlaying the more subtle and more beautiful energy centers. And if you will follow my direction here, you will see that they move completely up what's defined in the Earth as the spinal column until we reach the top here."

Peter finds himself lifting, rising up, so that he can peer down on the shadow form of the reader. "I've heard of those," Peter answers softly. "They're Eastern. They have to do with the philosophy that the body, or something associated with the body, is dependent on … what was it … seven or eight of these spheres of light, and that when they are treated in a certain way they result in good health for that one, and when one or more is amiss, that means that the one could be unhealthy or something of that sort. Is that correct?"

"It is good enough for the purposes here. They are often thought of as the steps to higher consciousness, for there is a correlation between them and the evolutionary spiritual growth of acceptance of a person, as well. But to come to the point here, if you will notice these energies at the basal and mid-section of the entity, they are having a imbalancing effect to these ... in the Earth they'd be called glandular centers and chakras, or a variation of combined terminology that builds upon these basic premises. Understandable, Peter?"

Peter nods, trying to absorb and equate all of this information.

"So now, the reader is being shown where the opportunity is, what in past is still influencing the present. And he is being shown this at this time because he stands before an opportunity in the Earth specifically for the purpose of providing a prospect to release this past karmic relationship."

"Fascinating! But what is causing that specific mass of color or energy there?"

"Just watch." Beu gestures to the vast "screen" before the reader.

Peter again is drawn back to another battle. He notices in this calamity of conflict a small sea of warriors striking at one another, thrusting, hacking, hammering, accompanied by groans, wheezes, curses, cries of agony.

"Good grief, this is like going back and living an historical event."

Beu nods with his gentle countenance. "It is precisely that, Peter, and for this one, it is very meaningful. Watch the next few events, pay particular attention to him over here." Beu thrusts a finger forth. A small orb of light illuminates one man with a twisted, grimaced face of hatred and anger, wrath, swinging a great axe on a massive handle.

Consumed by the intensity of the event, Peter winces as he sees the man's axe strike bodies. One falls, blood gushing. Again and again, he swings, the giant battle-axe continually in motion, cleaving all that comes into its path.

Peter thinks for a moment of the weight of the man's weapon and then studies the man who is stout and muscular. But the most powerful force the man seems to be emanating is this wrath and hatred.

Suddenly, Peter can sense what he remembers from the Earth as pain, and he sees that one of the man's opponents has struck their mark, having thrust a sword into the left side, rearward, of the man. He falls to his knees, one arm grasping the axe in desperation, wildly trying to swing again, and the other arm twisted back with a hand striving to cover the gaping wound in his back, cursing with a vehemence Peter can never recall having seen before.

Then there comes another blow to the man as he is on his knees, being struck again in the back, on the area just below the right rib cage. At that point, he drops his great axe, and both hands are now pressed against the lower back. Peter hears a strange sound and glances up to see a group of horsemen ferociously moving towards him. In the next seconds, the man's body is trampled repeatedly as this band of horsemen pass by.

In an instant, there is a bright flash, which Peter knows all too well is the man leaving that physical body, and the chaotic swirl of colors and density of patterns returns to the screen.

Peter turns to look at the reader, who is now overlit with the familiarity of that event. He looks closely and sees that the energy around the mid and lower back of the reader is now pulsing, as though it has some sort of living light or essence within it. The two guides are now positioned closer to his back, and the other two more luminous entities are frontward. Obviously, there is communication here, but Peter cannot discern it.

Beu turns to Peter. "There is no need for us to attune ourselves to that level of communication. They are simply attempting to help the reader remember this upon awakening sufficiently so that it will have an after-effect upon this one's current life."

Suddenly, Peter notices that the reader is beginning to dissipate, the particles of substance that were forming the reader's expressed form moving away molecule by molecule, bit by bit, until there is nothing, literally, sufficient left here. A swirling spiral of tiny luminous bits gather in a large mass of color (*almost like a comet*, Peter thinks, *though not nearly as bright*) and move away and down. "What is happening now, Beu?"

"Ah. The entity is waking up."

"You mean waking up, as waking up from sleep?"

"Precisely so. The interesting part will be how much is recalled. Let us try to observe here a bit."

Curious as to how Beu might just do this, Peter remains quiet and motionless at his side.

Beu extends a hand in front of him where there is still a small area of this screen-like substance. His hand slowly moves over the area of white luminosity, and Peter is surprised and excited to see, first, the rooftop of a dwelling in the Earth. As Beu's hand continues to slowly move over this, it is as though they are X-raying the house. They move down into it and can perceive a man sleeping in a bed below them.

The man stirs for a time here and finally opens his eyes, lying there, staring at the ceiling.

Curiously, Peter can hear the man's thoughts as he reviews this "dream" in the morning light of a new day. The dreamer is reflecting upon his strange dream. Peter can tell the man's thoughts to a considerable degree, and he knows that the man is thinking, *There's that strange dream again. I wonder how many times I've had it now, and why.* He turns on his side to see the luminescent dial on a clock next to his bedside. Peter hears the thought, *I may as well get up. Only a few minutes more 'til this thing goes off anyway.*

They follow the man's movement to another room where Peter recognizes the familiar activity of filling a coffee pot and activating it for the first cup of coffee of that day. The man seats himself on a stool by the coffeemaker and, rather absentmindedly at first, picks up a pencil and begins to write on a pad of paper the events of the dream.

"Oh, good," smiles Beu. "It's working this time."

Peter can feel a sort of uplifting light from the guides, though he knows not where the reader's guides are. Turning to observe the man again, Peter notices that, although the man is concentrating on writing, there are various colors and such that are growing in their luminosity in orbit around him. Gradually and then more swiftly, Peter sees that these are essences on the spiritual cloak of the man and there, suddenly, depicted right in the same position as in the reader's form, are those errant energies. "Are those causing him pain, Beau?"

"Yes, pain in the outward meaning of that term, and pain in the sense of the emotion, and also in terms of limitation and a lack of growth, so to say, in the overall sense spiritually. So, as you can see, it's an important point at this time for this man to rid himself of that or to convert it into some more usable form."

"How might he do that?"

"By simply understanding the meaning of the events he has just dreamed. Example: The warrior that was swinging the great axe was filled with hate and rage. Of course, his opponents were acting in the same manner, for this was a long-standing feud between these tribes, which, incidentally, was around and about the Black Sea in distant times. The people here continue to fight in sort of cyclic patterns, as though it is a part of their way of life, as though it is expected of them. Yet, what is gained? Here you see this man expressed in this lifetime, and what is the effect of that lifetime?"

Beu pauses here, and Peter finds himself a bit in the spot-light once again. He hears Zachary speak.

"What he's asking you, Pete, is for an objective evalua-tion based upon your recent and therefore more familiar Earth relevance to such an event. He wants to know what you would think would be the value of such an experience."

Peter, a bit mystified at what's expected of him, proceeds anyway. He begins his commentary based upon the battle. "There are many people, tribes, cultures, religious sects, and races, who have emotional reactions to other such groups for reasons most people don't fully understand. It just seems to be the way things are and the way things always have been, according to their family, the older members."

Beu nods. Peter takes this as an invitation to continue.

"So in this battle, apparently this man was simply doing what was expected of him in that lifetime. I can't truly answer the question as to why the great degree of hatred, but … "

Beu raises a hand, causing Peter to pause. Reaching out into the cloud-like screen before them, greatly diminished in size now, Beu moves his hand again, and Peter looks sur-prised to see another battle and another man who is being struck again and again. By what Peter can tell from the garb and the insignia and such, it is this same enemy. This man staggers, stumbles, and finally falls. And again, the appear-ance of the light, and Peter knows that the man has passed through the portal of death, as it's called in the Earth. Beu moves his hand again, and the vision is gone.

He turns to Peter. "A brother, who fell some several years previously. A brother well loved by this man, the dreamer. So this, to answer your question, was the source of his rage, his hatred, his desire for revenge. Yet you might ponder, Peter, in your current position of grace and love, how many other brothers, husbands, and such did the dreamer fell with his great axe? How many other karmic relationships might be thought of as being a part of the dreamer's life now, because of his actions, borne out of the desire for revenge?"

Beu pauses, and Peter reflects upon this.

"I see the meaning here. So the collage of color and energy around the mid and lower back of the dreamer, is this karmic energy, the results of his deeds? In other words, people he destroyed in battle?"

"Yes. But the curious thing here—and it's worthy of note for you, Peter—is that you will notice it is not individually oriented. The energies here are thought-form oriented. In other words, they are oriented towards the event, the attitude, the emotion, and not towards a certain person, with the exception of this one right here." At which point, Beu points to an energy Peter can tell is an expression of another entity over the dreamer's body. Peter knows that energy is part of an entity because of the way it vibrates and has light, even though it is expressed heavily, darkly, so to say, and unpleasantly.

"This is the energy of a foe in battle in that same time, to which the dreamer had a great awareness, and vice-versa. They were what you might call mortal enemies. They hated one another, and they were looked up to, each one, by their village, so they often met in conflict and battle. And the dreamer has this same entity in his life at present. Of course, they aren't bludgeoning one another with great axes and swords or such, but they are bludgeoning one another with emotion and conflict and frustration. For, you see, they work together, strange as it might seem, in a rather competitive corporate environment. Both are striving for advancement, both are striving to, as they call it in the Earth, get ahead.

"This dreamer would just as soon 'get the head' of his opponent in this lifetime, as he so often sought to do in the past. That is keeping this energy alive, so to say, and it is drawing the collective thought-forms of all those years of battle and hatred and anger as a sort of magnetic attraction, with this one energy here as the magnetic core of this condition of what I will define to you as dis-ease."

"Wow. Then I might conclude from this that the dreamer does have a physical dis-ease or pain with this?"

"Oh, yes. Indeed so. Has chronic back pain, occasionally so severe that he must take a holiday for repair and rest. If you will notice over here, there are varying types of medication, devices for support, and we can convey to you that he seeks frequent treatment for relief of this. The practitioners of healing, known in the Earth as doctors, have defined this as a degenerative spinal dis-ease and have urged the man to seek some forms of radical treatment. The man's guides are encouraging him, to the extent that they are permitted through Universal Law, to seek radical treatment in the spiritual sense rather than in the surgical sense. And as you can see, the man, in jotting down the highlights of this dream, is beginning to understand. He is beginning. He is opening the portal, so to say, to heal himself."

"Remarkable, utterly remarkable. Does every person have such opportunity when they have conditions of dis-ease? For that matter, do all conditions of dis-ease have similar root causal forces or variants of this? And is it possible for them to heal their dis-ease by knowing the causal forces and, by doing certain things to let those go, make themselves better?"

Zachary is now chuckling in the background. "I told you, Beu, he loves his questions. And he does well with them, wouldn't you say?"

"Indeed so," Beu smiles to Zachary. Once again, the sense of immensity and great presence from Beu is radiating and noteworthy to Peter and all the company here.

"To answer your questions in a summary form, for there are other things to be about for the moment, Peter, the answer is yes. Most all things in the Earth, or any realm for that matter, can be traced often, if not always, to some previous experience or action, some sort of root causal force. That is one of the beautiful opportunities that can be obtained through working with these beautiful records called the Akasha, or this place often referred to as the Great Hall of Records.

"Now, if you will stroll with me a bit, Peter," with which Beu grasps Peter firmly again, without waiting for his approval and sweeps Peter along. "Look about you here and ask as you will."

They move through what Peter perceives to be an endless array of massive volumes, others more diminutive in size but radiant in their craftsmanship, some appearing to be engraved, others multi-colored, some seeming to have jewel-like essences on them, others great in filigreed script and craftsmanship, and on and on. All the while, Peter observes other entities, some coming and going, some he notices with what appears to be the reader form, which is not fully expressed, some entities appearing to have clothing, which Peter notes is "modern" who are these are readers. Other entities of great light seem to be coming and going, and Peter can perceive a myriad of angelic forms moving into and out of these records with graceful ease. Sometimes Peter is aware of beautiful sounds. Other times he feels as though he and the group are being bathed in resplendent light, which vibrates within every molecule of his being. Other times he can detect essences of joy, of love, a collage of emotions that seem Earth-oriented.

And yet, overriding all of this is a sort of cohesive essence that inspires hope, that inspires forward thinking, that Peter would conclude, no matter how grave, how heinous, an event might be when re-observed or re-experienced from the past, there is the constant, gentle flow, almost like a current of light, a flow of loving light, all throughout all of this.

Finally, Beu pauses and turns to Peter. "Well, as you can see, Peter, so it goes, on and on. You will find that the Akasha has a mode or means of expression in virtually every realm. While you might perceive certain entities in and about the records as we have traveled among them, what you do not see are those entities whose vibrations are substantially less than required to be expressed at this level and others who, conversely, have expressions well beyond this.

"Are you saying that they are here right now, at this moment, but not being perceived?"

"Yes and no. Yes, in the sense that the records are eternal and, therefore, all things that are eternal are capable of existence and expression in a like manner. It follows thereafter then that these records could indeed be accessed eternally from any realm. Conversely, no, in the sense that the spiritual level of acceptance of you and your group and, equally so, all those who are present here now," and again he gestures with his arm in a sweeping motion around the great vast array of records, "all these entities are equal to or greater in their level of spiritual acceptance, comparatively speaking, to that which we are now manifesting.

"So it is that you, Peter, can perceive those of the angelic host, others similar to yourself, and numerous others who fall at arrays between those two points of reference, as well as readers who are being directed and guided by their guides. And there are those who visit these records for the purpose of benevolent works, like Zachary's comment with the tea leaf reader, but on a somewhat more elevated, we might call it (not judgmentally but with a loving intent) on an elevated level of service. Some of these entities are recognized in the Earth for their ability to reach this level and, having so done, to acquire information for others, as well as themselves.

"But virtually all entities in the Earth can reach the Akasha at this level of acceptance, or lesser or greater, depending upon their need and their willingness to perceive same. Entering into same as an objective with good purpose, with a high ideal, virtually any entity seeking in God's name, aided by those who guide, can easily attain these references and the powerful opportunities that they present. See?"

Peter, absorbing all of this as rapidly as possible, has

made numerous notes of questions and areas to explore, but at this point, Zachary speaks. "So you see, Pete, the fellow on the street that we observed prior to coming here has all of this available to him when he is ready to break free from the habit pattern. And as you saw in his records, aided by Beu, he's about at a point where we should think that sheer boredom if nothing else may be sufficient to cause him to cry out for a break, for relief. Perhaps when this occurs we, as a group, and maybe even aided by you, Beu," at which Beu nods, "can assist. We should think you will find that to be most interesting, Peter; and more importantly, it will be a good service that will bring all of us an opportunity for joy."

The group now moves back to their earlier position at the entrance to the Akasha, and they settle themselves to rest and perhaps to answer some of Peter's myriad of questions.

We shall leave them for the present, encouraging you then to consider more carefully your dreams, your visions. And though symbology may at times seem to be alien, make note of it. Review it. Compare it to past visions. And consider that one such just well may have been the result of a visit to the Akasha.

CHAPTER 18

A Gift to the Earth

DECEMBER 10, 1993

We have here the intent found in the heart and mind of our Channel to bring a gift to you in this season; and beyond that, the intents and purposes of each of you, individually and collectively represented. We reach out in these works to embrace your kind and loving thoughts and call upon Universal Law that these shall be returned to you many-fold over.

As the Channel has indicated his appreciation and joy for the information given thus far, so would we gently indicate to all of you the joy we have as workers in His light for the opportunity to present this to you. For while Truth has always been with you in the Earth and in all realms, we have such joy in expressing Truth perhaps in a different light, in another tongue, and in ways that are contributive to the current consciousness in the Earth.

As you consider the topic called "the Akashic Records", each might have a variant perspective. While Earthly logic cries out for standardization in order to be acceptable, you might look upon this as one looks upon art in its purest form considered a masterpiece because it is unique and innovative. So too, then, might we humbly suggest it well to consider this perspective as you look upon those things that move beyond the finiteness of the Earth and into what is called the infinite.

We shall attempt to tie this together while responding to the Channel's request to recognize the season, the holidays celebrated in different ways and lands. As we do, our intent is that it shall be regarded by each who shall perceive same, as an offering given to you in God's Name.

We rejoin Peter and his colleagues, now, at the point ap-

proximately where we left them, although some considerable exchange has taken place. Additionally, some actions have been engaged in that have had the intent and purpose of enlightening Peter in areas relevant to the Akasha and other similar works. The following is our translation of these experiences and those now unfolding.

Peter is commenting with excitement and exuberance. "It is incredible that such records can exist as those I've just encountered, and that they can be accessed from virtually any state of expression or any realm. I would really appreciate a further understanding of the mechanics involved … how entities access them and how the entities ascertain their meaning and how it all might be applied to them as individuals."

"Well, Pete, it has to do with the desire on the part of the seeker. If someone in, what we could call loosely, a less than illuminated realm were to suddenly realize that they are, indeed, in a less than illuminated realm, this very realization makes many things possible for them that might not be available to the others in that realm."

"So, if I understand you correctly, Zachary, you're saying that the need or the desire is a sort of key for that entity that opens the ability to access the records?"

Zachary nods.

"Well, what happens after that? I mean, once they have gained the willingness to know of the records, what takes place then?"

Paul is the one who responds to this question. "Any number of things can occur at that point, Peter. In our earlier experiences, there could have been many variations of experience we shared as we passed through what you call the *colors*. This is because events involving the Earth or other finite expression are usually heavily saturated in emotion, and emotion becomes a sort of agent that binds (if you will) the record itself.

"Once an entity discovers that their own thoughts, intents, and purposes are heavily involved in what they are experiencing and that the cumulative effect of that is, in a way, precursory to what shall be, then this realization becomes a sort of pathway for those who are serving that entity to bring knowledge to them.

"Taking yourself as an example, in order to make all this more understandable you have looked at some of your past experiences, and you have engaged in numerous experiences here with us and in other realms. All of these collectively have built a certain degree of understanding within you. In the example of an entity dwelling in a less than luminous realm, they too carry all of this within them. But their *willingness* to see, their willingness to know, needs to be dealt with before they can understand to the degree that you do."

Peter studies Paul. "Can you give me a specific?"

"Certainly. The case of the person we visited and then viewed his records with Beu brought us to a point of understanding of his habit and the consistency with which he had formed a continuum of lifetimes. That consistency, itself, tends to be a very valuable tool because, ultimately, he is going to reach a point where the very fact that things remain the same (in other words, do not change) will tell him something. And as he reaches a point of what he would consider to be sheer boredom about what his life has become—which is a microcosmic collective effect of all of his past lifetimes now focused in this current life—that boredom becomes pivotal. It becomes the opening.

"It is known that virtually all entities will arrive at a point where they're (to use your Earthly term) just plain fed up with the monotony of the experiences they are having. It is at that point that an entity can be brought insight, information, guidance, and all that sort. The entities we have observed in realms very close to the Earth who, to you, feel limited, that is their intent, their thought, as you have come to realize."

Peter nods.

"They have simultaneously amassed quite an accumulation of good potential, which grows to the point of being a counterpoint to the monotony of the continuum of their experiences. So the moment that the entity, of their own free will, chooses to change things, there is the light to dispel the darkness (colloquial terms used here, of course, Peter), and it takes actually very little to enable that entity to cross the threshold into less limited consciousness. Reminding you of Jack as a good example and the intensity with which he first approached us. Do you recall this?"

This reminder strikes a strong resonance within Peter.

Smiling at the strength of this memory in Peter, Paul continues. "Then, you also remember how swiftly, once he opened himself, he was able to make a transition from that dense experience to one of much greater light and into a joyful state of helpfulness and service."

"That was an excellent example. I doubt if I shall ever forget that Jack. What a turnabout that was."

A pause falls upon the group, then Elizabeth speaks. "There are many forces that could be defined in many different ways, Peter, numerous realms of expression that entities can be found in. Even in the Earth, there are numerous ways of thinking, levels of perspective and understanding. All of those things that make up the composite of each person could be thought of as little realms of awareness within that entity's consciousness. Do you understand what I am saying, Peter?"

Peter indicates that he does, and Elizabeth continues. "So there is an array of emotions entities work with, experiment with, discover and explore while they are expressed, for example, in the Earth. Of course, one of these is love. The capacity of each soul to know and to express love is unlimited. I might suggest here that you further explore these capacities and their relevance to the Akasha and the significance that the

Akasha holds for all of us and perhaps a return to the Earth or to a position in close proximity to the it."

Elizabeth pauses and looks to Zachary and Paul, and then to Peter. Of course, Zachary and Paul are immediately aware of what Elizabeth is intending and focusing on, and they respectfully and lovingly indicate their affirmation. So when Elizabeth's focus comes to rest solely upon Peter, though not fully comprehending her intent, she receives from him the emanation of utter faith in her, along with his love and high regard for those experiences they have already shared.

"Well," comments Zachary rather boisterously, "rather than having these philosophical and, if you'll forgive me, a bit dry conversations continue, let's have an experience that will illustrate all this. What do you say, Pete?"

"Yes! Let's do it." Peter turns to find Beu immediately to his left. "Oh, uh … thank you very much, Beu, for the, uh, tour and information."

"Indeed," adds Paul, echoed by Elizabeth.

Zachary finishes up with, "Well, Beu, you've done it again. We'll be back soon," a radiance beaming from him, synonymous with a radiant smile. He continues, with a bit of an impish grin about his countenance, "We'll contact you. In the meantime, if there's anything we can do to assist, of course you know we are at the ready."

Peter, inspired, by his dear friend Zachary, chimes in. "Yes, sir, Beu. I am deeply thankful and would be honored to serve any work that you would feel we," casting his gaze about his small group, "might answer for you in any way … " He sort of fades off with that comment.

Beu is smiling broadly, and an emanation of wisdom coming from his eyes, and Peter knows no further comment is needed. He knows that Beu will take Zachary, Peter, Paul and Elizabeth up on their offer, perhaps more than once.

All embrace and good energies are exchanged, and Beu rather abruptly moves from the group and up towards the entrance to the Great Hall of Records.

"My, that's an impressive entity," comments Peter. "Has an essence of the angelic realms about him and many other beautiful essences I don't have good descriptive terms for."

"Yes. Incredible fellow. For as long as I have known him, I have never seen him fail to respond to a need. Brilliant, masterful in his methods and knowledge. We'll see more of him, Pete, I can assure you."

Without waiting for Peter to respond, Zachary swoops up one of Peter's arms and begins to move off, Paul and Elizabeth along with them.

Peter laughs. "I always enjoy our journeys but, forgive me, Zachary, the times we sing together aren't as beautiful as the sounds I'm hearing at the moment in this journey. What is producing this beautiful sound?"

Peter detects from Zachary's broad smile that Zachary is about to engage in one of his favorite pastimes, which is to delightfully enlighten Peter. "Well, Pete, now that you mention it, I suppose I could say that it's some of my musical handiwork. But that would be less than accurate, for it would imply that I, as an individual entity, am responsible for its creation, when in fact, this is the collective representation of our group as we pass through these beautiful realms associated with the Akasha. You could say that the beautiful collage of music you are perceiving is the exchange of greetings, affirmations and such, between our group and all those entities and groups that we are passing by."

"What? Our greetings to the other entities we are passing by, did you say?"

"Good perception, Pete! That's almost precisely what I stated. Good work."

All laugh aloud with vigor at this little exchange.

"Okay, Zack. I'll rephrase. Are you saying that, as we pass along here ... " he turns to look about. "I don't see anyone we're passing by. All I can see is the beautiful light and colors. And I'm not aware of greeting anyone, much less someone greeting us."

"Well, then, Pete, what you need is a good change of consciousness. You know, redundancy tends to be a limitation once one has gained the value of that experience."

"What?"

"You know, repetition, habit. Once you've learned something and you continue to learn it over and over again, doesn't it get to be a little wearisome?"

"Well, yes, I suppose so. But I had favorite music and favorite things in the Earth, and I never got tired of them." Pausing for a moment, Peter responds further. "No, I suppose I could answer that unquestionably, I am not. I am in a heightened mode. My curiosity is sharp. I'm anticipating the adventure or outing ahead. I'm not in a bored mode at all."

Zachary chuckles softly. "Well, then, your state of mind, or consciousness more accurately, is not openly attuned."

"What? What do you mean, not openly attuned?"

"Simple. You are not looking, listening, perceiving, in a broad sense. You are focused. You are somewhat intensely focused on what is about to happen or may happen. Therefore, you are not aware of, or you are closed down to, current peripheral stimuli."

"Okay, help me be more open, then. I would like to know if I am being greeted and, even more importantly, as absurd as this might sound, I would like to know if I am greeting them in return."

This brings another round of laughter. "Good, Pete. This is a good, heightened state of ease. Nothing brings about ease more quickly and more fully than a state of joy. Now, go inside yourself and see if you can find the presence of all color and light."

Peter is about to respond, *How do I do that? Where is "all color and light?"* But before he can express it, Zachary reminds him, "Have the thought, the intent, the need. Then, create the action."

Dutifully, Peter closes down his perception in the outward sense and focuses within. As he does, he feels a marvelous fluid silken-like movement, ever so graceful and joyful. And he begins to perceive what he interprets as color and sound, first soft, muted, almost pastel in nature and, then, more swiftly, very well-defined, very individually expressed, and symphonically beautiful in resonance. "I have it, Zack," he comments without thinking, and at that point, his perception opens outwardly to his group.

In utter amazement, looking all about Peter can tell their motion, for he has references, and here and there is an entity or a group of entities, brilliant in their luminosity, resplendent in color, and as remarkable as Peter can find expression to think it. He marvels at the coloration of sound ... the collage of energy expressed (as he perceives it) as colored sound and light. "Beautiful," he whispers.

In the next moment, Peter perceives what he thinks must be a reflection of his group and, more specifically, of he himself. "Oh, how delightful! Now I understand that I am greeting them in return. My consciousness thought of greeting as 'Good day, sir, how are you? Nice to see you again,' and a handshake or a pat on the back. You know, things that would be a greeting in the Earth. I hadn't thought of the essence of one's being as radiating outwardly in the form of a greeting. But now I see that is so. Am I correct, Zack?"

Smiling and nodding vigorously, mimicking Peter's occasional vigorous affirmation of understanding, Zachary signals to Peter a yes.

Paul is barely able to contain his joy. "As you have come to know, Peter, Zachary's methods may not be thought of by some as, well, what they would consider to be spiritual. But what is spiritual, after all? Is it not the free-flowing expression of one's truthful Self?"

"I suppose so, Paul."

"Well, look about you and observe. Many of these entities are colleagues of ours, and many are about works just as we are, joyfully acknowledging our mutual bond, our dedication to service in God's name. And others of these entities, if you will note now, Peter," continues Paul, "have beautiful light and color about them. You have been feeling the intent or essence that that color and the accompanying sound, as you call it, musically creates within you."

"Let me try that!" Peter closes down his outer perception again and quickly flows along the silken path of grace within him and reaches a point of understanding, precisely so, of what Paul is conveying to him. Just as swiftly, he returns to his consciousness. "Paul! I have it. I have the understanding. In fact, with each of these groups we are passing, I get an essence of their work, of what they are doing, where they are doing it, and their intent or purpose. How beautiful."

Continued exchange passes throughout the group. Finally, the conversation reaches this topic. "I know we are upon a journey, and I am curious … It seems we have been in the midst of many colleagues or like-minded entities for some time now. Are we moving that slowly, Zachary? Or is it that the realm we are passing through is that immense?"

"Well, a little of both. But then, there's a new aspect to this that your question offers a remarkable opportunity for us to share with you, Pete." Zachary turns and gestures to Elizabeth.

Radiant with the light and musical essence of their just-previous humor, Elizabeth picks up the conversation softly, in a manner that stimulates Peter within. As he hears her words, he marvels at the healing nature that Elizabeth's thoughts, comments, and so forth seem to activate within him.

Without paying note to those thoughts within Peter, she continues. "We are journeying to the proximity of the Earth because it is in one of its greatest seasons of joy and openness."

"What is that?" asks Peter, his curiosity greatly aroused.

"We are approaching the religious ceremonies of highest esteem in the Earth for many people." She pauses to allow Peter to absorb this.

He responds, "Then it must be about Christmastime."

"Yes. We are near the celebration in linear time in the Earth of the Christ Mass and other equally reverent and joyful celebrations in other doctrines. But for this journey, I believe, and I know the others do, as well," comments Elizabeth, turning to gesture to them, "that the Christ Mass should be the focus of this journey."

Peter is excited by the prospect of returning to the Earth at a time that he so revered in his just-previous incarnation. "Something that piqued my interest in what you just said is about the openness of people. Does that have anything to do with all of these other entities around us?" Peter turns to confirm that they are still in the midst of many entities of lights, individuals, but mostly groups.

"Yes, it does," responds Elizabeth. "It has a great deal to do with that, for the mass-mind thought of the Earth tends to be what we might call a force that acts somewhat like a filter or a buffer, in that the intents and thoughts have much governing effect or control over what can be brought to the Earth.

"Under what we would call, clearly, our Father's Laws—and you know much about these already, Peter ... Universal Law, that is," and he nods, "we can only give to those to the extent that they are willing to receive. We can offer, or we can leave in place, some blessing in the hope that, ultimately, it might be of use to them. But we would not ever, as a part of our works in God's Name, force or coerce, or in any way get in front of the entity and their individual free will choice.

"But as you recall and know in your memory, during the Christ Mass season, people change. They become more receptive, more open. They are willing to see themselves in a different light and, consequently, their brothers and sisters, their neighbors, and even those who are enemies or foes to them during other times."

Peter responds. "That is true. I know that what you say is true. I remember the heightened fellowship around the Christmas season. People just become more tolerant, more understanding, more forgiving. It brings out the best in people … " And Peter's communication tapers off into nothingness as it draws former thought-forms into his consciousness.

Allowing Peter space or time, as you call it, to re-engage those thoughts, after a time, Elizabeth continues on. "So you see, we are in good fellowship here. All of these good workers moving with us have as their intent to offer many good things, many opportunities, to those in the Earth who might otherwise be quite closed to them. To an extent, the wonderful harmonics of music and color and light that you acknowledged moments ago could be thought of as the joy expressed by these entities for this opportunity."

"How wonderful." Peter turns to gaze about and perceives the great numbers of entities. They seem to be endless. "My goodness. All these entities are now moving to the Earth for this purpose, as a singular intent?"

Elizabeth nods. "As the primary intent, yes. Certainly, there are others in this group who have other specific works as a part of their intent, as well, but in the broadest sense, the answer is yes, you are correct."

"My! If we could only know this while in the Earth. If we could only see this as the window of opportunity that it is, and make what these beautiful entities are offering permanent, that it could live on as a living light that allowed us to release the old habits and attitudes, my, wouldn't that be something?" Peter wistfully peers off at the beauty and grandeur, the utter love and the feeling of grace that he knows these entities are preparing to offer as gifts to the Earth.

Soon, he can feel a growing transition, a feeling about

him of increasing finiteness. From his previous experiences, he recognizes this. "We must be nearing the Earth. I can feel a sort of diminishment of my joy, my potential."

"Yes," responds Zachary quickly, "and therefore it is well to prepare ourselves appropriately. Instead of being as open as I had assisted you in becoming previously, it is now well to center ourselves and re-focus our consciousness so as to not violate God's Laws as we move through these realms."

Peter nods and turns inwardly briefly (and this is considerably paraphrased, dear friends, for your understanding) to activate his cloak, and he can see the others do the same. Shortly thereafter, there is a combined essence or greater cloak-like orb of light that surrounds them as a small group. He turns to perceive that every one of those journeying with them, individuals and groups, have also done the same. *It is like a sea of lights, like looking down from an airplane on highly illuminated residential areas and their display of Christmas lights.*

"Quite a coincidental similarity, wouldn't you say?" comments Zachary to Peter's unspoken thought.

"Uh, er ... yes. Guess I drifted off there. I wonder if any greater correlation could be found here?" asks Peter further, not really sure about what he is asking.

"I suppose there could be. Perhaps it could be that no matter how far away they have taken their memory or their consciousness, perhaps every person at some level remembers having seen such as this ... " He gestures about them at the armada-like array of lights in motion flowing towards the Earth.

"Oh-h, what a beautiful thought," responds Peter, with an almost weariness.

"Not to falter. Not to falter now, Pete. Eternity is before us all. Don't think in terms of finite time and weary yourself at what appears to be the long continuum of less than luminous consciousness that you perceive to have befallen the

Earth. Remember, there are many entities of goodly light in the Earth, expressed in physical body and nonphysical form, alike. The hope is great in these times, Peter, and the potential even greater."

"Thanks, Zack. I needed to hear that. For a moment there, I remembered how quickly the spirit of the season passed and how, all too quickly, people moved back into old habits once Christmas was over."

"Well, be of good cheer, Peter. There is more to be seen and more to be experienced here just ahead."

Peter perceives them to begin to move with certain swiftness, passing through the realms of less than brilliant light that surround the Earth, and now they are within the Earth's atmosphere itself, perhaps only several thousand feet above. He peers out, noting that it is night here, and he perceives the many luminous twinkling of multi-colored lights. "Oh! That is so lovely. Christmas is so hopeful, so spiritually uplifting. It was ... well, one of the closest things I can associate to being here with all of you and in the other realms of great light."

"I wish we could put you on a national TV program and have you state that to everyone, Pete. Of course, most of them wouldn't believe you or any of this. They'd think you are whacko or some weird person recently released from an institution. The best we can do is be ready when a person is open or calls. And we can do a little more in this season because the mind-set, the mass-mind thought, opens itself. It's better conditioned to receive in the unlimited sense than it is most all of the rest of the time, though there are exceptions.

Elizabeth interjects, "If we might, I should like to move to a position for a specific purpose."

Peter can feel their movement in relationship to the topography of the Earth, which he observes with interest and familiarity. In a short moment or two, they come to a pause. "Where are we positioned at present, Elizabeth?"

"At the moment, Peter, we are over what is considered to

be a place of holiness. It is the birthplace of the man called Jesus, of course, known to you and most all who follow the His teachings as the Master."

"Oh-h … " This awareness triggers many emotions deep within Peter.

"Good," notes Elizabeth. "Those are good topics of discussion here, and I should like to engage them, Peter."

"How do you mean that?"

"Rather than my attempting to communicate that to you, let us observe, if you will."

Slowly, slowly now, they move, coming closer and closer to the Earth.

Peter hears occasional outbursts, which he recognizes as gunfire. "What is this? I thought we were near to the, you know, the Master's place of birth."

"It is, indeed, what you perceive," Elizabeth replies, with a detectable hint of sadness. "But let us not focus upon this. Look, if you will, over here, and over there and there and, well, just look about you, Peter."

Peter turns to look and joyfully perceives several great resplendent groups of light, each of them somewhat unique in their manifestation, but very, very beautiful. "Other groups such as ours!"

"Yes, and more," explains Elizabeth. "These are entities who are, what we would call, soul groups. They are not in physical form. They are unlimited in many respects, some of them very much so. There is great joy among them, for there is an opportunity just ahead for a great transition in consciousness."

"What is that?" Peter's excitement is awakened.

"It is that a healing is in the offing here. Though limited in some respects, it is of major significance to the Earth and to the future of it."

"A healing? Do you mean a person is to be healed?"

"More than one. Many peoples, races, theosophical

groups. And the outcome of it could mean healing of a magnitude not seen in the Earth for hundreds or thousands of years."

"Goodness! Then this is a potentially historical event?"

"Yes," nods Elizabeth, smiling, her hopefulness radiating from her as an angelic light, which Peter duly notes.

Turning to look at the greater groups, which seem to be geographically positioned over some point, almost as though they were tethered there in a manner of speaking, Peter notices around their periphery many other lights, some seemingly representing groups, others seemingly more individual.

Elizabeth explains. "The greater groups, Peter, represent certain ethnic or theosophical mind-sets. These are, if you will, the soul groups seeking to help those who have differing beliefs to find a bridge of understanding and communication between one another, to hopefully end the hundreds of years of conflict and hatred that has gone before, and to truly embrace the concept that we are all one under one God."

"Oh-h, my. That is incredible."

"Yes. So you see, the other groups, great and small, on the periphery of the larger groupings, are here just as we are, to offer assistance and help to the greater soul groups who have done such a fine work and who are so hopeful and contributing so much to attempting to end the time of darkness between these peoples."

"Then we are speaking of the Israelites and the neighboring peoples, the Holy Land. It would be something if peace could reign there! It truly would."

"It would be so, Peter," comments Zachary, "in more ways than your consciousness is aware of at this point."

"Indeed," adds Paul. "The potentials of this, Peter, are brilliant. It is a beginning, one of several that have recently unfolded in the Earth, which many of these groups have served long and faithfully to attempt to contribute ... the unfolding of these realizations upon the Earth in general. And not only upon the Earth, but in the realms adjacent to same."

"Then this is a unique time?"

"It is more than what you would consider the individual uniqueness and beauty of a single Christ Mass, Peter. It is more likened to the approach of a great spiritual Christ Mass that has been building for many centuries but has accelerated greatly only in the last decade or so. And the acceleration is amplifying daily, to the point where entities in all walks of life, in all conscious levels of perception and interaction, are becoming aware of it."

"That is incredible, beautiful."

There is a pause, a time wherein Peter and the others simply observe and participate in the joy that is emanating from the other groups and the contemplation of the potential that lies ahead.

After some time and more exchange of conversation, the group begins to move to another position, not too distant from the Earth but to a point that is beyond Peter's current ability to perceive in finite detail, though, if he wanted or needed to, he easily could.

"We would like to share with you now, Peter, a very, very beautiful blessing, a blessing that is not ours alone, although we shall participate in it, if you choose."

There is a pause, and Peter, realizing that his affirmation is important here, asks softly, "Is this a work in the Master's name?"

"It is, indeed," responds Elizabeth. Paul and Zachary nod in affirmation.

"Then, of course, I would joyfully participate."

"Well, then, center yourself as I lead you, Peter."

Peter does not question, but he wonders within himself precisely how Elizabeth is going to lead him. Knowing this, Elizabeth answers Peter directly, *Follow and do as I do. We shall become formless. Remember how?*

Yes, I remember.

The group moves into a position where they become light, indistinguishable in the individual sense, but one radiant orb of light, within which there is the characteristic and uniqueness of each of the entities in a harmonic overtone.

Easily following Elizabeth's lead, Peter becomes ecstatically joyful. Soon he finds himself sharing the consciousness of his group. Utterly, they are without form. There is light and laughter, rivers of it, as Peter might use the term to define his experience.

Open yourself now, Peter, utterly. Keep your form without definition. Keep your consciousness as one with all that exists.

Without comment, Peter follows Elizabeth, who he perceives to be moving as a radiant expression of something that has no term for. He finds himself being transformed until it seems to him that he is vibrating in every molecule of existence—that all of expression is him and all of he is all of expression.

Let your consciousness change just a bit, Peter. Follow as I lead. And Elizabeth becomes so subtly focused in the individual sense that Peter perceives a collage of ever-moving, undulating light and color and sound.

Oh, you are so beautiful, Elizabeth. He turns to observe Paul and Zachary similarly expressed. *Oh, and each of you! How majestic.*

You, too, Pete. Looks good on you, too.

A rivulet of beautiful soft pastel reddish-rose color sweeps over the group, indicative of their humor.

Now, Peter, here is the blessing, the gift to the Earth in this time, coming in its most pure form.

In what could be measured in mere moments in the Earth, Peter feels this incredible essence of all manner of stimulus. Every part of his being sings out with joy. The collage of symphonic colors and lights seem to *be* him! He feels the love, the forgiveness, the sense of peace and oneness, so much so that he feels he might truly lose himself completely and forever in this. It is a state of ecstasy that Peter can find no measure for expression.

It continues for some time. Peter feels It moving and flowing, as though It is like a river reaching out to find those paths that It might follow, offering Itself to any such as would be willing to accept It.

Time passes in the Earth, and each in the group focuses themselves somewhat.

Peter states, *This is the gift offered to the Earth, correct?*

Indeed so, reply the others.

Then I have but one prayer ... that all would know of it and accept it. For I know this to be the Light of God.

And so, dear friends, we echo Peter's prayer and wish you all a joyful Christ Mass—wherever you might be expressed, in whatever form, in whatever time.

Remember this: The Master is a powerful force. That same force is within each entity, a spark of life, an essence that is of the purest nature. It is, in fact, that pure nature upon which all of existence is built.

CHAPTER 19

Healers, Watchers, and More

JANUARY 1, 1994

In the works that have been a part of Peter's experiences since our last meeting with him, there have been many discussions regarding the immensity of that light and beauty flowing to the Earth. As we rejoin Peter and his companions, we believe you will begin to comprehend the broader meaning of what Peter experienced and also understand the opportunity that is now presented to all of Earth in the approaching times. This shall be a part of our prayer, ever offered.

The group is still rejoicing and in wonder of the just-previous experience, and Peter finds himself with an inner glow that he treasures in an embrace of his own thought and heart. "I doubt that there is any part of my being that was not in resonance, in harmony, with that experience. Perhaps it's due in part to being formless. Since it is one of your favorite expressions, Elizabeth, you might be the best to answer that question."

"What you say is true, Peter. The resonance of your being, once you have moved into the formless state, enables you to be a part of all expressions. As such, every aspect of you was and is still in harmony with the experience. And that is one of the reasons I find formlessness so delightful." She radiates the rosy light of her nature towards Peter.

After a pause, Peter becomes a bit more centered, immediately visible to all present.

Zachary asks softly, "What shadow of thought passes over you, Peter? You have perceptibly changed."

"Yes. I was just thinking about how much the people of

Earth are missing ... something this majestic, this beautiful. And I suspect the greater that one shares this, the more profound it becomes."

"Very true," adds Paul. "But then, there is the Law. How would you see us contributing such a blessing to the Earth, using the understanding you still retain from your previous Earth incarnation?"

Peter wistfully looks off into the distance. "I just don't know. But there must be a way." A sort of melancholy emanates from him.

Zachary quickly advises, "That should be about enough of that energy, Pete. The better path is to sustain a hopeful, expectant attitude. Remember, like attracts."

"Yes, of course. I didn't mean to generate something less than joyful, certainly not in the afterglow of that wonderful experience. But can you understand why I feel as I do?"

"Most assuredly, Pete. And supposing we just presume that there is something we can do, what would you say to going forward and pursuing that as an objective?"

Peter is brightened by Zachary's suggestion. "Are you saying that there is a way within the Law, within Universal Law, that we could help bring this beauty to the hearts and minds of people in the Earth?"

Zachary laughs softly. "Well, of course, Pete. There are many things we can do, and many things that others, individuals and groups, are doing. No different than our works in the past have certainly contributed."

A bit of disappointment passes across Peter's countenance as he absorbs Zachary's communication to him.

Zachary studies Peter for a moment and smiles. "Oh, I get your drift, Pete. You don't want to wait too long before presenting the Earth with the majesty of your recent experience. Is that the point?"

"Yes. I'm a bit impatient, I suppose. Goodness, we have this grand experience that is too beautiful not to share or be able to tell someone about."

"Well, then, let's get on with the journey."

Zachary swiftly gathers up Peter and begins to move him without waiting for Peter to reply. The rest of the group follows Zachary's lead.

"This movement feels good. It feels that, as we move, I am leaving those somewhat less than joyful thoughts behind."

All the while, they are moving more and more swiftly.

"There's truth to that, Pete. Truth, indeed. For matters of one's heart, one's mind, especially so in the Earth, tend to become a part of the environment in which they are dwelling. Therefore, moving from that environment, even if but for a brief period, can have a significant effect on the power of those limiting thoughts or attitudes. So what you say is true to a far greater degree than one might surmise."

"Interesting … " Peter is shifting moreso into a mode of curiosity.

"Ah, that's the ticket, Pete. That brings back the flavor of the true Peter."

Laughter resonates within the sphere of light of the group as it continues to travel, now at a remarkable pace.

Then, as swiftly as their movement began, it slows, until Peter realizes that they are now stationary. Quickly glancing around and opening himself, he realizes that they are back in the Control Center. He rushes forward, followed quickly by the remainder of the group, each chuckling to themselves at Peter's zealous movement.

Over his shoulder, he hears, "Uh, Pete. If you don't mind, where are you going?"

"I'm looking for Zeb. He's got the answers. I can feel it."

"Oh, okay," comments Zachary. "Just checking."

Soon, Peter perceives the radiant glow of his friend Zeb and a variety of others who are gathered nearby. He also notices several other groups that arc distributed out across a broader area of the Control Center realm than Peter had recalled in the past as it having.

Then there comes Zeb's booming greeting. "Hey, Peter! How are you and your friends doing? Come over here and let us give you an embrace." Peter and Zeb virtually collide, and Zeb reaches out to each of the others with equal joy. "So, Peter, you had quite a good time, so I have seen."

"Yes, to put it mildly. I've had quite an indoctrination into some of the inner workings of being unlimited. And I must tell you, Zeb, I have a far greater respect now for what you and some of the others here are doing." He casts a glance around the Control Center. "By the way, Zeb, who are these other groups and those other entities over there? I don't recall seeing them before. In particular, I notice one way over there." Peter leans way back, extends an arm and points.

Chuckles murmur throughout the group, and Zeb's booming laughter fills the envelopment in which they are presently expressed. "Well, travel hasn't changed you in the least, Pete. You are still filled with curiosity, questions, and a desire for growth. How wonderful. I do hope you'll keep those qualities."

Zachary, rocking on his heels now, is looking down, somewhat controlling his mirth.

"Well, dear Peter, let me just take you over here and introduce you to some of these entities and groups, now that you have so keenly noted their presence." Without a moment's pause for Peter to comment, Zeb swiftly and with irresistible power sweeps Peter along, followed immediately by the remainder of his group. Reaching the first group, Peter is introduced to each of them, and then Zeb asks one of them to explain to Peter briefly what they are doing.

"It is wonderful to meet you, Peter. We have been with you here and there, though you may not know it. Do you remember Cara?" questions the spokesperson.

"Remember? I don't think I can ever forget her."

Smiling gently, the spokesperson continues. "That is

good, for we have other works ahead that we would like to offer you and your group, hopeful that you will agree." The spokesperson turns to one of the others who comes forward, and Peter senses a degree of familiarity, not so much the entity but the countenance. "You are aware of my companion here, I gather?"

"Uh, well, not so much so that I could give you a name or anything, but do I sense something familiar that is recent."

"Would you like to identify that for yourself? Or shall I comment on it?" Glancing over to Zachary, the spokesperson pauses, as though seeking from Zachary some sort of indication as to how to proceed.

"If you will, my friend, let Peter find it for himself. It's good practice, and it will, as you know, strengthen the communicative link."

Turning to glance at Zachary, puzzled why the spokesperson would ask of Zachary in the first place, Peter asks, "Communicative link? What is that, Zachary?"

"Find it, and you'll know, Pete. Take a look inward. And by the way, focus on the other entity right here, as you do."

Peter, turns to look at the spokesperson's companion, and receives a remarkably familiar warm smile. Following Zachary's guidance without question, Peter centers down a bit and moves upon a velvety line of light between them. Swiftly finding a resonance, he perceives the Great Hall of Records and before him is Beu.

Greetings. Beu startles Peter beyond words.

"Wh-what?"

I said greetings, Peter. You have found one of our workers, I see.

"Uh ... yes. But, Beu, how is it that you are speaking to me inside me?"

Oh, that is no significant thing. We do have a bond, a communicative link, do we not?

"Well yes, uh, and I remember that, once we have made

contact and moved into harmony with one another, thereafter we have some sort of a light between us."

Yes, what Zachary called the communicative link. But perhaps we should conclude our conversation here. You might want to return to the others in your complete consciousness, with which Beu smiles broadly at Peter.

Peter, now somewhat flustered, moves back to a consciousness of full expression in the Control Center with the group. As he perceives openly now the entity before him once again, Peter blurts out, "You are a co-worker with Beu!"

Nodding, the entity simply smiles at Peter.

"Not bad," comments Zachary. "In fact, wonderful work, Pete. Keep up that sort of thing and … well, who can say?" Again, Zachary looks down and begins rocking on his heels, obviously delighted at this event.

Zeb clasps Peter firmly and embraces him with an exaggerated hug (spiritually speaking). "Indeed, Peter, well done. How is Beu these days, anyway? Haven't spoken to him for a time in the direct sense. I must make a note here to remember to visit him soon. He's an old friend, you know. We've worked together a great deal here and in other realms."

Peter looks at Zeb full-on. "You know Beu?"

"Oh, yes. We go way back."

Zachary can no longer contain himself and bursts out in delicious merriment and laughter. Peter turns to look at Zachary and immediately is caught up in the mirth. Then laughter cascades in rivulets of color all about the Control Center, so much so that all the others join in.

"Goodness, Zeb! I didn't mean to take over the whole Control Center."

"You gave us all just the lift we needed. In fact, just the other day we were praying for something light and mirthful like this to come our way. As always, our prayers were answered, and here you are."

Then the entity standing next to the spokesperson of the

group turns to Peter. "I would like to help you by being a contact between Beu and the Hall of Records and some of your future works. That is, if you will permit me and my colleagues."

"Assist me? With Beu and the Hall of Records? How would it happen that I should be so honored to ... " He stops himself, remembering the lessons given him regarding self-worth, self-appreciation. "Yes, of course, I'll take your help. What is it that we'll be doing, anyway?"

Zachary is chuckling. "See? Just like I told you. You'll love working with this fellow. He's so refreshingly spontaneous, and so utterly without limitation. Such a joy, a delight. We all love him dearly, and I'm sure you shall, as well."

The new group nods in affirmation to Zachary.

Then Zeb states rather abruptly, "Well, there are others to meet here. We'll meet you all a bit further down the light."

Peter does not understand Zeb's comment, but Zeb, once again rather deliberately, moves Peter forward. "A bit further down the light, Pete ... that just means further into the work, that's all. It's not to be taken in the literal sense, but then, on the other hand, if one were to take it in the literal sense, it would certainly be revealing. That's to answer your unspoken question." Zeb lets go a rivulet of delightful, melodious laughter. Before Peter can respond, they come to a single entity, who is busied about something, though Peter can't perceive what it is.

"Greetings!" comments Zeb. "If I might interrupt for just a moment, I should like to introduce Peter and his companions. They will be working with you and the others in the planned work just ahead.

Before Peter can ask about any of this, the entity steps forward without a word and embraces Peter in a manner that stuns him momentarily. It is as though the entity probes his being in many places, as though tiny little rivulets of energy emerge from the entity and enter Peter. As they do, it stimulates him. He feels electrified, enlightened in a remarkable way. He is reveling in this resplendent experience, and shortly, the entity releases him and steps back.

In awe, Peter moves awkwardly aside as he feels Zachary step forward with a hint of humor in his countenance. "Here, old friend, I'll have one of those, too, if you don't mind." He and the entity also embrace, and Peter can see dancing spirals of beautiful energy cascading all about them, erupting here and there, as though Zachary has just stuck his finger into a light socket on Earth. Then next come Paul and Elizabeth, each embracing the entity as long-lost friends.

Finally, the entity turns to Peter and states in a resonance that, in a way, echoes within him. "Yes, Peter. Much has been shared of your works and your progress, and I should like to speak on behalf of my group, that we shall be honored to serve with you in any commission that you should choose and that you should ask us to participate in."

Peter, in wonder at the uniqueness of this one, comments softly, "And, uh, your, uh, group ... is it nearby?"

"Oh, yes," again reverberating within Peter. "We are all here right now."

Glancing this way and that, Peter cannot perceive another single form within close proximity of this entity, whose radiance effervesces a quality, almost rejuvenating in nature, sort of spiraling off the entity. "Forgive me, good sir, but I cannot perceive any others. Are you maintaining a link, a line of communication with your group? If so, might I ask what realm they are in their current position?"

The entity radiates beams of what Peter would describe as delightful electromagnetic energies. "No, we are here. The form or expression I am manifesting for you *is* our group."

Peter is without words for a moment or two as he digests this information. "Wow! I think I understand! You are expressed as the group or, no ... you in the singular sense are actually the group ... uh, but the singular form of yourself is what I perceive ... but really there are many of you ... or is it that the many of you are singularly formed into the one you?"

Zachary can no longer contain his humor. It reverberates all about, and the group again shares in the delight of Peter. The entity, in his effervescent radiance, also shares in this delight and, as he does, Peter notes that this adds a remarkable new quality to this experience of laughter and joy. It is like little rockets of energy seem to shoot about, and whenever one of them strikes Peter, a marvelous rivulet of energy transcends down and up throughout his entire expression all at once. Again, this is joined in by all the others in the Control Center and shared equally by each.

Finally, the group comes back to a centered communicative level.

"You are correct, Zachary, in your description of Peter. He is every bit as delightful as you have expressed."

Zachary simply nods and rocks on his heels, arms folded, glancing at Peter, giving him an exaggerated wink, as Peter wonders, *How is it is that this single entity, Zachary, could know so many others and have had so many experiences?* Pretending to be a bit taken aback by Peter's thought, Zachary raises his hands. "Well now, wait a minute, Pete. Paul was there, too, weren't you, Paul?"

Smiling broadly, Paul nods to Peter, and then Peter glances at Elizabeth, as Paul states, "Yes, she was there, too."

They all laugh a bit longer, and Peter returns to focus on the entity, whose countenance is utterly delightful and curious to Peter, simultaneously.

"Let me help just a bit here, Peter." Without waiting for a response, the entity begins to glow. The glow swells and expands and, suddenly, before his eyes, Peter perceives within the sphere of the glow many individualized expressions. They swirl about and begin to take slightly unique differentiating forms, one from the other, until Peter can perceive so many, many entities, he cannot count them all. They suddenly emanate a love, a greeting, to Peter. Then, just as quickly as they expressed themselves, the group comes together in the singular, individualized form that once again stands before Peter.

"Incredible!" exclaims Peter. "I'm reminded of when we ... " and he turns to glance at Elizabeth and the others of his group, "when we entered into a formless state. I think somehow this is how this group is now expressed, but they have managed to, uh, well, I wouldn't know how to describe it or understand how they did this. But what I see," turning back to look back at the singular entity, "is actually an expression of the entire group. Am I correct?"

"Excellent assessment, Peter, and actually, there is little that we could contribute to that or embellish upon it."

"Wow! I wonder if sometime you could ... "

Zeb interrupts. "Forgive us, but there are several others for him to be introduced to here. We'll be back to see you shortly down along the path of light."

The entity embraces Peter and steps back, and Peter, once again, feels the rather forceful engagement of Zeb moving him and his colleagues along.

"Goodness!" remarks Peter aloud, "what a resplendent entity, or, uh ... group, I guess I should state. Who or what are they? What do they do? Where do they come from? And how is it possible that we'll be involved with them in future?"

A quick glance over his shoulder, and Zeb gets a broad wink and an *I told you so* type of shrug from Zachary.

"Good questions, Pete," states Zeb. "We call them, very loosely here, the Healers. They are focused almost exclusively on healing works, and I must say they are remarkably skilled at it. Of course, all healing is between God and the individual, but these entities carry God's grace like the rest of us might carry a few packages. Utterly dedicated. You'll see. You'll get to work with them, and I have no doubt you'll enjoy every single moment with them."

Peter, dwelling on each morsel of information, sort of

files these comments inwardly. "Incredible."

"Not really," responds Zeb. "Just focused. Very, very focused. And consequently, very good at what they do. But look over here. I want you to meet this group now. They're delightful, too."

They step forward and wait for a moment while the group obviously concludes something they are doing, something that they are looking downward towards. Peter imagines that, should Zeb so wish to do, he could wave a hand and allow the Earth to be visible.

One of the entities, who Peter perceives to be remarkably tall in stature, turns, smiles, and with another booming voice, greets Peter in a manner as though he had known Peter for some considerable time. "Hello, Pete. How are you? And you, Zachary and Paul, Elizabeth? Come over here. Let's have a big hug."

Peter is again taken aback at the familiarity and the rather earthy tone with which the entity greets them. But without hesitation, he goes to the entity and receives a hug.

"Here, greet my fellow workers." The large entity thrusts Peter into the arms of one after the other. As he does, Peter smiles inwardly, as it feels as though some great grandfather might have brought him to meet the rest of the family tree.

"Good assessment, Pete. You could think of this as one big family."

And Peter realizes again that his thoughts were as spoken words.

"Oh, not a bit of shyness here, Pete. We're the Watchers, … constantly aware of opportunities taking place in the Earth. We spent a good deal of time with you and, of course, your guides. But as we were just working here … " he turns to direct Peter's focus to the beautiful white luminosity before them. In an ever so subtle motion, he sweeps the whiteness apart, just as Zeb has done many times before for Peter and his group, and Peter finds himself looking into what seems to be someone's home.

"Here's the chap over here." With his long arm, the entity thrusts a finger of light and focuses on a man who is obviously aged, slouched down in a well-worn, overstuffed chair. "This fellow's got about two or three steps to go, in terms of Earth time, before he does one of two things: either he joins us all over here," pointing his thumb backwards over his shoulder, "or we can reach him and help him to do some good works and build his soul's light, instead." But let's take a look over here. Here is someone I think might be able help."

In just the passage of a split-second, Peter perceives the scene of a city. It zooms in, as though the tall entity had some sort of magical remote control for a giant television.

"Why, that's Cara!" exclaims Peter.

"Well, yes, of course, it's Cara. And there's her friend over there … Tim, I think you called him, although we've got several names for him here. But notice over here … " The tall entity sweeps his hand across the scene, and Peter perceives the grandfather, several other souls and, to his delight, there are Hope and Rebecca. "Old friends of yours, right?"

"Oh, yes, dear friends. Do they know I'm perceiving them?"

He looks at Peter. "Why don't you ask them?"

Peter turns, awestruck, to look to see Hope and Rebecca wave and send warm, loving energies to him.

"How does all of this work? It's like a two-way television set."

"Oh, it's better than that, Pete. Wait until you get with some of the other Technicals. They have things that they can show you that you simply won't believe. Well, on the other hand, experience will probably bring belief to you. It has always done so in the past, hasn't it?" He bursts out in such laughter that it fills Peter, a booming, melodious sound that stimulates him from what would be his toes (if he had them) to the top of his head. He hears Zachary join in, and the others, as well.

When it subsides, Peter asks, "Technicals? Did you say technicals, sir?"

"Well, yes, but then that's just my pet term for them. Some of the others might have different terms. It's just something I use to identify them lovingly, in respect and honor to the dedication of their work."

"Do I know them, or have I known them?"

"Well, you know part of them. The group you just left performs a part of that work, although I wouldn't call that technical in the literal sense, like some of the others. They are moreso practitioners of the Law of Grace."

"They are?"

"Oh, yes."

"Well, do they ... "

Before Peter can finish, Zeb sweeps him along again. "Okay, then, we've got to go. Thanks a lot, everyone. We'll be back, as you know, a little bit further down the path. Thanks so much for pausing. And greetings to you there." Zeb waves to Hope and Rebecca, who Peter now realizes have observed and participated in the whole unfolding event.

The tall entity then closes the veil of light over the perception and goes back to the other members of his group, and Zeb swiftly moves Peter along again.

"Good grief, Zeb, this is incredible! Were all these entities here before?"

"Well, they come and go, you know. This is just a wonderful place where we all gather and share and work in accordance with the light, and not disrupt anyone else in adjacent realms. As we move and adjust the Control Center, we work together in positioning it properly."

"Move the Control Center? Position it properly? What does that mean?" Peter queries. "And would you tell me more about the Technicals that that fellow commented about. And who *is* he, anyway?"

The group struggles to keep their laughter contained, as they continue to move along.

"All in good time, Pete. You'll have answers to that and more. But I think you'll truly enjoy this next group. These aren't the Technicals. They're sort of free-lance. You'll find Technicals here and there, and when we do I'll stop, and we'll greet one of them, but for now, let me introduce you to this group."

Peter turns to focus his attention upon what he perceives now as a beautiful collage of wondrously soft, pastel light, swirling colors, so beautiful it would bring tears to Peter's eyes, were he in physical form. He is immensely moved by the delicate warmth and the emanation of profound trust and acceptance coming from this group.

Zeb greets them. "Greetings, friends. Might we take some forms here, in order that we could communicate in a manner that is more familiar for our friend, here?"

In a split-second, Peter perceives many beautiful forms. Some of these, Peter recognizes without question as being angelic. Others, he perceives to be just simply radiant, having a quality of light that he remembers but hasn't found in recent times among his journeys. Then ... "Bobby! Is that you?"

Peter surges forward, without realizing he is so doing, and embraces his old friend.

"Yes, it's me, Peter! And these are my friends." He turns to introduce a wondrous array of entities, almost magical in their quality of light and peace.

"Oh, goodness. You are all so beautiful," Peter comments to the angels who are scattered all about. The love they are emanating to Peter is an identifier that no one could possibly mistake. He feels an essence of familiarity from several of them, and he exchanges it equally so from a level of his experience with the angelic host. Greetings are exchanged as they all embrace.

Bobby begins. "Come here, Peter, if you would. Let me

explain to you some of what we do. It is so joyful. I know you will find it most endearing."

Peter feels movement, as though they are moving a considerable distance in the twinkling of an eye. Suddenly, he is confronted with a massive array of souls of all different luminosity and qualities.

"These are the Potentials," explains Bobby, softly. "They have been called here because they are being offered incarnations in the Earth."

Peter is utterly stunned, utterly without speech.

"You see, Peter," continues Bobby, as though he had not noticed Peter's reaction, "there is a continual movement of entities to the Earth and from it as, of course, you know. What we are doing here is counseling those souls who are being considered for entry into the Earth to help them clarify their purposes, individually and collectively, for returning, and where they might *intersect*, so to say, to accomplish mutual intentions. As with the others, you have met (and some you have not, as yet) who have invited you and your group's participation, we invite you as well. You will discover those areas of potential that are of particular interest to you, and you will begin to gravitate towards those."

Bobby embraces Peter now with his perception, and Peter returns the loving exchange.

"I would consider it an honor of the highest accord to serve with you, Bobby, and your group, and all of the others. I don't, in my present perception, know how best I can contribute, but I'm sure that will evolve."

"That is received in the humility and selflessness for which you are noted, Peter."

Zeb steps in. "Well, then, I think that's enough introduction here for the present, and I know you're occupied, Bobby, you and your group, so let us share a bit of light between us, and then I'll take Peter to make one more stop before we allow him to express what must be a mountain of questions at this point."

A bit of laughter comes from the group, and Peter notices that, from Bobby, there comes not laughter in the literal sense, but a quality that can be found, he recalls, only in the eyes and spirit of a child in the Earth. This warms Peter in a center of his being that he had forgotten existed. It reminds him of the unquestioning level of acceptance and joy that are the precious jewels borne by the children of the Earth. He cannot contain it and he hurls himself to embrace Bobby, feeling an in-pouring of the quality that the Master loves most of all in all entities: the beautiful child within.

With some communications of exchange and greetings and embraces amongst all in the group, Peter and the entourage move again. Peter perceives that they are moving back towards their point of original contact with Zeb.

Zeb comments softly to Peter, "Are you balanced, Peter? Are you able to absorb all of this as rapidly as it has been presented to you?"

"I feel wonderfully good, Zeb, thank you."

They are moving at a more moderate rate than previously, when Peter is startled by a swooshing sound, and a bright array of lights burst forth in front of him. Zeb grasps Peter and they come to a stop. Zachary is chuckling over Peter's shoulder.

"Well, there's one of them now, one of the Technicals I told you about."

"Uh ... I don't perceive anything but a beautiful display of bursting light."

"You will, Pete. Just a moment until they settle in here. They have a habit of moving about and then showing up."

"Hey, Zack. You serve as a Technical, right?"

"Well, Peter, there are several titles, several names. I'm not so sure that there is much to be taken from a title or name, but, yes, I have ofttimes found it particularly joyful to be in this particular form of service. But if you don't mind, one of my friends has just come before us here," pointing to the mass of sparkling light that is now settling down and becoming formed.

Peter stands amazed, in wonder at the Technical and the lights that are crackling and popping. As they settle in, there forms an entity. Peter's first impression from this one is of delightful humor, a quality he immediately recognizes as always having been present within his dear friend Zachary … a sort of pixyish, child-like, playful, delightful quality, but one that seems to have no barriers, no limits, and loves everyone with a sort of puppy-like embrace of existence.

"Really?" asks Zachary over Peter's shoulder "Puppy-like? You can't do better than that?"

The entire group again bursts forth in laughter.

The Technical who is now almost formed laughs the loudest. "That's a good one, Zack. But I would say that was a not a misnomer, either. It's probably one of the best truisms I've heard in some time. Aren't canines loyal? Are they not patient and forgiving? And are these not qualities that we share, Zachary? Good compliment, Pete. I'll take the best from it, and if Zachary wishes, he can have the rest." He lets out with a hearty, playful laugh

"See what I mean, Pete? One of my own. Difficult to top that chap. He's quick and good at what he does." Zachary moves forward and collides with the form of light before him. Good to see you again, old friend."

The merging of these two entities in an embrace causes Peter to move back several steps in awe, as there is a resplendent burst of lights and laughter upon laughter as these two friends are obviously delighting in rolling about and sharing, what Peter discerns, must be many mutual memories, a vast array of past experiences cascading past him.

From Zachary, he hears with mirth, "Well, time is not relevant, Pete."

Peter is amazed that even from within this level of activity, his dear friend is aware of his thoughts and can respond.

Then, immediately before Peter, stand the two forms. The display of sparkling light is gone. One is looking like the other, arms folded in front of them, both rocking on their heels.

Peter looks from Zachary to the other. "Goodness, I would never have dreamed there could be two so similar as you, Zachary. How delightful to meet you, sir."

Zachary steps aside. "Wait a minute. I want to get out of the path here, in case you guys let off a display of any sort. He's been known to do that."

The Technical feigns innocence about Zachary's comment. "Come over here, Peter. Let's have a hug from you, too."

The collage of light sweeps Peter up, and he feels himself spiraling off through time and space, laughter echoing all about them. *This must be the Realm of Laughter,* he thinks to himself.

"If you think it's so, it is so, friend Peter," replies the Technical, both of whom now are formless, cascading through colors. Peter is caught up in the warmth, the utter friendship, from this entity.

After a passage of what seems a great deal of time but is actually but a few moments, Peter and the Technical are once again standing before one another, and there are the others of the group. Zeb is smiling broadly, as are Paul and Elizabeth.

Zachary is standing off to the side, pointing at them. "See? I knew it would happen. Spiritual fireworks. He does it every time."

Peter is filled with the joy and with sharing Zachary's ... he doesn't know what to call it ... Background? Heritage? Soul group? *Whatever it is,* Peter thinks, *I like it.*

"Well, thanks, Pete," comments the Technical. I'm quite fond of you, too. Incidentally, Zachary has let me and a number of us follow along with you all throughout. We've offered

---

a suggestion here or there ... some he even accepted." Laughter pours forth from the group again. "We would all be delighted to assist you in any way we can. But, if you'll forgive me, one needs to be mindful for whom one is working, and I have a call. See you all later." There is a barrage of light and color, and a flash where the Technical stood spirals swiftly towards the Earth and is gone.

"Always a bright spot in the events at hand, that fellow," mulls Zachary. "Perhaps a little innovative around the edges, but hey, creativity is the ticket, I always say."

Peter is still in shock at the possibility of there being more like Zachary. Slowly, he perceives the communication. "Oh, uh, what was it you were saying? I agree, whatever it was."

A gentle rivulet of humor resounds from the group as they begin to move back to the point where Peter initially entered the Control Center.

He is chattering away about the angels and Beu and the others until they reach a point where Zeb states, "I suggest we all have a time of rest and focus, a time for easeful exchange. What would you all say to that?"

All affirm their agreement. Zeb casually tosses himself into a horizontal position, settling in on what appears to be a billowy, multi-colored luminescence. "I always like to pause in this flow of consciousness. It's so energizing. It displaces any little segments that aren't charged properly into a state of utter harmony. Would you like to join me here, Pete?" Zeb reaches out pats the billowy swirling colors, which seem to respond, as though they were actually matter.

Peter, saturated with joy and wonder at all the new experiences and potentials that lie ahead, accepts Zeb's offer and hurtles himself head-first beside Zeb. He feels a responsiveness from the billowy substance, as though he, too, had physical form and was being supported by it somehow. He notices that the others have done the same and are all scattered about here and there.

"This is wonderful! What a fitting closure to what has been a most wondrous series of experiences. And, by the way, Zachary, I'm still not over the fact that there's another one like you. It just does not seem possible."

Laughter reverberates within the sphere of their focus, and so we shall slip away here and allow them their time of joy and rest.

We have been most joyful to have been with you in these works. We should like to assure you that we shall all, including Peter's group and each of those he has just met, dedicate ourselves unto any works that you would perform in God's name. Our dedication extends, as well, to you, each of you.

What lies ahead now may provoke even the most inert portions of your consciousness into action. You should find new vistas of realization, and perhaps many new opportunities for your own awakening, as well.

Fare thee well for the present, dear friends.

We pray that this work as has been given herein, and those that follow in the continuation of Peter's journey, might promote an understanding with which you can meet and manage each event or circumstance during your sojourn there on Earth.

We pray, further, that these shall thus make the way that much more passable for you, as you move beyond this incarnation and into realms beyond.

–Lama Sing

A Note from Al and Susan Miner...

The complete works of the Peter Project include more than 200 readings and take place over a period of ten years.

The Project includes two components.

One of these is comprised of the Peter Chronicles, the readings following Peter and his experiences.

The second component is comprised of questions about the Chronicles submitted to Lama Sing by project members for answers.

Many people have told us that the great wealth of information, beyond the excitement of Peter's story itself, lies within the Q&A readings, which actually make up more than two-thirds of the Peter Project.

We are very pleased that these Q&A readings are currently being made available as companion workbooks, as a research tool to each of the Chronicle books.

Books by Al Miner & Lama Sing

The Chosen: *Backstory to the Essene Legacy*
The Promise: *Book I of The Essene Legacy*
The Awakening: *Book II of The Essene Legacy*
The Path: *Book III of The Essene Legacy*

In Realms Beyond: *Book I of The Peter Chronicles*
In Realms Beyond: *Study Guide*
Awakening Hope: *Book II of The Peter Chronicles*
Return to Earth: *Book III of The Peter Chronicles*

How to Prepare for The Journey:
       Vol I. Death, Dying, and Beyond
       Vol II. *The Sea of Faces*

Jesus: *Book I*
Jesus: *Book II*

The Course in Mastery

When Comes the Call

Seed Thoughts
Seed Thoughts to Consciousness

Stepstones: Compilation 1

The "Little Book" Series:
       The Children's Story

About Al Miner

A chance hypnosis session in 1973 began Al's tenure as the channel for Lama Sing. Since then, nearly 10,000 readings have been given in a trance state answering technical and personal questions on such topics as science, health and disease, history, geophysical, spiritual, philosophical, metaphysical, past and future times, and much more. The validity of the information has been substantiated and documented by research institutions and individuals, and those receiving personal readings continue to refer others to Al's work based on the accuracy and integrity of the information in their readings. In 1984, St. Johns University awarded Al an honorary doctoral degree in parapsychology.

Al conducts a variety of field research projects, as well as occasional workshops and lectures. He is no longer accepting requests for personal readings, but, rather, is devoting his remaining time to works intended to be good for all. Much of his current research is dedicated to the concept that the best of all guidance is that which comes from within. Al lives with his wife in Florida

You can read more about Al's life and works at the Lama Sing website: *www.lamasing.net*.